Ben

A Jacana book

A Jacana book

OPERATION VULA

CONNY BRAAM

First published in 2004 by Jacana
5 St Peter Road
Bellevue
2198
South Africa

2004 © Conny Braam
English translation © Richard Blake

ISBN 1-919931-70-8

Cover design by Adele Prins

Printed by Formeset Printers

See a complete list of Jacana titles at www.jacana.co.za

To Oliver Tambo and Joe Slovo

ACKNOWLEDGEMENTS

I WOULD LIKE TO THANK ALL THE PEOPLE INVOLVED IN OPERATION Vula who assisted me in refreshing my memory and have given me so much of their time in telling me the story of their lives. I also owe gratitude to the Dutch writer Adriaan van Dis who encouraged me to write this memoir and to my Dutch publisher Tilly Hermans who helped me to become a writer.

And last but not least my daughter Tessel, who sat for long hours next to me, playing with her toys, without a word of complaint. I am still in her debt.

JOHANNESBURG – WINTER 1992

"LUCKY BASTARD!" THE WHITE DRUNKARD SPLUTTERS THROUGH his conspicuous lack of teeth, and slaps the black man on the shoulder. The old black man is staring at the silver rand coin he's just found on the street. He quickly clenches his fist around the coin. A few yards away three policemen in grey-blue uniforms, revolvers on their hips, are watching the pair. The drunkard staggers, regains his balance and disappears around the corner with no further comment. The black man straightens up and turns to a fruit stand. He picks up an orange, glancing at the young seller. From under his balaclava, pulled down low, the boy keeps his eye on the closed fist. But the old man just briefly smells the fruit.

It is early morning, still very cold. The trees are bare, their dead leaves rustling across the street in the breeze. A dog sniffs at a pool of blood, dried black at the edge but still fresh in the centre. Someone has bled heavily during the night. On a white wall which conceals the nearest house hangs a sign: "Armed response". No sign of a trail leading away from the blood – the victim's departure must have been straight upwards.

Most of the shops are still closed, but the café where you can get everything except coffee is open, and I buy a loaf of bread and a newspaper. The Star reports that negotiations between the African National Congress and the government are deadlocked. It seems such a short time ago that I saw Mac Maharaj on television, participating in a new round of negotiations for the ANC. That was amazing. Little more than a year before, Mac had still been in prison, accused of inciting armed revolt, charged for his role in Operation Vula. It had seemed, briefly, that South Africa would soon be eased onto the road to democracy through talks, with some reason and good will at the table. But the cynics have been proved right: in Pretoria the people who kept the system going for so long have gone on pig-headedly working out a

9

new form of apartheid. Meanwhile, in the townships a great deal of blood has been shed.

In the Weekly Mail *I find new revelations of torture and murder by the police and state security apparatus. The opposition press is tirelessly collecting evidence and searching out witnesses. There are millions of witnesses.*

The butcher opens his doors. I need to buy meat for the braai. This evening I shall again meet the friends with whom I've worked for five years on Operation Vula. Almost everyone is now back from exile or from prison, or has finally emerged from life underground.

AFTERNOON – BOSKUIL 1992

IT'S GOING TO BE A LONG DAY. WITH THE BOEREWORS SAFELY IN THE refrigerator I leave with Ronnie Kasrils for Boskuil, a small village to the southwest of Klerksdorp. The villagers are threatened with eviction, under pressure from the white farmers who own the surrounding land. There has long been a rumour that the ground under the huts and shacks is rich with diamonds, and the farmers want to get their hands on it before it's too late – before all the apartheid laws are gone. The villagers have asked the ANC for help. After hours of driving across mining country, we approach the village. Apart from an occasional tractor the road is deserted. Signs with Dutch names announce that there are farms here, but they can't be seen from the road. A group of villagers wearing ANC T-shirts stands waiting for us where a dirt track crosses the asphalt road. We drive very slowly down the track to the village, surrounded by craters and mounds of freshly dug earth. Farmers, gold prospectors and other whites in the area haven't bothered to wait and are already excavating around the houses, gnawing away at the village like rats. "But they haven't found nothing yet!" a young boy shouts to Ronnie, laughing.

Perhaps a hundred people are gathered in the centre of the village. A bench has been reserved for us, a single plank, and we are each given a glass of lemonade. A few old men sit in the shadow of a huge tree which still carries its leaves. As we set down our empty glasses one of them speaks. He does not know how old he is, he begins, and holds one hand three feet above the earth: he was that high when his parents brought him to the village, and others have lived there even longer. There is silence. Everyone waits; what more is there to say, in fact? The old man waves towards the trenches and earth heaps. "Why?" he asks. "Don't they have enough? Do they ever have enough? Do we have to be thrown out because of that?"

Ronnie listens attentively. He too, like Mac, has been involved for a year in the negotiations, from the moment he could leave his safe house. Before that the police and security services had been hunting him for months. He had become known as the Scarlet Pimpernel, his photo was shown on TV, captioned "Armed and Dangerous". He was wanted by the police for his work in Operation Vula.

Others take over from the old man. They explain how they have complained to the local authorities and how powerless they are because almost all of them depend on work as farm labourers, working for the very men who are trying to evict them. Emotions are running high.

Ronnie stands up, looks around the half-circle of villagers facing him, and starts to speak. His voice is loud, occasionally strained. His words are carefully chosen to reach everyone; sometimes he translates a sentence into Tswana. "They," he cries, as his hand describes a wide circle over his head, "they are trying to grab everything while they still can, because they know it too: things will never again be the way they were." There are nods and cries of approval. He warns, however, against expecting too much. "They are tricky Maburo – those Boers." It's not over yet. There is still much to be fought for, and not least the great and painful issue of land ownership. When will these farm labourers ever get their own piece of ground on which they can feel secure?

Suddenly there is a commotion at the back of the crowd. Troop carriers, Casspirs, have been sighted. Then we see them too, coming through the mealie fields in the distance. On their high wheels they make light work of the rough track. They come to a halt about a hundred yards from the huts. The leading vehicle turns, showing its dangerous cargo – about eight heavily-armed soldiers. Ronnie ignores them. He continues speaking, but now with a slightly louder voice, and I become aware that he is repeating himself. A woman admonishes the children not to look at the soldiers, and the young man who has organised the meeting walks towards the first Casspir. Ronnie closes his speech by urging the young men to protect the village by patrolling the area at night, and calling the ANC branch in Klerksdorp if danger threatens. Then he turns and introduces me: chairperson of the Anti-Apartheid Movement in the Netherlands. He waves me forward.

I have not prepared for this, and I feel my face redden. In the front row two women with babies on their backs nod to me in encouragement.

I thank the people of Boskuil for welcoming me to their village, *but all my experience of public speaking has suddenly deserted me. I look towards the Casspirs, and so does everyone else. "I feel so ashamed," I say.*

They look back at me in surprise.

"Ashamed, sick to my stomach that your existence is threatened by people who have the same names as my neighbours in Amsterdam. Even the name of your village sounds Dutch: Boskuil – a hollow in the woods. But right now I'm seeing the hollows around this village, and I won't forget what I have heard here today! I will tell the story in the Netherlands, to journalists, members of parliament. I shall make sure that the Dutch government complains about this to Pretoria."

How dare I say this, all these clichés? Face to face with these people, where am I finding the gall to make these promises? Holland seems like a self-centred merchant far away, with very different concerns in his mansion with its neatly tended garden. "I will do everything I can," I add hesitantly. Haven't we always, damn it, done what we could?

"Viva international solidarity!" I finish, militantly.

They respond as one: "Viva!" retorts like a cannon shot. Everybody stands. The young man returns to say that the soldiers want the names of all those present. There is laughter, and the crowd turns their backs to the army vehicles.

After a while the Casspirs drive away, and we take our leave of the villagers. I need a toilet urgently, and a few women accompany me to a corrugated iron privy. Inside is a hole in the ground, perfectly circular as if turned in clay. When we leave, the children run beside the car all the way to the asphalt road, calling out after me: "Bye-bye Holland!"

Evening – Soweto

The boerewors hisses and sputters on the grill over the fire. Jabu sits on his heels, swiftly turning the meat with his fingers before it burns. He sees Little John staggering towards us carrying a huge pot of pap thrust upon him by Totsi, and flashes me a grin. Boerewors and pap – a South African meal to celebrate our first gathering on South African soil. Most are here, with their children. Only Mac and Joe Slovo are out of town, and Ivan is stuck in Durban for a meeting.

Earlier, before we began cooking, I accompanied Jabu and Little John to the cemetery in Mamelodi. We wanted to visit the graves of three of their friends who were hanged in Pretoria in 1983: the Moroka Three, as for a short time they were known even far outside South Africa's borders. The graves stretched as far as the eye could see: endless rows of low sandy mounds, with small wooden crosses everywhere. Most graves only carried reminders of the deceased: a teapot, a cup, a plate, sometimes a medicine bottle. "There are a lot of comrades lying here who were sentenced to death," said Jabu. "They were hanged in Pretoria Central Prison, and buried here."

Finally we found a big headstone carrying the three names: Thabo Marcus Motaung, Thelle Simon Mogoerane and Semano Jerry Mosololi, all with the same date of death. Jabu bent his head, his hands folded in front of him. Little John, standing on my other side, closed his eyes briefly. The words on the stone read: "You have sowed the seed from which generations will take inspiration and courage ... Maatla ke a Rona, Amandla Ngawethu." After a few minutes Jabu raised his head and softly said: "Thank you." He walked away among the mounds, looking for other friends, but most of the graves were unmarked.

On the way back he was quiet and tense. He drove at high speed past the hostels, long barracks where frustration could easily be brought to the point of explosion. For months, the violence had been flaring up almost every day. As we joined the motorway I saw Jabu relax a little. Little John put the radio on, and Jabu tapped his fingers on the steering wheel.

A short distance before the Soweto exit a Jeep pulled alongside us, staying dangerously close. A white man stuck his head and shoulders out of an open window, staring wide-eyed at Jabu, then at me. The Jeep came still closer. Jabu's hands gripped the wheel tighter. "Don't let them provoke you," I said softly, leaning forward. He slowed down a little. The Jeep shot ahead, and the white man jabbed the air with a rude two-fingered sign as it cut across in front of us, staying just ahead until we pulled off for Soweto.

It was almost dark before we at last arrived at Jabu's home, the house where he was born, a safe refuge, secure despite being so small. The sun wasn't yet quite below the horizon yet, and its rays beamed like searchlights through the thick smoke which hung above Soweto at mealtime. All the cooking and heating fires of millions of households were contributing to the thick, heavy mist, which above Jabu's house was joined by the yellow-gold dust blowing over from the nearby mine dumps. For over a hundred years the mines around Johannesburg have spewed out mountains of worthless minerals and sand. The golden dust covers everything – grass, scrub, walls, houses, the remains of a car in the front yard. I saw Gebuza standing there beside it with a glass in his hand. Most of the guests were already there and our reunions were loud with laughter. I greeted Gebuza last. Once again I had to stand on tiptoe to plant a kiss on his cheek. And once again he didn't bend forward as much as an inch.

It's getting cooler now. The others are standing round the fire warming their hands, eating and sharing reminiscences. Gebuza has joined them and tells the story of something that happened in Swaziland. More laughter, but his own face remains serious above the glass he holds against his teeth. Little John walks with me to the path in front of the house. He has just a week ago returned to Soweto after seventeen years underground in the struggle. "We've travelled a long road to come home, but we still can't even see our own houses clearly," he says, waving at the thick smoke. Shots echo in the distance. No-one even looks around; there is shooting every night.

Ronnie and Chota, off to one side, are deep in conversation. Chota has just returned from a meeting with people from various groups, discussing ways of getting the deadlocked talks moving again. This is the first time I've seen the two of them together inside South Africa. The last time was in 1986, in Lusaka, on the eve of Operation Vula.

LUSAKA – SPRING 1986

IN LUSAKA, YOU JUST DIDN'T GO OUT IN THE EVENING. ONLY AN urgent reason to see someone justified the risk of being on the streets after dark. Armed *kabalalas* roamed the district on the lookout for a driver careless enough to stop for a red light, or for an unwary pedestrian new to the dangers of the city. I knew that other dangers lurked, too.

At eight in the evening the flat was already very quiet, no sound of music nor voices – except Dora's. She walked restlessly about the room, dropped herself into a chair, and ran a hand through her graying hair. "You don't know what it's like to live here." The Cockney accent gave her words a rough, foreign tone. "You're afraid of raids, afraid of strangers, afraid of everything."

Apart from Dora, an Englishwoman who had married a South African years before, everyone I knew in Lusaka was in exile. The city was a staging post, a waiting room. They were all troubled by a longing to be somewhere else.

For a few, life among the Zambians had even brought its own strange appeal. One remained an outsider, after all, bearing no responsibility for the misery around you. But the majority simply lived with their dreams, of some place in South Africa, in the township of their youth, where everything was more beautiful, warmer and greener, where the scent of the flowers on the rubbish dump nearby was more intense than anywhere else on earth. The bitter memories of poverty and barbarity had to be deeply repressed, so as not to cloud the yearning for home.

But the exiles' natural inclination was towards the South, whereas Dora was consumed by a growing longing for the North.

She was sitting beneath a framed photograph of Cape Town's Table Mountain and a watercolour of a Welsh landscape. Her husband, an ANC veteran, was in hospital for stomach surgery.

"You're staying here!" she insisted. "Hotels are much too dangerous. You can sleep in the study – I'm expecting someone else to arrive, but we'll manage somehow." She stood up and rummaged in a cupboard to find me a glass. A revolver lay on the top shelf.

"Are you really that scared, Dora?" I asked.

She let her head rest for a moment against the cupboard door. "You know, it's crazy, but those bombs – that's something so unspeakable, you almost get used to it. It's more the other things: like when there's yet another unexplained death, and the rumours start. 'It was poison,' they say. 'He drank something from an open bottle, or his clothes were poisoned. Do they know who gave him the bottle?' No-one trusts anyone else any more. Even if they find a bomb before it goes off, it'll explode anyway a hundred times in their minds. Then the fingers get pointed again. If you believe some of them, there are more spies than exiles in Lusaka. Sometimes I think it's the fear that'll beat us in the end."

The doorbell rang. Dora turned quickly, and moved uncertainly to the hall. Staying a safe distance from the door she called out, asking who it was. I couldn't make out the reply, but apparently the caller was well-known to her, because she threw off all the locks and I heard her delighted cries mingle with soft laughter from someone else. She came back into the room with a radiant smile on her face, followed by a tall Indian man with deep-set eyes and unruly hair. I quickly sat up and put my feet on the ground, looking for my shoes. He shook my hand, and sat in the armchair beside me.

"How was Harare?" called Dora from the kitchen. She was warming up the pan of curry which had been ready for days, waiting in the refrigerator.

"Wonderful," he answered quietly. His voice sounded a little hoarse. I saw that his hair was dyed; the grey was showing at his temples. He leaned forward, looking at me with frank curiosity, and asked where I was from. Amsterdam? His eyebrows lifted with interest:

"Do you know Helene Passtoors' children?" he asked.

Helene had been jailed in South Africa seven months earlier for treason, even though she was not a South African citizen, but

Dutch. I happened to be carrying letters from the children in my luggage. They'd brought them to me just before I left. On the envelope was written, in small letters, "Chota".

He smiled, "That's me."

Dora brought him a plateful of food, and spread a napkin over his knees. He continued to watch me from the corner of his eye, and laughed softly at the surprise on my face. "Such a big continent and such a small family," he said, and offered me his fork. I took a burning mouthful of the curry.

Chota – Ebrahim Ismael Ebrahim. I knew very little about him; I had come across his name in a book about sabotage missions in the early years of armed resistance. For that work he had spent fifteen years in prison on Robben Island, and now he was stationed in Swaziland, with an important role in the underground resistance network organised from there. That was all I knew. Except that Helene had been arrested while trying to smuggle him out of South Africa after a clandestine mission.

Chota put his plate on the table, held the letters under the standard lamp and started reading. Dora's eyes darted from me to the half-empty plate, then carried it off to the kitchen to keep it warm.

He laid down the letters and removed his reading glasses: "I'm worried about Helene. Seven months' solitary confinement..." He was stuttering slightly, and said nothing more. I wondered how it must feel if someone is arrested while trying to help you. Would it be possible not to feel guilty? He shook his head when Dora asked if he wanted more to eat. She turned away abruptly and went to the study.

"How is Klaas de Jonge doing?" He had a little trouble pronouncing the name of another of my compatriots. I could tell him no more than that Klaas still sat, lonely but uncomplaining, in his little room in the Netherlands embassy in an office block in Pretoria. The tale of Klaas's escape from the South African police had swept through Lusaka as the story of a victory. Arrested for arms smuggling, he had promised to lead police to an arms cache. Instead he led them to the door of the Dutch embassy and slipped inside. The South African Police seized him and took him back to prison, but after the Dutch government threatened to recall its ambassador for this breach of the inviolability of diplomatic premises, the police were forced to return Klaas to the sanctuary of the embassy. Everyone enjoyed the story, and because I was also from the Netherlands I was obliged to retell it again and again in colourful detail. "He's asked if he can have a cat to keep him company, but the Dutch ambassador said no," was my most recent report.

Chota clapped his hands: "A cat to stroke, did you hear that, Dora?" he called, laughing.

But Dora was busy dragging my luggage through to her own bedroom, returning with clean sheets and towels. My offer of help was shrugged off dismissively as she strode past with sponge bags under her arm, a dress on its hanger over her shoulder and both hands full of notebooks.

"We're going to bed. Chota is tired," she called out to us.

He waved a half-hearted denial, but seemed to have long ago given up resisting Dora. From now on I would have to share Dora's double bed – the only remaining sleeping place in the tiny flat.

When I got up the next morning he was already sitting in the living room listening to a little transistor radio. Every hour he followed the world news, and then quickly tuned to a South African station to catch the last of the reports from home. Dora had already left for the ANC offices where she worked. We brewed a pot of tea. Chota moved silently around the house. Even if he was washing up, which he did every time a cup was used, he scarcely made a sound.

We each pottered about the flat, staying politely out of each other's way. I had no urgent appointments and felt no desire to go out. He read the newspapers and I went through my notes again. Several times we both looked up at the same moment, smiling briefly as our eyes met and then going back to our reading.

Around midday he heated up the curry and presented me with a plate piled so high I could eat no more than about a quarter of it. The radio went on again: in South Africa black pupils were boycotting the schools in protest at the inferior education offered them. Three people had been wounded the day before when the police broke up a banned meeting.

Chota came to stand near me while I cleaned up the kitchen. He leant against the refrigerator and again talked of Helene.

"She hasn't even seen a lawyer yet," he spoke so softly I could barely make out his words. "No one at all. That can break you. Very slowly you go out of your mind." He spoke with the familiar expertise with which a ship's doctor, after thirty years in the tropics, might answer a question on the symptoms of malaria.

He looked so worried that I had an urge to put my arm round his shoulder, but instead I handed him a tea-towel and put the water on for tea. We returned to the living room and sat side by side, in the same chairs as the previous evening.

"How old were you when you were arrested?" I asked. It struck me that it was not this man of almost fifty who had been carted off to Robben Island back then, but a young man.

"Twenty-four. It was August 1963."

"What went wrong? Or would you rather not talk about it?"

"Oh, why not? I can still see it as if it was yesterday. I'd been picked up so often by the police, but that time it was different. Maybe my memory of it is so sharp because those were the last moments of freedom before I started those fifteen years." He hesitated, leaning back; his stutter had become more noticeable, but he needed no further prompting.

"It was about noon on August the fifth. I'd missed the train in Pietermaritzburg that morning, so I'd had to take a bus to Durban, where I was to meet a comrade. The police were closing in on us; a couple of our group had already been arrested. We didn't understand what could have gone wrong. I arrived at Kloof Station, right on time. I saw straight away that we were in trouble. A plainclothes policeman called Captain Grobler – I knew that face well – was standing there. I turned away, but I had the feeling he'd recognised me.

"I walked quickly to the washroom to get a drink of water, hoping that Grobler would disappear. I was still drinking from the tap when I heard someone say my name, turned round and found myself looking down the barrel of a revolver." Chota fell silent.

"And then?"

"Grobler screamed 'Don't move!' Outside there were more than fifty of them, guns at the ready. I saw my friend get out of the train – straight into their arms. He was beaten up on the spot, they went on kicking him after he went down. The pack of TNT he was carrying rolled across the platform, but they didn't see it." He shook his head at the memory.

"Did they beat you too?"

"Yes. 'We'll break you – you'll talk!' they said, and drove to an out-of-the-way place, dragged me out of the car. 'Where is Ronnie?' they wanted to know. That seemed to be their main concern. Lieutenant Steenkamp was there, and Prins, and Van Zijl. They kicked me and beat me. I didn't say anything. Lieutenant Prins said: 'He's no good to us, let's drown him.' He was the most impatient. Two of them picked me up and threatened to throw me into the water. I can't swim. Prins just went on asking: 'Where's Ronnie?' they were in a hurry, they were afraid he'd escape."

He turned towards me, and lightly stroked my arm. "Those people really hate whites who join the ANC. They hit me so hard that I passed out. The beating went on for two weeks before they gave up."

We talked all through the next day, and the day after that. I made no more appointments, and Chota's meetings at head office kept getting postponed for one reason or another. We relaxed in those chairs or hung around in the kitchen.

During one walk to the market I told him how I had come across South Africans by chance during the late '60s, and how that had influenced my life afterwards. He listened patiently while I described the loss of my first South African friend, who had committed suicide after giving up hope of ever being able to go home. And he smiled at the crazy events and silly misunderstandings I had encountered over all those years of conferences, seminars and committee meetings.

We bought fruit at the market and he took me to an obscure little shop where he ordered two huge, watery ice cream cones. On the way back to Dora's flat he hesitantly began to tell me about the underground mission inside South Africa from which he had returned a few weeks before. It had gone badly. Helene and several others had been arrested, and he had had to lay very low for months before he could escape to Swaziland. In Durban there was still a full-scale hunt going on for him. Now he was in Lusaka for the debriefing, but he wanted to return as soon as possible to Swaziland; there was so much to do there, he had been away for so long...

He was hesitating more now, stuttering and interrupting himself, until finally his words died away in an introspective mumble. He was silent for a while, looking straight ahead as we walked. Then he seemed to pull himself together. He took my hand, led me into a small side street and asked me to wait for a moment on the corner. Five minutes later he returned, with two even bigger ice cream cones.

Two days before I was to fly home to Amsterdam, Ronnie Kasrils arrived in Lusaka – a coincidence. He never stayed in one place for long, and our visits to Lusaka seldom coincided. I had known Ronnie since 1974 when he came to Amsterdam with a group of South African poets. I shall never forget my amazement when I later learned that he was also the ANC's head of military intelligence, and since then I have always seen poets in a different light.

I asked Chota to track Ronnie down and make a date for my last evening. Ronnie used various addresses which were all kept very secret. He was one of the most important targets for the South African state security apparatus; but if anyone would be able to contact him it was Chota.

Chota and I took Dora out for my farewell dinner in one of Lusaka's very few restaurants. A couple of glasses of wine helped change her mood to one of noisy gaiety, but soon, after a hair-raising ride in her car and our half-sincere invitation for her to come with us, she again became dejected, dropping us off with cursory goodbyes. I was not to see her again; when I got up to leave the next morning she had already left for work.

Ronnie spread himself comfortably on the sofa, a glass of whisky in his hand. He was obviously delighted by this unexpected meeting. Under the heavy eyebrows his eyes twinkled in curiosity from Chota to me. It was pleasantly cool in the room, the curtains were closed and a Chopin concerto was playing softly in the background. Chota sat beside Ronnie with a bottle of poisonously green soda–pop – he didn't touch alcohol. Ronnie lifted his glass to his old comrade–in–arms and looked at me: "You do know that I just escaped arrest, thanks to Chota?"

Chota laughed but looked uncomfortable. "If he hadn't kept his mouth shut I wouldn't be here." Ronnie swirled his glass, listening to the sound of the ice. They had to be about the same age, both with reading glasses in their jacket pockets, both trying to keep their stomachs flat.

"How long have you known each other?" I asked.

Ronnie laid his hand on Chota's shoulder: "How long now, friend?"

"A long time; more than twenty-five years. Since July 1960. I first saw you during the state of emergency." Chota had an exceptional memory.

"We were experts in blowing up all sorts of things." They looked at each other with pleasure. "When MK was started we joined straight away." Ronnie enjoyed talking about those days. "We were trained by Second World War veterans, and believe it or not, Chota blew up a track under the Victoria Street bridge with fourteen sticks of dynamite." We all burst out laughing, because Chota appeared so gentle. But Ronnie wanted me to share the image of the other Chota – running into action with explosives.

"But the best operation back then was the power pylon in Montclair."

"First of November 1962." Chota added.

"It was on a Thursday evening," Ronnie said. "I know that because right afterwards we went to play cards at Kate's place as usual. We drove there, tied the dynamite round the base of the pylon and set the detonator. We were so cool then and such amateurs! Just as we got to Kate's place the lights flickered a couple of times, and suddenly went out – all the power was cut. Half of Durban was dark."

24

"The Boers just didn't believe it could be the work of Umkhonto," laughed Chota, in a louder voice than I had ever heard him use before. "They thought the Cubans had landed!"

They exchanged more reminiscences, with Ronnie continually making sure that Chota's role received due credit. But close to eleven we decided we couldn't stay longer. Ronnie had no car to take us home, and although the house was not far from Dora's flat, it was not prudent to leave our walk through the streets any later.

Ronnie rose with us. "I'll walk along with you. There's something I want to talk over with you," he said to me. He put on a jacket and a cap. Outside, by the garden gate, he stopped me.

"We need your help," he began. "We're very hard pressed now. It's getting more and more difficult to operate from the front-line states. The Boers are trying to drive us further north, so contact with our people inside South Africa is becoming almost impossible. What they want eventually is to cut us off completely from the resistance inside the country. Pretoria has forced concessions and treaties on the front-line states by keeping them under tremendous pressure, then promising that there'll be no more attacks if they withdraw all support for us, or worse – make our work impossible. It's been especially hard recently for people like Chota and me; we need friends who can provide safe hiding places, who are prepared to operate as fronts for us."

He fell silent, as if giving me time to draw the obvious conclusion for myself.

"And we need them urgently," Ronnie continued, "people who can organise safe houses – a house where a comrade can live inconspicuously, a safe place we can work from. Far too many of us have been picked up because we had no secure refuge. As South Africans, ANC people, we can't just go out and rent houses all over the place; that would attract attention very quickly. It's far too dangerous. So it's safer if other people do it for us: foreigners, political friends, anyone prepared to give us that extra bit of help."

I opened my mouth to speak, but he took me by the shoulders, determined to finish his story. "I'll try to describe the kind of person we're looking for. It has to be someone prepared to take a job in one of the front-line states, and to live as normal a life as possible there, with friends, hobbies, everything. Most importantly, this person of ours must always be able to justify being where he is, with a good cover story, be prepared for any question. That's actually not too difficult. There are so many reasons for someone to want to live in another country, after all: the climate, escape from an unhappy love affair, and so on. The story just has to hang together consistently and logically, and be practised and tested until any question can be answered."

He paused for a moment, but now I waited calmly.

"You'll have to try and find someone who is not already known as a political militant, no-one with a high-profile role in any political movement, no-one who's always marched at the front of a demonstration. That won't be easy, you need very special people for this kind of job.

"And then the house; that'll have to be carefully chosen. Our comrades can help with that – the house has to fit the story, too. Wages in the front-line states are often low, and rents are high. Sometimes we'll have to help financially to be able to rent a house that fulfils our needs. But the difference between income and rent can't be too conspicuous.

"Once everything's ready, job and house, then a comrade can move in. One room needs to be separated off so that the comrade can work undisturbed, and so there's still some privacy, because they could be together for a long time. They agree on security precautions with each other, they're dependent on each other after all; they have to guard one another's backs."

Chota moved closer to us: "Don't forget that a white face has many advantages," he explained softly. "It means that fewer questions are asked; salaries for whites are mostly higher, they have better houses – even in Swaziland. They're less likely to be stopped at roadblocks. They are just not so likely to be suspected of helping us. Whites are still very much a protected species in southern Africa. We must use that fact to our advantage; we have no choice. And that's how you'll have to explain it to people who are prepared to come here. It's not something to feel bad about."

"We need somebody right now in Swaziland," Ronnie took up the thread. "Someone's got to be in place inside a couple of months. But we're going to need a lot more people, in Botswana as well, and in other places. Do you think you can help us?"

It was so quiet that I heard myself swallow. I nodded. But I also felt, and not without some fear, that the safe boundaries of my own familiar patch of territory were being permanently shifted; that organising conferences and demonstrations, collecting money and signatures on petitions, might now cease to be my main concern. I was being drawn closer to the battle lines.

Ronnie said goodbye and hugged me. "I'll be in London next month; after that I can come to Amsterdam if you've found someone."

Chota and I walked back to Dora's flat, keeping to the middle of the road. It was a clear night, and there were hardly any street lights. I looked up at the huge black sky where thousands of stars blended into patches of light between the few bright individual stars whose names I knew. "One day I want to sleep outside in Africa, under a sky like that – but only when all the poisonous snakes and Boers are gone." Chota laughed, put his arm round my shoulder and whispered: "I'll give you a post office box number in Maputo. Write to me ... it's so fine to get a letter now and then when you're underground."

AMSTERDAM – WINTER

I RETURNED FROM THE HEAT OF LUSAKA TO THE GREY DEPRESSION of a Dutch winter. Amsterdam seemed to greet me with cool reserve, as I walked shivering about, re-stocking my kitchen and attempting to feel at home. The linden tree hung frozen against the window pane, and the lock on my bicycle was rusted fast. It took days for the long-unused heater to make an impression on the chill in the house, and I sat wrapped tight in a blanket watching my daughter, back from her stay with grandma, rediscovering her toys with as much delight as if they had all just arrived.

By now Chota must have returned to Swaziland. I was unable to form a mental picture of how he lived there, how he spent his days; that was not something he had told me about. I had no idea either of how Ronnie lived. He would have faded out of sight again somewhere in southern Africa; Angola or Mozambique, Swaziland maybe, or Zimbabwe, or Botswana. South African resistance fighters moved through the front-line areas around the borders of their own country as nervously as antelopes cut off from their watering hole.

For me, Africa was unreachably distant from the moment I walked out of Schiphol airport. I couldn't phone anyone because telephone numbers were unknown, and nobody could, would, or was allowed to say where someone else could be reached. A letter, even if there was an address to send it to, could only be about day-to-day trivia. Out of Africa was indeed out of Africa. Contact with the South Africans was broken until either I went there again, or they came to Europe.

But this time Africa seemed more distant than ever. The longer I thought about what Ronnie had asked of me, the more impossible, the more ridiculous even, his request seemed. How, in the name of anything, could I find someone within such a short time who would be prepared to leave the Netherlands and plunge into the unknown in Swaziland? Where should I begin, and above all, how? There was so much more I would like to have asked Ronnie, and oh, how much easier it would be if he could be close at hand to help me find my way.

I tried to form an idea of the person who would match up to all the criteria. In my mind I made rough sketches of a house in which someone would have to live in hiding – a safe house, a shelter for a long-term resident.

I had seen my father in hiding from the Germans who were rounding up all the young men and forcing them to work in German war industries. He was concealed by my mother and sister in a pit dug out under the floor, and later in an old-fashioned chimney-piece above a stove, standing on two wooden supports he made for himself. The story was very much a part of my parents and their past, and as a child I had found it completely normal, my admiration being mainly for my father's inventiveness. It was only when they had grown old, and I had grown older too, that I understood that escape and hiding go together with survival and the fear of death, and that it can be easier to go underground than to come back out into the open.

However difficult I thought my search for this person would be, I underestimated the fact that many of my generation, born as I had been under the shadow of war, were quite familiar with ideas like resistance and hiding. When I cautiously asked a friend if perhaps he knew of anyone suitable he came up with a name straight away: Andre, a builder, who had just returned from Nicaragua where he had been building houses in the war zone.

A few days later Andre stumped his way up the stairs to my flat. He seemed rather dour and non-committal, as in a roundabout way I tried to explain what I was asking of him – carefully not mentioning names or places. I wanted some kind of reaction before revealing too much. I did draw him a comprehensive picture of the very difficult conditions under which the ANC had to operate in Swaziland. I had an uneasy feeling that I was over-dramatising – trying to play on his feelings.

When I had finished he raised his eyebrows, looked past me, and said:

"No. It's bad timing. I can't go away right now."

After a short silence he went on: "I'll think about it all right, but not yet. But maybe I can help. I'll put you onto a mate of mine, he's in construction too. We were in Nicaragua together. He could be right for you."

Before the week was out they came back together, Andre and Joop. Two strapping great fellows, filling my living room. Joop had an impressive belly, huge hands and traces of cement on the edges of his work boots. His face was surprisingly young above the great body which looked more like that of a fifty-year-old. Beside him Andre appeared taller and wirier than he had on his own.

After gruff introductions they thumped down together onto the sofa. Cigarettes were rolled first, the ceremony leaving shreds of strong tobacco around their feet. They waited in silence for me to begin.

"Has Andre told you why I wanted to see you?" I asked.

"He just mumbled something like 'It's-another-kind-of-a - Nicaragua-thing,'" answered Joop. He waved at the images and masks I'd brought back from Africa over the years, and said: "But this is an Africa house."

More directly and concisely than with Andre – I was more businesslike about Swaziland in particular – I explained what it was all about. The tobacco reappeared.

"I've never had anything to do with South Africa. Or with the ANC. I don't know anything about that kind of work," Joop muttered, and with some effort crossed one leg over the other. "I hope I'm not going to have to explain about how much I'm against apartheid, because I don't feel up to it."

I laughed, to put him at ease.

"How did you end up in Nicaragua?" I asked, looking for common ground.

"Oh, that wasn't so special. A couple of years ago a few of us were doing up a bar. One of the girls working there had just come back from Nicaragua. One day she sailed in and asked, 'Hey Joop, why don't you go and build something in Nicaragua?' We laughed, but I told her, 'Hey, you might just see us do that.' We talked it over – the guys on the crew. Andre was there too. So we were in Nicaragua for three months, building houses and a community centre. Right under the Contras' noses – there was fighting just a couple of miles further up."

"Come on, you don't make those decisions just like that." I exclaimed in disbelief.

"No, of course not. But it wasn't as if it was something new for me. I've been working with solidarity movements since I was a student. I was with them all – Anti-Nato, Greece, whatever ... I lived on the Nieuwmarkt, with all the old Spanish Civil War fighters and Spanish workers. We hung around all the time in the same bars, and we talked..."

He had dropped his studies to find work in a factory, on a production line. He claimed that on the assembly line he'd learned to understand much more about himself and those Spanish workers than he would ever have got from his books. There was something defiant or stubborn in the way he spoke, as if he expected argument and was defending himself in advance, unwilling to discuss decisions taken long ago.

As they drank their beer from the cans, the glasses stayed dry on the table, abruptly Joop said: "I certainly want to give it some thought – what you're asking. I reckon it might just suit me."

Andre looked at me with 'I told you so' in his eyes.

"I can't give you much thinking time." I said quickly, "I've got to get someone out there within a couple of months."

"I don't need much time – just got to talk to my mate. We've got a little construction business. Can't just walk out on him. I'll call you in three days."

During those three days I concentrated my attention on the search for other candidates. I couldn't pin all my hopes on Joop; there were too many reasons why he might pull out. But as I was wondering how I was to find another go-between, chance came to my aid.

As I cycled down the Sarphatikade I saw Wilma in the distance, coming the other way. I didn't know her well, but what I knew was enough. She was a crane operator at a steel mill, and very active in the trade union – a left-wing girl who spoke her mind, straightforward and with plenty of nerve. I'd seen her at a party a while before, and she'd told me how she very much wanted to go to Zimbabwe, because it was an independent African state still being built up, and she needed a change of air anyway.

As we passed I stopped her and asked if we could set up a meeting.

"Of course," she said, cheerful as ever. " What's it about?"

"I'll tell you when we meet."

Before I had even finished my story the next evening her fists were clenched in triumph over her head.

"I knew it!" she burst out, eyes shining, "I knew you were going to ask me something special! I've always known – if I'm ever asked to do something like this, wherever it is, I'll go straight away. I've just been waiting for this!"

"Why?" I asked, thoroughly taken aback.

"Come on! You of all people must understand – internationalism, the international brigades. That's always been really important for me. When Klaas de Jonge was arrested I just wished I'd been asked to do that work! And now you are asking me! And it's come exactly at the right moment; I've had it with the job, and I'm sick of the shift work. I want something else."

She told me about her schooldays, her friends and her work. There were many similarities with Joop. After a time at university she too had left to find a job in the steel industry. During the 1970s that choice had been made by a fair number of political militants, especially those from the radical left. I had never really been able to understand how you could give up a place at university; but it certainly took courage, and that I admired.

I insisted that she take at least a week to think about it. It was a big step, after all, and not without danger. She looked at me a shade disdainfully. She wasn't the least bit worried, why should I be? Halfway down the stairs she stopped, turned a radiant face up to me and said: "Oh, I know already. I'm going!"

I'd sent word to Ronnie via London that I was waiting for him to come to Amsterdam. And Joop called: he wanted to go, even at such short notice.

Before Ronnie came I approached a third candidate: Lucia. She had worked for years with the *Anti-Apartheidsbeweging Nederland* (AABN), the Anti-Apartheid Movement of the Netherlands, which was of course completely at odds with what Ronnie had said about being known in political circles. But she had been away from the organisation for some time and had not joined any other political group. I had been very impressed by the dedication and commitment she brought to her work.

She had also maintained long-term personal friendships with several South Africans, was very discreet and her knowledge of the political situation in southern Africa might well turn out to be useful. We would just have to find some way to camouflage her past connection with the AABN.

Years later, as we walked together through the market in Lusaka, she told me she had been exhilarated that I had asked her to take on such a task.

"You warned me so strongly of the risks, almost as if you felt guilty about them. But it didn't scare me off at all. To me it was worth the risk. You wanted me to take time to make the decision. I did – but only for your sake. Even before I got home that evening I was already saying yes – I remember I was already working out solutions for all sorts of practical problems, like what to do with my house, what to say to my mother, and who gets my bicycle..."

Ronnie and I waited for Joop on a corner of the Rijnstraat. He was to pick us up at exactly seven o'clock. We stood under the awning of a travel agent's shop, and Ronnie asked if I had any news of Helene Passtoors. Her trial had begun in March, and only then had it become clear what she had endured: endless interrogation sessions, and a long time in solitary confinement. Her mental state had deteriorated so badly that she had needed four weeks' care in a hospital psychiatric ward. Now she had been charged with high treason and terrorism.

"What about her children?" asked Ronnie. I had no more news of Helene herself than he had already heard from her lawyers.

"I see them now and then. They're having a hard time."

"And Klaas's children?"

"The same. They all get together sometimes."

He pulled his cap further down over his eyes.

"It's important for families to be well informed if something goes wrong. You'll have to make sure you know how to reach parents and other next of kin, for these new people as well."

A van pulled up in front of us, and I saw Joop sitting high above us in the driver's seat. I clambered up into the cab, and Ronnie slid in beside me. We drove out of town, along the Amstel river, until we found a suitable coffee shop in Ouderkerk, not busy and unlikely to be frequented by anyone we knew.

Ronnie was experienced. For almost thirty years he had been asking people of the most diverse characters and backgrounds to participate in South Africa's struggle for justice, but there was no sign at all of his enthusiasm or persuasiveness wearing thin.

I listened to him avidly, wondering how much self-confidence you had to radiate in order to presume to ask others to resign from their jobs, invent stories to satisfy family and friends, and trust their fate to the hands of complete strangers, these people with whom they share no more than political conviction and ideals. But people commonly put themselves in danger for far less, of course.

It all sounded so ordinary, now that I heard him talking, while in fact the whole idea really verged on the insane. A double life in a land where you've never been before. Living every day in danger and insecurity. No chance to talk about what you're really doing, not with anyone, not even when things become almost unbearable; not even when, from sheer desperate loneliness, you'd talk to a perfect stranger.

Ronnie knew just how Joop must be feeling:

"If you've lived your whole life in the country and you come to the big city for the first time, the traffic seems deadly dangerous. But after a while you realise that you've become a part of the city. You've learnt to weigh up the dangers. You cross the street almost without thinking, and become a part of that same traffic. That's what will happen down there. All the things which at first seem impossibly difficult will be easy once you've settled in."

With a friendly smile he waited for Joop to react. Joop just nodded, and when Ronnie asked if he wanted more time to think, he replied with a brief, stubborn head-shake. "No. I'll do it."

In April I received a letter from Chota. His letters reached me by various roundabout routes. Sometimes there were two envelopes, one inside the other, closed with sellotape, bearing stamps from Zimbabwe, Nigeria or England. He probably gave the letters to one man, who passed them on to another. Finally they were taken in to a post office somewhere in Africa, or carried by hand, covered in huge postmarks, all the way to Europe.

He complained of hearing nothing from me for a long time. I couldn't understand it – I always sent my letters to him at the box number he had given me. A courier was supposed to take them on to him.

But in a hurried postscript he wrote that three of my letters had just been brought all at once. They were probably being stockpiled at the postal address – as if three letters were more worthwhile to deliver or receive than one!

"I shall read them again and again, especially when I feel down. It is so very lonely here, and I don't seem to handle that so well anymore. When shall I see you again? I have so much to tell you, and there's so little I can put on paper."

He signed himself: "E".

At the end of April Mac Maharaj phoned me; he did not say from where, and I couldn't tell from the noises on the line. Sometimes I could hear from the static and the echoes, before the caller spoke, that a connection was being made with Africa; as if I held my ear to a pipe through which the sound hissed across thousands of kilometres to reach me. He didn't say who he was, just chatted on to give me a chance to recognise his voice. When I let him know I knew who he was, with a long drawn-out "Oohhh hellooo!" He explained briefly that he was coming to Amsterdam and gave me his arrival time and flight number, adding that he was coming especially to see me, and not as a guest of the AABN.

I had first met Mac in 1977 in Nigeria, during a United Nations conference. A few weeks before that he had secretly left South

Africa, after twelve years in the cell next to Nelson Mandela, waiting for his freedom. After his release he had been put under a banning order, which again severely curtailed his freedom of movement. But his fighting spirit was unbroken, and there had been nothing for it but to search outside the borders of South Africa for space to apply his enormous energies.

We had met in a bare, unbearably hot hotel room in Lagos, as cockroaches scuttled to and fro and the distant noise of a crowd reached us through the window – a thief was being flogged in public. Mac had sat on the edge of the bed and talked with us, the anti-apartheid activists from Europe. He was short and slender, and had one immobile glass eye behind his spectacles. A permanent friendly smile almost succeeded in concealing his natural guile; if one watched and listened carefully, a dangerous under-layer revealed itself, which was better left unchallenged. His kindly and obliging tone of voice disguised a sharp tongue, which he only used with good reason. That day with us, however, he was all charm and grace. He listened attentively; we wanted his opinions on a thousand-and-one things, like a well-behaved school class sitting at the feet of a favourite teacher. He was very much the centre of attention.

After that I came across him fairly often, mostly by chance: at a meeting in London about political prisoners, in the ANC office in Brussels, and once we kept each other company on a flight to New York. I was reading Joseph Conrad's *Heart of Darkness* for the first time; he had already read it three times on Robben Island.

Mac inspired confidence, we shared many political opinions, and he treated me with consideration and warmth, as if I were one of the family. Nevertheless, I was never to quite work out just how much distance he kept between himself and me or others, nor manage to guess what was really going through his mind.

Early one evening I picked him up from Schiphol airport. In my flat, over strong coffee and chicken from the late-night store, he demanded full reports on my child, the AABN, and how I myself was doing. We talked trivia for a while. I made fresh coffee and set myself to wait. He took his time, pushed his plate aside, cleaned the last of the chicken from his teeth with a broken match, hidden behind the other hand, and then began to speak, almost casually, carefully choosing his words.

Within the foreseeable future – nothing was definite yet, everything was still at the planning stage – he was to go underground in the front-line states, or more probably in South Africa itself. We were talking about an operation led by a very small group, known to as few people as possible, for security reasons – not more than five. The operation was under the direct command of Oliver Tambo, president of the ANC.

Mac lit a cigarette, pulled at his beard, and once more emphasised that this was a very confidential discussion indeed.

"A decision was taken some time ago," he said, "that the ANC leadership should go into South Africa, underground, to unite the resistance and give political leadership. Of course an operation like this needs careful preparation. There are all sorts of technical problems involved."

He stood up and walked over to the bookcase. Running a finger over the book spines, he explained that one of the problems facing them was that he was well-known to the South African security police. He had been in prison, they had photos and other information on him in their files. They had detailed descriptions of other comrades, too, who were to be involved in the operation – information gathered by spies, or defectors.

The security police noted any changes in the appearance of ANC members they were interested in, and their computers could in minutes give a description of any wanted person. He didn't know how far this actually went, but it was better to allow for very advanced police methods. If Mac was to operate underground with any success then he would have to drastically change his appearance.

He turned, looked at me with a slight smile on his face and asked if I knew of people, professionals, who could help him to build a good enough disguise – not just a quick change of moustache, but a thorough disguise to change him completely, and which he would be able to use for a long time – years maybe – with no danger of being recognised.

I nodded, more to show that I understood what he had told me than because I had an answer ready. At the same time I was allowing my wide circle of friends and acquaintances to parade before my eyes, searching out actors and theatre people. That was the world where I would have to find the necessary experts.

"You'll have to give me some time, but I'll find someone," I promised, and just then a face appeared in my private parade – the sad clown's face of an actor with whom, years before, I had had a brief affair.

Mac sat down again, opposite me at the table, lighting another cigarette. There was more: did I know experts in communications, computer programmers? It quickly became clear to me that this could well become the most important, but at the same time most difficult, element of the whole plan. Reliable contact with the people outside, with the ANC leadership in Lusaka, would be of critical importance. He wanted to be in direct contact with them, but with no danger that his messages could be intercepted by the enemy.

Communication in particular had always been one of the weak links in resistance work. Telephone lines were tapped, the mail was unreliable and it often took couriers too long to deliver a message. Mac wanted a communications system he could depend on from moment to moment of every day.

Gradually it was dawning on me that he was planning a major operation. Everything seemed to fit into some comprehensive and well-thought-out scheme that he had been working on for some time. He would talk for a while, and then lapse into silence.

During the days he stayed with me he went late to bed, and was up again before six. He paced the house restlessly, with an eye patch over his empty socket. He spoke only of his plans now, and leapt from one subject to another. His mind was working at full speed.

There had to be bags and suitcases, with secret compartments or false bottoms. Disguises, communications, technical devices, everything would have to be better than it had ever been before, every detail would have to be re-examined. Above all, and this seemed to excite him most of all, each of these elements to be integrated into the building of the operation must carry its own element of surprise.

To plan this he took the enemy's world as his starting point. They had to be enticed into the trap of their own narrow prejudices, so that a veil could be drawn over reality. He was searching for a balance between what the opponent expected and assumed, and what he wanted to achieve. He weighed up their strengths against his ability to deceive them by creating illusions which he himself could control.

Floris was a designer, inventor, dreamer and visionary. When he was asked to create the sets and escape tricks for an opera about the American illusionist Houdini, he had been able to bring all these qualities into play, and had immersed himself fully in the world of visual deception and manipulation of appearances.

His work bench was always covered in cardboard boxes which could be folded in many different ways; you couldn't work out precisely what you were seeing, where the opening was, how mere square sheets could fit together so flawlessly. I couldn't see the secret even after he had explained it to me.

When Mac returned after a few weeks – he had given me just enough time to make some appointments – Floris was the first person we visited. He had understood immediately what we were looking for, and he produced books about Houdini to show us that a trick is always based on a simple idea. The true power lies in the illusion – how can you lead someone to believe that what is seen is also true? Floris was in his element, and sketched for us a trick which had been described to him by Houdini's aged assistant.

"The lid of the chest is closed, with Houdini inside. The chest is further secured by locks and huge keys. Then the keys are thrown away with a big dramatic gesture. Two men with axes stand on the stage, ready to hack the box apart if something goes wrong. The audience hold their breath ... will he make it or not? A cloth is thrown over the chest, and after another few seconds he reappears, beside it. Voila!

"You only have to imagine a kitchen cabinet, with a sliding section that can be opened from inside, and you understand the illusion. It's a bit of a let-down to know how it works; believing is much more fun than knowing!" Floris crumpled his drawing into a ball and threw it over his shoulder into the wastepaper basket. Mac laughed, and leafed through the books with interest.

Floris described an illusion for which he had constructed the scenery himself – the disappearing woman.

"The conjurer stands on the stage, with his beautiful assistant beside him. He announces that she is about to disappear. There are some steps worked into the set, up which the magician climbed to reach the stage. Dramatically he holds up a huge cloth in front of his assistant, talks and talks, then whips the cloth away and voila! The beautiful assistant is gone! She's hidden in the steps, which visually appears impossible – the steps only look about ten centimetres deep – but that's where she went!"

Mac became very interested.

"How small can a space be and still hide a human being?" he asked.

"Very small. Just the same as if you want to crawl through a small gap. With a person of reasonably normal shape if the head and shoulders can pass, so can the rest."

Mac nodded and made a note on his pad. "Can you apply these theories if you want to disguise someone?" he wanted to know.

"Of course," Floris replied. "The South African security services have a certain image of an ANC guerrilla. Some people are stopped at the border, others aren't."

"What if I disguise myself as a businessman?" asked Mac.

"Perhaps. Something like that. A smart businessman doesn't fit their impression of a dangerous terrorist. Business people have other interests, they belong on their side. But that kind of disguise will only work if you've thought about it carefully, worked it out to the last detail. It's always the little mistakes which attract unwelcome attention – some detail you've overlooked. A disguise can be very simple. Even slight changes can really disrupt someone's preconceived idea of you."

Floris took a raincoat from the rack and pulled it on.

"There was one time I'd agreed to meet a friend at a bus stop. I stood there waiting, wondering where on earth he'd got to; but he'd been standing beside me all along. He's a pretty hefty, good-looking man. The bloke standing beside me was a rather pathetic little chap; all he'd done was put on a waterproof jacket with the hood up and the drawstring pulled tight around his face. He stood slumped, withdrawn into himself. And that's all he needed to do!"

Floris straightened up and pulled the hood off his head, adding: "But for the actual technical work of creating a disguise you'll have to go to someone else. That's a very specialised skill."

I had called my old friend, my tragic actor, and agreed to meet in a bar after his show. As always he'd had enough, wanted to leave the profession and go sailing away on his boat. I waited patiently until he remembered that there was something I wanted to ask him, and once I'd awakened his interest he thought hard for a while about trustworthy make-up artists, wig makers and costume designers.

"Not especially political types, eh?" he said first, then suddenly sat up in excitement and cried: "Winnie! She's the one you can ask. Winnie Gallis – make-up!"

After that we both drank a few beers too many, and I left quickly before I could again fall in love with his sadness.

On the Prinsengracht, up among the rafters of an old canal-side merchant's house, Winnie shared a studio with a colleague.

Ahead of me Mac climbed the stairs which became progressively narrower, the ceilings lower on every floor we passed. The last flight was so steep we had to pull ourselves up by the bannisters, ducking our heads.

The studio looked like a wigmaker's workshop from the eighteenth century, as if the period's white-powdered wigs had only yesterday been removed. Wig stands were everywhere, curling irons hung from the rafters, false moustaches were clipped and pinned in rows on strips of cloth. Dozens of delicate pincers, scissors, brushes and combs were strewn around, amongst hanks of hair sorted by colour.

With lightning movements of their fingers the two women were planting little tufts of hair in nets stretched over wooden spheres. I watched carefully over their shoulders, but couldn't see exactly how they made the knots.

"If I try and do it slowly, it goes wrong," said Winnie, and let her hands rest. She had found it the most normal thing in the world to offer her skills to the ANC, and now sat looking with curiosity at Mac as he settled back surrounded by the wigs, completely at ease. While he was still explaining to them how he wanted to accomplish a complete change of appearance, they were already prowling around him, plucking at his hair, running their fingers through it to check the thickness, and pulling at it. His hairline was low at the front, and apparently this was a problem; the women discussed it over his head. Mac resigned himself to their attentions. The edge of the wig would have to begin above the hairline; otherwise it would be obvious the hair was false. They decided to use light grey hair, with strong curls, in a distinguished cut suitable for the older businessman Mac wanted to become. He would be able to keep the hair in shape with curling irons, and they would teach him how to put a wig on and how to take it off, so he could also quickly divest himself of his disguise to meet people to whom he must be recognisable, as he had told them would be necessary.

The moustache and short goatee beard, so characteristic of his face, would have to come off. Winnie took Polaroid photos and made drawings in order to be able to reproduce them exactly.

"A chic businessman," said Winnie, "an affluent older gentleman."

Her colleague produced an expensive black silk suit belonging to her husband. "He won't miss it anyway," she said, not entirely convincingly. Her husband must have been unusually tall, because the trouser legs were at least twenty centimetres too long. The suit would have to be altered everywhere; taken in here, let out somewhere else, a bit more padding in the shoulders. Pulling and stretching, they pinned the suit around Mac, until it fitted remarkably well. Extra pockets could be made in the shoulder padding, to hide papers or money.

"I'll ask Yan Tax to alter the suit," Winnie said, and without looking up quickly added:

"Yan's all right. I only ask people who are all right."

I found later that Winnie judged colleagues simply in terms of "all right" or not. The criteria she used for this judgement varied from personal friendship to someone's ability to make her laugh during a long, boring film shoot. Nevertheless we agreed that she would always consult me before anyone was asked to help, and that new people would be told as little as possible.

They took measurements of Mac's head, jaw and shoulders, while I was given instructions on buying expensive shirts with matching ties. Once more Winnie anxiously examined the hair. The black hair at the front, which would remain visible, would have to be dyed. That was a tough job, because grey to black is easy, but to change black to grey a real hairdresser would have to be called in.

"I'll ask Michiel. He's the best I know." She looked at me sideways, with a glint in her eyes.

"He's all right!" I ventured.

At last all the measurements had been taken, sketches and photographs taken, and I was given a substantial shopping list. Winnie was to let me know when everything was ready.

A broken shower, a frame for an AABN exhibition, or a loose bridge in my mouth: if I ever had technical problems, I never wasted much thought on them, but called Diederik straight away. He was one of those irreplaceable friends who would always have just the right little bolt to fit just a particular little nut. I had met him when he was a dentistry student who played bassoon in a classical orchestra. Now he was my dentist, and he played saxophone with a big band.

For some time Diederik had been working on the development of night-vision glasses. After my visit to Lusaka I had talked to him about what Chota had described to me so vividly – how in the front-line states the danger came at night; how the comrades in their houses or in the bush had to trust solely their ears because of the limitations of the human eye. The enemy usually struck after sunset; houses were surrounded in silence, and cars approached without lights. Night-vision glasses could give you the eyes of an owl.

On his days off, Diederik would snuffle around flea markets or look for obscure little shops in side streets full of army surplus equipment. Now he'd found a dealer who sold the components he needed to build the night-vision glasses.

Every so often I called round to see how things were progressing, and during one such visit he told me he had made a set of dummy front teeth for a friend of his, an actor. They had been used for a film, and the results had been surprising. I told Mac about the dummy teeth, of course.

When we left Winnie, Mac and I strolled together beside the canals and over the bridges to the Lauriergracht, where Diederik lived in a converted warehouse dating from the eighteenth century. He inhabited this monument with casual flair. His floor of the building consisted just of one great space crammed high with musical instruments, radio components and mysterious scrap metal objects piled on every surface. A collection of cameras stood on a shelf up by the ceiling, a piano against the wall, mounds of clothing and towels on the bed. I always felt very much at home in this magnificent junk store; it was a fine and familiar environment. Years before, when I had been at the AABN office every day, I had come here if I was tired or had a headache, to take a daytime nap on his bed. The house was opposite the office.

With one arm Diederik swept aside a mountain of letters, nuts and bolts, angle irons, latches, reeds for his bassoon and coffee cups. Smiling shyly he made delicious-smelling espresso coffee in one of the many machines in his kitchen, while two cats wove an intricate pattern around his legs.

Mac looked round with amusement, asking what things were, and what they could do. Diederik gave exhaustive replies, with a slight air of apology. Within fifteen minutes Mac had developed a warm liking for him. I could hear it in the tone of his voice.

After the coffee, the subject of teeth was broached. Diederik carefully lifted Mac's upper lip, pushed his bottom lip down, and looked inside with a dentist's swift glance. With his fingers he traced a possible construction for Mac's mouth. It would have to look very natural. Diederik hesitated; it would also have to be very thin, but not too weak.

"For it to really look like tooth enamel you have to use very hard material," he explained. "Material that you can polish to a high gloss. Not plastic – that's not strong enough." He sighed and looked thoughtful. It must not break.

He wanted to try and make a front set to clamp over the real teeth, and follow the unevenness of the side teeth, for firmness. It would have to meet the gums exactly. That way you automatically get thicker teeth, which changes the whole face, and that was the idea; the character of a face is strongly determined by the position and size of the teeth. Along the bottom set he would be able to build in small packing-pieces, to broaden the look of the jaw; this would also change the sound of Mac's voice.

We agreed that the next day he would make plaster casts of the top and bottom set in his surgery. Now he wanted to cook for us. He talked, petted and fed his cats, did things with saucepans, poured us a glass of wine, and cooked something absolutely delicious and totally new to me.

Later in the evening I reminded him of the night-vision glasses. He looked through a box in the bottom of a cupboard, retrieving a metal tube which he laid on the table. Mac picked it up. Diederik explained that the light of the stars, or even the reflection of city lights on clouds would give enough light for an acceptable image in the dark. Good enough to see people at long range.

"May I try it, can you switch it on?" asked Mac. The lights were turned off, curtains closed, and Mac put the viewer to his eye. I tried it as well, and saw one of the cats jump up onto the kitchen counter and lick a coffee cup. Everything was green, clear and sharp.

Maputo – summer 1986

I had been to Maputo once, years before, but this time I found I was able to enjoy the city's rather dilapidated beauty: the grand avenue with its softly rustling palm trees, and the skilfully-wrought iron balconies standing out against the pastel colours of the houses. I discovered the strong, briny smell of the Indian Ocean, and in the evenings its salt was in the sheen of oil on my skin. War was still being waged outside the city and the poverty was becoming steadily more visible, but this visit to the city was so much more pleasant than my last. Perhaps it was because I now was waiting for Chota.

As soon as it had been clear that I would have to fly to Lusaka to sort out some AABN business, I had let him know by courier that we would be able to meet in Maputo. I had no idea if my message had reached him. I had now been waiting for almost a week, during the day inspecting the façades of the old colonial buildings and the murals dating from the revolution – new to me, because I had never before had the time to look at them. They also served as an excuse to avoid meeting the eyes of the many beggars, and of the war-wounded queuing silent and resigned in long lines outside the local hospitals and government offices. I kept my eyes on the architecture as I passed these queues, mainly so as not to look like any other nosy westerner. Bitter complaints and anger would have somehow been more bearable than the palpable silence surrounding those sad little crowds.

Ideally I would like to have gone to the beach for a swim, but I had been warned that South African saboteurs had buried land mines in the beach sand to remind the Mozambicans that Pretoria did not approve of their government's support, however discreet, for the ANC. These mines had already claimed victims.

Still, there had been hope, two years before, when the Frelimo government had signed an accord with Pretoria. The South Africans had promised to end their support for the rebel groups which were keeping the country in a state of war, and had promised economic aid. A few South African trucks had arrived, loaded with apples and powdered milk, and that was it. The South African government didn't honour the agreement; in the countryside the Mozambicans were slaughtered by Renamo, and in the towns they were close to starvation.

The government of Mozambique had stuck by the terms of the treaty, however, and had expelled large numbers of ANC fighters – with apologies. This shouldn't be seen as a betrayal of brotherhood, they said. The South Africans had forced them to this at gunpoint. The ANC's representation had been cut back to a handful of people.

But the continuing stream of young blacks leaving South Africa was not to be contained. Every day groups of them arrived via Swaziland, bringing news from home. Nearly six thousand people had been arrested by the South African police under the state of emergency which had now been in force for just seven weeks. They had defended themselves, organised street committees, driven back the troops with stones, and had dug pits to trap police vehicles. But the police had hit back hard, had sent criminals in against them, and in the school compounds armed soldiers had appeared, with dogs. The young people had strengthened their self-defence groups, but eventually, exhausted and with too many friends lost, they climbed over the border fence to ask the ANC for weapons and training.

In Maputo they had to await whatever the ANC leaders decided for them. Would they be allowed to go to Angola for military training, or would they be sent to Tanzania for schooling? What they wanted most of all was a military crash course so as to be able to go home with guns and dynamite and pay the Boers back in their own coin.

There was always plenty of activity around the newcomers. Cars drove back and forth between the border and the houses where the newcomers were received. All of them wrote their life stories: where they came from, the organisations they had worked with, who their friends had been. They were being screened. It was hard to tell who was a rotten apple or a potential asset.

Sometimes I sat with them in the garden. Just boys, they kept their faces hidden under their caps, but you could see by their bodies that they were no older than fifteen or sixteen.

"Have you ever met Tambo?" they would ask, or: "Is it cold in Holland?"

Everyone was in a hurry. There was too much to do for too few people. Every morning before breakfast Bobby, who had shared a cell with Chota for ten years, would come rushing in before breakfast, just to announce that Chota might arrive any day – everything was ready to smuggle him over the border, and it really couldn't be much longer now. Then Bobby would rush off again to distribute food packets to the ANC houses, or give a lift to someone with no transport.

Maud called by, an English woman who had been married to a South African. She had come to pick up the money I had smuggled in from Lusaka. It was a lot, they had told me, carefully packed in luxury soap boxes. They were desperate for it – South African currency for the comrades going home. Maud tore the boxes open, counted the money adroitly, and cursed: yet again too little. I asked her if she knew when Chota would arrive. She shrugged; she had no idea. She rushed away again, leaving me feeling very uneasy. Surely he had received my message. Why didn't he arrive?

Finally I was invited out for a day by the sea. Albie Sachs, a South African lawyer who had lived in Maputo for years, knew of a stretch of beach guaranteed free of mines, and Jeremy Brickhill, a friend from Harare on a visit to study slurry pit projects in farming cooperatives, also fancied a swim. On Sunday morning we all dragged beach chairs, blankets and ice water out of the car, and set off in single file behind Albie who strode confidently ahead.

Jeremy and I dropped our clothes by Albie, who was content with his deck chair and book, crossed the burning sand with a few great leaps, and cooled our feet in the water. We went for a long walk at the edge of the surf, where the only danger was from a few unfriendly blue jellyfish.

Jeremy spoke of his time in the Zapu liberation army, and then endlessly about the great importance of slurry pits for the farming cooperatives that were to be the salvation of Africa.

He was amusing and cheerful, and I enjoyed the swimming, and the feeling of the sand between my toes.

I had the taste now, and the next day I was back at the safe patch of beach, this time with Joy Harnden, an activist from Johannesburg. We sat in the shadow of the trees, as it was very hot that day, even by the water.

She told me enthusiastically about the anti-apartheid organisation she worked for; about the picnics they organised in city parks, raising money to help children in the townships. I found her rather endearing, perhaps rather naïve, but then I always very much enjoyed meeting young whites who had broken loose from their protected environment and who weren't afraid to take risks. We swam, ran back across the sand, and while we dried ourselves she told me that her dream was to come to Amsterdam to see how we worked there. She asked for the office telephone number, and promised to do her best to get in touch with us as quickly as possible. I dozed in the shade for another fifteen minutes, then heard a car horn: Bobby had come to fetch me.

But my pleasant memories of the beach at Maputo were wiped away by events which took place not long after those couple of sweet days.

One year after our walk, Jeremy was blown up inside his car parked outside a shopping centre in Harare. He was very seriously burned all over his body. Six months later, on a Mozambican public holiday, Albie again decided to go to the beach. Just after nine o'clock his car was blown up. He lost his right arm, and the sight in one eye. Since then the names of the South African security apparatus agents who carried out those attacks have been made known.

And then on February the third, 1989, the South African newspaper *Daily News* reported that security police Major-General Basie Smit had proudly announced at a press conference that Joy Harnden was one of his trained intelligence agents. He said that Harnden had worked for five years as an infiltrator inside the ANC and its front organisations, where she had been entrusted with sensitive duties. She had provided the state with very important intelligence.

I had only a couple of days left of my stay in Maputo when Bobby pounded on my door very early one morning. Breathlessly he shouted through the window that Chota was coming. He had crossed the border in the night and might arrive in the city at any moment. I dressed quickly, combed my hair, and took up a station by the window.

It was another three hours before the doorbell rang. I opened the door to a mass of people crowded into the yard, with triumph on their faces as if they had finally tracked down someone long missing, and brought him home. Some of them I had never seen; they had come along to join in the welcome. Behind them, only visible because he was the tallest by a head, stood Chota. They poured inside and I put my arms around him. He looked like a tramp, in a suit several sizes too big, covered in dust. Bobby giggled like an excited teenager, slapped him on the shoulder, and winked at me. The crowd had made its chattering way to the living room and settled there, with Maud dominating the conversation. Everyone wanted news from Swaziland. Chota let go of my hand, found somewhere to sit, and wiped his face with a tired gesture. He didn't answer their questions, just looked at me, laughing. The questions kept coming, about bomb explosions in Wimpy bars and raids in the Transvaal, and when he still did not react they started a discussion amongst themselves, provocative and loud, trying to tempt some reaction from him.

I wished they would all go away so we could be alone. When the noisy crowd did finally leave, curiosity unsatisfied but bearing his promise that they'd meet later on, he slumped back, exhausted. Beside the chair lay three small tattered plastic bags containing papers and documents which wouldn't fit into his suitcases. He felt dirty and wanted to take a shower; his luggage was supposed to be arriving soon with clean clothes.

I made coffee, and he asked how much longer I could stay. I told him.

"Only three days..." he repeated in disappointment, and explained that my message had only reached him two days before, at a moment when he couldn't easily leave. Then everything possible had gone wrong before transport was organised to take him to the border. He had crossed over on foot through the grass, and been picked up by another car on the Mozambique side.

The suitcases didn't arrive that evening, and Chota fell asleep early. In the morning the doorbell rang – Maud. She shoved at the door before I'd got the security chain off, stamped inside, and banged her handbag down on the table.

Her mouth was pulled into an angry line.

"It's not my fault," she shouted in her piercing voice. "It's not my fault!" She looked dishevelled.

We looked at her enquiringly.

"I got home late last night, dead beat. I just didn't have the energy to lug your bags up the stairs, or to bring them over here. I left them in the boot of the car."

There was a long, painful silence.

Chota groaned.

"Oohh, nooo …"

"Yes, they stole everything. Other stuff too, much more important than your clothes," she exclaimed defensively. Chota said nothing.

"Don't worry," she was already by the door, "I can get some money together and buy you new clothes."

Chota was just staring straight in front of him, crushed. In those suitcases had been everything he possessed: a suit given to him by his family, a pair of shoes belonging to a friend, all his cassette tapes, and a present for me.

The next day Maud picked us up in her car, and drove us to the Foreign Currency Shop where with foreign money one could purchase clothing which was not to be had anywhere else in Maputo.

She strode along the racks of shirts, pulling out armfuls to look at.

"I'm pressed for time," she said coldly. Chota protested. He did not want bright, conspicuous clothing.

"I'm underground," he pleaded in a whisper, and pushed the shirts back on to the rack. Maud sighed as if she was dealing with a difficult child, pulled a face towards me and pushed a dark blue shirt into his hands, pointing to the changing room. I hurriedly searched through the trousers and jackets for something he might like, but when I was ready to suggest a smart and practical combination, the bill was already paid and Chota was standing by the exit with a bag full of clothes.

Maud dropped us off at the house, and once inside we stood together, looking out of the window at the ocean which that day was flat and grey. A few low fishing boats moved across it, seagulls crowding behind them. Chota held my hand in silence. The bag of clothes stood in the kitchen, beside the cardboard box we were using for rubbish.

"Let's go to the beach tomorrow, it's peaceful there. I know a safe place." I said.

There was an old Volkswagen we could borrow. I just had to pick up my swimming costume from Bobby's house, where it had been left behind after the last beach expedition; he had given me a key. I unlocked the door, pushed it open – and set off the alarm, a deafening continuous bell, locked in a steel box on the front of the house.

We looked at each other, horrified. I opened the door further and pushed Chota inside. That hellish noise must be audible over half of Maputo. Chota had no papers, had entered Mozambique illegally, and could under no circumstances attract any attention. How could we turn the damned thing off? Perhaps it stopped automatically after a time, perhaps not. We pulled drawers and cupboards open, looking for a screwdriver to open the box.

The alarm howled mercilessly on, making my head ring. On the street by the garden fence a few children and an old man appeared. They stood quietly staring at the house. Sunday morning in Maputo. Deserted, as if everyone was in church. Oh God! The police might come at any moment!

Chota had to go, out of the house. I had a valid passport, I was a foreigner and could justify my presence: a tourist, just visiting, and an alarm no one had told me about. But he had to leave, we decided. I stood looking at him as he walked down the street, but he stopped and waited at the first corner as if he was hesitating, unwilling to leave me alone. I waved him further away. The children and the old man were looking back and forth between the two of us.

I ran back into the house and tore at all the electricity wires I could find in the corridor, but with no effect. I found a screwdriver which was far too small, and went outside to sit on the step and pull myself together. How long had the bell been ringing? Fifteen, thirty minutes? I felt exhausted, but I couldn't stay sitting there and went to the kitchen to make some coffee, determined to just ignore that hysterical noise. It would surely stop of its own accord eventually. My hands were shaking so much that I dropped the coffee pot, which shattered on the floor.

I ran back outside. There was now a substantial crowd gathered. The old man had lost his prime position, and the children had made themselves comfortable on the bonnet of the old Volkswagen; but there was still no sign of a uniform.

From the kitchen I brought out a chair and a pair of scissors, climbed up, opened the box with the point of the scissors and pulled out some wires. Suddenly the noise stopped. The silence was shocking. Exhausted, I sat down on the chair. After a minute or two the spectators drifted away and the street was empty. I heard a bird singing. Chota approached, walking fast, pulled me inside and sat me down at the kitchen table. I laughed at him, and then burst into tears.

Bobby and Chota brought me to the airport. I was tired and shivering. I had not been able to sleep all night, and had kept Chota awake too. With severe stomach pain I had gone to sit in a chair by the window, wanting to talk to rid myself of a feeling of disappointment, but not knowing how. I felt betrayed by my expectations, nurtured in Amsterdam, of long walks along the beach and meals together in restaurants looking out over the water. Our time had been far too brief, and the reality of Mozambique did not permit such delusions. I was angry with Chota, too; he had grown used to being satisfied with so very little. Every disappointment, every setback, he just swallowed calmly as a matter of course, as if he had in advance relinquished any right to comfort.

He had come to stand behind me, softly massaging my shoulders but saying nothing. Then I had felt I was being unreasonable, but had tried to convince him that he too had a right to some personal happiness. He had gently twisted my hair into a braid and kissed my neck, saying softly that for now all he could try to do was to survive from one day to the next.

And now I was going, leaving danger behind; he was staying. The distance between us would involve far more than just those few thousand miles.

Chota sat beside me in the back seat of the car and spoke in a low voice of Joop and Lucia. They would soon be flying to Swaziland and he was very much looking forward to their arrival. I watched his face with its great dark eyes and felt relief that there at least was something I could do for him.

"I'll try to come to Amsterdam for Christmas," he said. He put his arm round me and pulled me close.

"Then we can spend lots of time together."

I laid my head on his shoulder and without hesitation transferred all my dreams and expectations to Christmas; with snow halfway up the windows, an icy wind whistling around the house and a glow of heat from my gas fire.

I was breaking my journey for two days in Lusaka, then flying home via Rome, where I had to wait a few hours in transit for my connection to Amsterdam. We landed in Rome at four in the morning. I waited listlessly in the huge transit hall for my flight to be called. My hand luggage stood beside me. Inside, in a plastic bag, carefully wrapped in paper and cushioned by magazines, were plaster casts I had made of the teeth of two ANC people who were soon to come to Amsterdam for disguises. Mac had warned me before my trip that I should bring everything I needed to make the casts, and Diederik had in one evening taught me to make the paste in a rubber bowl, and shown me how to use the metal forms which would fit around the teeth. The two men had reported to my hotel room in Lusaka and had watched my preparations suspiciously, as if they were being forced to undergo surgery performed by a first-year medical student. With a flourish I had smeared the paste into the forms. They had each obediently opened their mouths, and I pressed the forms down around their teeth, let it dry a little too long, and then had to use all the strength I possessed to pull the whole thing loose again. They had felt around with their tongues to make sure everything they had come with was still there, and departed with at least as much relief as if they'd been to the dentist.

Diederik would be able to begin the preparatory work for their new teeth.

In Rome airport I dozed off, jerked awake, fell asleep again – until I was woken by shouts of "thieves, thieves!", in several languages. A man and a woman were looking around them in despair, and the consternation was spreading. Everyone had had something stolen. I pulled my bag towards me and felt for the plastic bag ... gone. Gone! The bag with the plaster impressions was missing, stolen. I went quickly to ask at the information desk about the chances of the stolen goods being recovered. The Italian stewardess merely threw up her arms and lifted her eyes in despair.

AMSTERDAM – AUTUMN 1986

JOOP SPENT HIS LAST EVENING BEFORE LEAVING IN HIS LOCAL BAR, and for the last time explained to everyone where Swaziland was on the big map of Africa. His mates drank his health repeatedly, with reminiscences about how whenever Joop worked on a roof, he couldn't take his eyes off any plane that flew over until it disappeared into the horizon. They understood it all right – you can't keep a bloke like that in one place, couldn't chain his sort down! So Joop was going to Africa, on a development-aid project, to... What's the place called again?

It was late September. Everything was sorted out; his partner would be able to keep the business running on his own, and his upstairs neighbour would forward his mail. Just before he left the doubts hit him: such a long time away from Amsterdam!

"I'll lose my whole circle of friends," he grumbled to me. "I'll have to build it up all over again when I come back."

"It's only for a year, and if it doesn't work out you just come back," I encouraged him.

"We'll see." But his face was still long. He wasn't reassured.

A Canadian nun, managing a building project in Swaziland for a development organisation, had written to Joop saying that there was a vacancy for a teacher in primary technical training at a school for boys who had failed at other schools – problem cases. Joop thought it might be all right. To convince the nun that Joop was the right man for her, we added to his letters of recommendation a glowing testimony from a community centre on Amsterdam's Nieuwmarkt where they dealt with problem children, and where Joop had in fact sometimes put in some time. I gave him one more encouraging thump on the shoulder, and he left. He was the first to go.

Wilma had resigned from her job at the steel mill and could now at last get on with organising her move. She was impatient.

Everything was taking much too long. The ANC in Lusaka proposed that she should go to Botswana, where they urgently needed someone for the "heavier work" as it was described to me – exactly what Wilma wanted.

She would be away for three years.

"Won't you find that too long?" I asked.

"Don't worry about me, I'll be fine," she answered, laughing.

As it was very unlikely there'd be a shortage of female crane operators in Botswana, I put together extra paperwork to help her land a job; although this was hardly necessary, as she had followed a wide variety of evening courses – in welding, draughtsmanship and much more. "As long as I don't have to teach. I hate that more than anything," she told me.

On the morning of her departure we met in a coffee shop in the Van Woustraat, near the market. She was already in her travelling clothes, and her face looked a little tense. Her long blonde hair was pinned up, and she was wearing make-up – completely unnecessary because Wilma's natural beauty needed no accentuation. She was biting her nails.

We went through everything one more time. She was to fly to Harare. We had already agreed which hotel she would use, and we checked there were no misunderstandings about the date and time when she would be contacted, the recognition signals and the passwords to be exchanged. I had discussed and arranged everything in Lusaka a month before. If anything should go wrong she would warn me through a friend.

She gave me a letter for her parents, in case of arrest or worse. In it she told them why she had taken this decision, and why she had not been able to confide in them. Suddenly she became restless, in a hurry to go. She rose, gave me a hug, and at the door turned once more to wave.

Lucia had a ticket for November 20. Her family and friends believed that she was going to travel for some time through southern Africa, and that she would work as she went to finance her trip. In her letters home she planned to postpone her return home, again and again, until she had completed her three years.

The problem of her long connection with the AABN had been largely solved. Over the previous months I had searched through card files and archives at the office, and had come across her many times in photographs, marching under banners with texts such as: Boycott South Africa! Freedom for Helene Passtoors, and Down with Botha! Or she had surfaced as the author of articles on the women's struggle, and political injustice. Together we had planned a route which would lead her to anonymity. She stayed away from the office, from demonstrations or meetings. I removed her name from the card files and threw away the photographs. Gradually we let Lucia the activist fade away. She no longer kept in touch with her friends on the political circuit, and stopped corresponding with her contacts in South Africa. This last decision was very painful.

"The time will come when you'll be able to explain it to them," was all I could say to soften the blow.

From the proceeds of some work cleaning houses she had built up a new wardrobe, because we had had to drastically change her appearance. Her clothes were always sporty, a bit tomboyish – sweaters and jeans, with hair cut short and round spectacles. Now she had to pass as a typical secretary. Neat, middle class, slightly dowdy and above all, inconspicuous. In any case, very different from how she had been known. Diederik changed the set of her front teeth, her hair received a permanent wave, and she changed her glasses for contact lenses.

Her work history was unusable. We had to think up a background which would help get her work as a secretary. I asked some friends, without letting them ask questions, if I might type a letter of reference under their letterheads. A sympathetic photographer wrote a fine letter extolling her virtues as an assistant.

But the main problem was still her surname, rare and therefore easy to remember. The only solution was for her to get married. She sounded out her circle of friends for a suitable candidate. The first man she asked turned her down, but the second choice was good. For this special purpose he was prepared to lend her his surname. In complete privacy, they were married; no family, no friends. Just two witnesses we had roped in the day before. Now she could apply

58

for a new passport, and we sat down with her new husband, a medical student, to discuss his future role in the masquerade. He would have to stay in touch, as a husband would, and write her letters that she would leave lying around to allay any suspicion.

I was continually amazed by the casualness and persistence with which Lucia worked to prepare everything for her departure, as if all this was the most natural thing in the world. Once she had left as quietly as she did everything, I missed her. No one asked after Lucia any more, so effectively had we arranged her disappearance.

During the preparations for the departure of Joop, Wilma and Lucia, Mac arrived. I had spent a lot of time on the telephone to arrange and co-ordinate all the appointments I wanted to make for him, and it was only now that I realised that these were all very busy people with overflowing appointment books. But they were all quite willing to rearrange work schedules or cancel meetings so that we would lose as little time as possible.

Winnie had put me in touch with Louis, the wigmaker at the Opera. She wanted a wig which fitted perfectly, and Louis had developed a special process which made the wig fit the head like a tight bathing cap. I had briefed Louis on what we were trying to do, and he had immediately agreed to be involved. More than that, he had stressed that he very, very much wanted to do something to help the struggle against apartheid. Again, no long discussions were necessary, and virtually no persuasion. Thus far, no one had raised any objections to supporting this clandestine operation.

Louis was to make a plaster cast of Mac's head. He would use it to make a model over which a net would be heat-shrunk to carry the hair of the wig. This was his speciality.

He settled Mac into the barber's chair in his studio, threw a cape over his shoulders to protect his clothes, closed the door to the rest of the studio against the curious stares of his colleagues, and pulled a tight plastic cap over Mac's head, leaving the ears free. Strips of fabric saturated with plaster were then laid over the cap, layer by layer, in two halves so that once the plaster was dry the shell could be lifted off. My job was to pass the dripping strips to Louis as he moved around the chair with the grace of a dancer, although he was big and sturdily built. He wore fashionable spectacles with gaudy frames, and talked non-stop to Mac and I.

Half an hour later he lifted the two hardened half-shells from the head, and I picked the last traces of plaster out of Mac's hair, until, groaning and laughing, Mac pushed me away because I was pulling his hair out with the plaster. Louis would now be able to make a perfect copy of his head.

Next he brought out great coils of hair in various colours; real human hair, specially prepared and very costly. He held them up beside Mac's face, to work out what the best colour would be. More and more hair emerged from drawers and cupboards, as his eyes watched the mirror looking for a good blend. The shade would have to exactly match the moustaches and beards which lay ready in Winnie's studio. Finally he picked out four different hanks from which to blend the perfect wig.

Diederik had the front denture set ready, and lifted the fragile thing gently from the plaster form, rinsed it under the tap and pressed it over Mac's own teeth. With a click it engaged over the molars. Not only did it fit and look very natural, but it also immediately changed the shape of the face. Mac had to stay prone in the chair while Diederik filed and scraped to achieve even greater perfection. Then the plate broke. Diederik cursed softly; Mac lit a cigarette.

Diederik worked on through the evening as we sat peacefully waiting, reading old magazines. He strode in and out of the laboratory, reassuring us each time he passed that it would soon be fixed, and at about midnight it was ready. He had reinforced the denture with a small invisible metal rim. Mac contemplated the impressive result in the mirror. The front teeth were large, and pushed the upper lip forwards. The two side-pieces beside the teeth on the lower denture widened his jaw, and changed the sound of his voice. Mac was very satisfied, and said so. Diederik took off his white coat and we drank a glass of cognac to celebrate success.

On Floris's work bench lay a wooden board with a large clip at the top to hold the notepaper.

"During a meeting you just make your notes," explained Floris with visible enjoyment. "But if you're unexpectedly forced to hide

them, in a police raid or something, then you slide this rivet over..."
– he moved something on the clip and pulled out the middle veneer
of the three-ply – "and you can fit three or four A-4 sheets inside
the board. You leave some innocent scribbles on the outside."

Floris closed the secret compartment again. It was impossible to
see that the thin wooden board was not one solid whole.

Mac laughed at the ingenuity of it, and Floris glowed.

He had also thought about the communications problem. A café
acquaintance of his had developed a machine on which you could
type a message which would then automatically be put into code by
an inbuilt scrambler. The machine could then send the message by
telephone within a couple of minutes. Whoever received the
message only needed to know the code word, and he or she could
decipher the contents using the same type of equipment.

The machine had been on the market, but in its original form
had been withdrawn from the shops – at the request of the Israeli
intelligence service, according to whispers in the café, because the
thing could be used for clandestine communications purposes, and
they found it difficult to break the code quickly. We figured that it
must be very effective. If the Mossad had problems breaking the
code, the South Africans had no chance. Instead of the scrambler
the machine now had a calculator; the young inventor had merely
changed the chip and now the things were again on sale.

"Perhaps I can get my hands on one of the old models," said
Floris. "After all, they were in the shops for a while."

Floris and Mac talked over the possibilities the machine could
offer. You could split a message in two, say with every alternate
word, and send it to two addresses, in code. If one half should fall
into the wrong hands they'd only have half a coded message. The
gadget had a lot of advantages; it was small enough to carry in an
inside pocket, all you needed was a telephone, and even a public
booth would do, because you just held it against the mouthpiece
and the message was sent. It sounded almost too good to be true.

Floris would try and get hold of an old model for tests. He had
to go to Japan on business, and he would send a message from there
to two different answering machines.

Mac was satisfied, and a week later he left for Lusaka. In January someone else would come to Amsterdam who also needed a disguise – one of the men whose teeth impressions I had lost in Rome. Mac had also asked me to search as quickly as possible for a suitable person to set up a safe house inside South Africa.

At the end of October an unknown messenger left a letter from Joop in my postbox. He had got a job with a construction project, he wrote, but the wages were very low. He was staying with someone else for now – finding his own place with so little money wasn't going to be easy, but there was a chance that the Canadian nun, who could be fine when she hadn't been drinking, would help him find something quickly.

"I'm already in touch with the family. The day after I arrived, someone came. The friend who told me he was coming made me close the windows and curtains, and my contact slipped in so quickly through the back door that I didn't hear a thing. A tall shabbily dressed man in a very baggy brown suit, very polite, with no fuss. He asked for letters from you straight away, so I knew who he was. Now we meet regularly.

"Sometimes we just drive around in his old car – a wreck held together with string and sticky tape. He listens well, and gives me advice. He doesn't care for too many words – just like me, as you know. But recently he's been looking tense and nervous. Samora Michel was killed in a plane crash. Nobody here believes it was an accident. He came in, put the radio on, and listened to the news. 'If this can happen, just like that,' he said, 'what can we expect from now on?'

"But most of the time he's very easy-going and level-headed. As for everything else, we muddle along somehow. No need to worry about me. If you're sitting close to the fire you feel the warmth, but at a distance you just see dirty smoke."

In December I heard from Lucia. A fair number of Dutch people travelled to and fro between the Netherlands and Swaziland and she'd found someone prepared to carry a letter home in his inside pocket. She had kept scrupulously to the code we'd agreed. I decoded it, and read the following:

"I've found a house, but as yet no job. How are you supposed to manage here on the tiny amount of money you can earn? How do the Swazis do it? Your friend with the dark eyes keeps my courage up, he's really very kind. Anyway, I've already found a house, and that's the main thing. Now at least I can be a front for a comrade.

"The ideal house that we talked about so much is virtually impossible to find. There must be some in the rich areas, with closed garages and several entrances, and a wall so nobody can see what's happening in the garden, but I haven't found one. My house certainly doesn't meet the criteria. It's on a dead-end street, close behind a police station and surrounded by apartment buildings mostly occupied by police officials and soldiers. But luckily there are some footpaths around the house so you can get to the back door without being seen, through the trees and bushes. It's well back from the road, and it's not easy to see in. To my surprise your friend approved it, and a comrade moved in with me very quickly. So we're here now with the two of us.

"I've made curtains (by hand!) and they gave me some money for furniture. I moved in here last weekend, when the person I stayed with for the first few weeks disappeared for a few days because there were rumours that her house might be raided. Nothing happened, but things are still very tense here."

It would be two years before I saw Wilma again. In the meantime we had no contact, and I could only ask about how she was doing when I was in Lusaka. Usually I was told nothing more than that she was fine, and that she was a fantastic girl.

When she visited Amsterdam briefly in 1988 she told me about her arrival and her first weeks in Botswana.

"In Harare I met my contact, just as you'd arranged, and the next day I took the train to Gabarone. Someone came to the hotel the very first evening, so that all went very smoothly. We agreed that I was to go off looking for a house and a job, and I was lucky. I saw an advertisement offering a house for three months while the owners were away working abroad. I made an appointment, and they thought I was the most suitable and the nicest of all the seventy applicants. So I had a house straight away. When he gave me the keys, the owner warned me about African men – they're often ANC people, he said, who use this kind of house to hide, or to store things. I asked him what he meant exactly, but he didn't want to say any more. He just wanted to warn me. I settled in with my bags and my suitcase, five books, the few clothes I had with me, and of course my radio. After a few days I got the first weapons to store, in the wardrobe.

"I had good luck finding work, too. There's a technical school in town, and when I went along to have a look, I bumped straight into the head of the mechanical department. He's a little stocky Englishman, wears shorts, knee socks and brown boots – a real colonial. I didn't think his type existed any more. I asked him what courses they gave. Maybe I could start by learning something – you know how I love taking courses. But instead of answering he asked me all about where I was from and what I'd done. After that he hustled me into the office, grabbed the head of another department by the collar, and said 'This lady is here on holiday; she'd like to stay longer, and I think she could teach for us.' The other man jumped up, just as enthusiastic, and cried 'Can you teach? Can you teach?'

"Of course I can teach," I said. They were a bit overwhelming. 'Oh, fine,' he cried out. 'We need someone desperately!'

I was a bit taken aback. I'd never taught anyone, and I didn't want to, but according to your paperwork I was supposed to be able to. The colonial in the shorts dragged me with him through the school and begged me: 'Please come back tomorrow.' I looked around a bit, and listened in on the lessons, and thought 'I can do that too.' Actually I thought: 'I can do it better!' That Thursday I started – a bit nervous, but it was exciting too. A couple of weeks later I made my first trip into South Africa."

LONDON AND AMSTERDAM – WINTER 1986

CHOTA WAS SENDING ME WORRYING LETTERS, FULL OF HIS ANXIETY about everything that was happening around him in Swaziland. His return there, a few weeks after our parting in Maputo, had been hard. A comrade known as Sebide had just been picked up by the Swazi police and taken to a police station close to the border. The following morning the South Africans raided the station and kidnapped Sebide. He was not the first case that year. Shortly before, one Sidney Msibi had been kidnapped

"Try and make sure it gets some publicity. I don't know how long we can hold out here. A few days ago the Boers attacked the house of some comrades; luckily they weren't at home, but half the house is in ruins. The international press really must give it some coverage. A lot of the comrades have already had to leave the country, and I'm holding the fort with a few others. We can't give up this post, but we won't last long if things go on like this. It's good that your two friends are here to help us. They're both fine."

With a different coloured ink, and in a different mood, he wrote in the margin that he had high hopes his passport would be ready in time; he was so looking forward to a relaxing stay in Amsterdam.

"I've never been to Europe, and when I'm in a bad mood I try to imagine the city, and the landscape, and you riding your bicycle."

In mid-November I received a short letter via a friend in London dated October third. He wrote in a gloomy and depressed vein that his passport had still not been sorted out, and that he wondered if anything at all was actually being done about it at the ANC office.

"Call comrade Kay, and ask him to hurry. He must understand that I can't travel to Europe on my old passport with all those forged stamps. Their equipment is much too sophisticated there. The last thing I want is to spend Christmas in an Amsterdam jail."

But at the bottom he managed to add: "Let's not be too gloomy; this is the way it always goes. At the last moment everything will sort itself out and we'll be together again before the year is out. Very much love, Chota."

On December 14th I travelled to London. During a telephone conversation about something completely different, a friend at the ANC office there had casually mentioned in passing that Chota was expected there any day. I had hurried to leave as soon as I could, because I wanted to meet him in London so that we could enter the Netherlands together. That way I could take care of any possible problems with Customs, for I was not going to allow him even for one moment to feel unwanted or unsafe. Nothing was going to spoil this visit. A vase of chrysanthemums stood on the table in my house – they should last at least a week – the refrigerator was packed with things he liked, and the whole house now had curtains which closed properly.

As always in London I was staying with Anne, and as soon as I had deposited my bags in her spare room I went straight to the ANC office, hanging around for hours in the hope of picking up more news about his arrival. The exact date wasn't known. It might be the fifteenth, or the sixteenth. But that day he didn't come.

On the morning of the sixteenth I took the bus in order to avoid the oppression of the London Underground, and because the ride through overcrowded London took longer, it cut the time I would spend waiting in the office. I imagined to myself that he had already arrived, and was sitting waiting in the office while someone looked up Anne's telephone number for him.

In Penton Street I announced myself breathlessly on the intercom, rushed up the stairs, and collided head-on with Dora. She was carrying a huge pile of reports, and looked smart and well. So she had managed to get out of Lusaka. She related cheerfully that she and her husband had a flat in London, and she was working in administration.

"What brings you here?" she asked with her usual amiability.

"I'm waiting for Chota," I replied artlessly.

"Oooh, my God!" she began, but before she could say any more a door opened, and Wolfie, an old friend, came swiftly out and took

66

me by the arm. He propelled me past Dora into a storage room, and pushed me into a chair. He hadn't even said hello, and there were beads of sweat on his forehead although it was cold; there was ice on the inside of the windows.

He wiped his face with a handkerchief, and spoke:

"Yesterday Chota was kidnapped from his house in Swaziland. The South African police have got him."

I didn't understand. Chota was on his way, he could walk in at any moment, this was a misunderstanding, a case of mistaken identity. Wolfie leant forward, trying to hold my eyes with his, and repeated what he had said, but I didn't react. I stood up and walked out of the room, looking for the official ANC representative. Then I went to Ismael, whom I'd also known for years. But they all just repeated the same thing:

"Chota was kidnapped yesterday by the Boers."

I searched the offices for any other familiar face. Everywhere were heads bent over typewriters or piles of paperwork, but it was quiet as the grave; no work was being done. By the photocopier an old friend of Chota's from Robben Island stood staring out of the window. I went upstairs where visitors were always received and sat on the worn-out sofa. Slowly it dawned on me what those words meant, what the kidnapping of a man must be like: cars racing from the scene, in one of them a terrified human being who has just been dragged inside, hands tied, forced into the back seat at gunpoint. In a flash I saw Chota's face, and felt such a wave of fear that my stomach cramped tight and I screamed. Wolfie came leaping up the stairs, sat next to me and stroked my knee, but I pushed him away and screamed again through my tears: "Where is he now? What are they doing to him?"

Others came to sit with us. I felt arms around my shoulders and Wolfie gripped my hand hard. Someone brought coffee for me.

"How can you all be so sure?" I shouted, suddenly very angry. "Maybe he's just gone into hiding. Why do you all just always assume the worst?"

"Other people were kidnapped as well," said Wolfie, "A Swiss couple, and a woman called Grace Cele. Chota's friend Shadrach

Maphumulo was murdered by the kidnappers. They shot a child dead as well – they took his father away with them. There's already been official confirmation. [Foreign Minister] Pik Botha has admitted that they've been seized." He held me tight, said: "You are going to have to believe it."

Suddenly the reality hit me. "They've got their hands on him. My God, what are they doing to him?" I looked from face to face.

"Don't think about it. We don't know, we don't even know where he is."

"Maybe he's already dead?"

"They're not going to be gentle, but they won't kill him before they've got every bit of information out of him," said Wolfie firmly. "You know he's never talked under interrogation, not even under torture."

"But that will just make them even worse!"

"Try not to think about it."

That evening, in some East End district where I had never been before, I visited a man who was to give me information about computers and modems. I wanted to work in the company of a total stranger because I hoped it would occupy my thoughts, and because I no longer wanted to inflict my tears on Wolfie and the others, or my questions for which they had no answers anyway. Wolfie protested when I left, and made me promise not to spend the evening alone.

I didn't manage to stay long. I looked dully at brochures and listened without interest to the explanations; after half an hour I was ready to go. The man offered to take me to the Underground station. It was dark, he said, the weather was terrible, and on top of that, he warned me, skinheads sometimes hung out along the road. Recently someone had been mugged. But I wanted to be alone, and said I could still remember the way I'd walked – it wasn't that far.

Wet snowflakes were already falling. Thin brown slush covered the pavement, and the visibility was bad. I walked down the long street – and missed the side turning which led to the station. After ten minutes I no longer had any idea where I was, could see no building I recognised, and became more and more lost in drab streets where all the houses looked the same.

I walked aimlessly, long past caring where I was going; I'd given up looking for the station. I wept continuously, and tried to suppress my agonising thoughts of Chota. Right then, at that moment, as those seconds crept by, he was sitting or lying somewhere; in pain, perhaps, or hungry. Or was he being beaten? Perhaps right then, as I stood still and looked up through the thick mist of falling snow, right then he was terrified for his life.

I remembered how I had teased him in Maputo, biting his shoulder, very gently, just in love. He had pushed me away laughing – he couldn't stand pain.

Shadows moved on the other side of the street. A group of youths, skinheads perhaps. It didn't matter to me. I walked slowly on; if they wanted to attack me then let them. They crossed over and came towards me. When they were closer I realised that they were older, two couples, arm in arm. I heard them push open a squeaky garden gate behind me.

The road came out into a street of shops. The fiercely-lit window displays were blurred into a colourful mist by the snow. Everything gleamed and dazzled, my eyes were burning, I could see nothing clearly, and I felt utterly exhausted. I no longer knew where to go or what I wanted, and with no further thought I sat down on the edge of the pavement, in the slush.

Not long afterwards a taxi pulled up, a mini-cab. A young black man, cap tilted over his eyes, threw open the door and called to me: "Hey, what's wrong? Where you gotta go?"

"Nothing. Leave me alone." I looked the other way, weeping again. He watched me, and I went on sobbing with my chin on my chest.

Then he got out of the car and pulled at my jacket. "You can't stay sitting here. You'll catch pneumonia. What's wrong, man?"

I stood up.

"Come in the car." He pushed me gently to the cab.

"Why are you crying? Did your man leave you?" he asked, trying to see my face.

Then I told him about Chota, everything, in an incoherent flood of words.

"Those bastards!" was his only reaction. "Where d'you want to go? I'll get you there."

I could no longer remember Anne's address, and I tried to find it in my diary, but my eyes were so swollen I could hardly read. Some time before I had stopped entering South Africans or important contacts under their own names, and first I had to remember what name I had used for that address. The young man waited patiently.

"Something ordinary, a very ordinary English surname," I said.

"Jesus," he said, "I wouldn't know anything about English names either."

"Smith." It suddenly came back to me. He started the engine, and drove – and drove; the journey seemed endless. Sometimes he stopped to look at the street map. Every so often he repeated:

"Those bastards!"

Just as I felt myself about to slip away into a strange sleep, I recognised the street. We stopped in front of the house, and quickly he came round to help me out of the car. I rummaged in my handbag to find my purse, but he was already ahead of me, leading the way up the garden path, then helping me search my bag for the house keys. He produced the key and opened the door. I fumbled in my purse, but he was already halfway down the path, calling: "Leave it. No way. It was my pleasure to bring you home."

New Year's Eve. I stood at a window, as the year turned, looking out over a small inner courtyard. Rockets exploded into showers of light against the black sky beyond the houses, and in a side street a Chinese chain of bangers rattled out its hellish noise. A cat slunk away terrified behind the dustbins. There were hundreds of people out on the street. I could not see them, but was aware of them out there. I just heard the fireworks and the car horns, and smelled the gunpowder.

The friends with whom I had just had dinner had all rushed outside, carrying with them the last of the champagne. I preferred to stay behind close to my child, who was somehow sleeping through everything.

Beside me, on the table, stood the telephone.

I had asked my friends not to talk about Chota, and they had complied. I no longer remember what we spoke about. I was just waiting for one moment – midnight, when they would all go outside and leave me behind with the telephone.

Over the last days I had waited anxiously for news, but had heard nothing. Chota had disappeared into thin air. We couldn't even discover if he was still alive.

Just after midnight I picked up the telephone and dialled a number in Lusaka which I had recently been given for urgent business. I dialled slowly, trying to break unobtrusively into the international lines, overloaded with New Year greetings. After three attempts I heard the telephone in Lusaka ring softly. Nobody answered. I let it ring on until the line was broken, then tried a number in Maputo – seven times. The engaged signal sounded each time even before I had an international connection.

London then – that was closer. I heard the bell clearly, as if it was in the Netherlands. I knew where my friend's telephone stood, in the kitchen beside the refrigerator. I knew also precisely how many seconds it would take her to walk there from the living room. I wouldn't hang up, even when I knew she'd had enough time to cover the distance four times over.

I opened the window. The bangs, whistles and howls continued unabated; the city still had enough fireworks for a good half hour.

I did not dare to call Swaziland, although Joop now had a telephone in his new house. I didn't know how things were with him and Lucia. The silence, which had lasted weeks, made me very anxious.

In mid-January a letter from Joop was finally delivered, hidden in a small parcel. In scarcely legible handwriting, with no greeting or preamble, he had written:

"Contact with the family has been completely broken. You'll have to try and set it up again. We can't do it without exposing ourselves. Find the man with the cap, the one I met. He'll know what to do."

The next day he had added:

"Bad news. The one who came to take stock and look into the disappearances has disappeared himself; picked up in broad daylight by the Swazi police in Manzini. No idea if anything's known about me now.

"I can't describe to you how I feel. I think about him, our friend, so often. The last time I saw him I'd just moved to my new house, and had been celebrating it with colleagues from school. I'd had a fair bit to drink and was just drawing the curtains to go to bed when I saw him standing in the bushes under the mango trees. I could see his eyes, looking round nervously, and I waved to him to come in. He was very tense. That day several people had been kidnapped, and one had even been killed. I hadn't heard anything. He wanted a chance to talk about it, and he left a whole lot of stuff with me, envelopes and papers which he fetched in quickly from his car. In the end he stayed a good hour, which is a long time for him. He didn't make another appointment with me when he left, but he rarely did. Usually he'd just turn up, and then suddenly be gone again. Now I can't stop thinking how he's shut up somewhere, in that awful isolation. It's a horrible thought. If I believed in praying, I'd be doing it now.

"I talked to Lucia, by the way. She's only just arrived, and now this! I know we weren't supposed to get in touch, but we hadn't bargained for this. You've got to understand that she's alone and nervous. It was a little while before we got round to talking about it. First she asked carefully if I'd read the papers, about the man who'd been kidnapped. The paper called him Ahmed or Roynie. We knew him as Roy. But pretty soon we were both sure it was him. We wondered if we should expect more raids. In the end all we could really do was give each other some support."

At the bottom of the letter was a short postscript. He had no time to write more, someone was coming for the parcel, to take it to the Netherlands:

"Better news. Someone from the leadership has arrived and contact has been re-established. The word is that the lawyers now know where Chota's being held. So he's alive!!"

72

Soon after I'd heard from Joop, one of the men whose tooth impression had been stolen in Rome arrived in Amsterdam. I had to pick him up from immigration at Schiphol airport. He was questioned by a young official about how much money he had with him, what exactly he was doing here, and whom did he know in the Netherlands. His passport, with a current visa, was lying on the desk. I held out my hand, but he hugged me. Then I was allowed to take him away, on payment of fifty guilders – administration costs. I once had to pay forty guilders for Mac. Indians were, it seems, cheaper than Africans for the Dutch Immigration Service!

This visitor was a calm and very unassuming man, who wanted to be known as Sabata. He had chosen the name especially for the project, to honour Paramount Chief Sabata of the Transkei, who had died shortly before. Chief Sabata had been an old and highly respected member of the ANC, and for many years had fought tirelessly for the rights of his people. He had also been a strong advocate of the clandestine return of exiled ANC leaders to South Africa.

I decided to call my guest Jack, however, as it had been agreed that I would give my visitors temporary names which would only be used while they were here. Nothing else occurred to me at such short notice, so Jack he became – after no-one, and only for other people. To me he was Sabata.

We got to work straight away. My task was simply to disguise him as well as possible. He was not hard to please. Mac had said that everyone should have at least two disguises, in case something went wrong with one, but Sabata thought that one was perfectly sufficient, and came up with a suggestion. He wanted to be disguised as a priest. This struck me as a good idea. In South Africa men of God are treated with respect, and are easily recognisable by their clothing.

"Do you know anything about religion?" I asked him.

He told me that he had grown up during the 1950s in the Karoo, in Cradock, where he had been a member of the Anglican Church. The vicar of that congregation was none other than James Calata, a former Secretary General of the ANC, who had taken care that the boy not only learned his scriptures, but also received a solid political education. I could well understand that he would feel at home, during his political mission, in a clergyman's apparel.

We discussed the idea with Winnie, who had her hands full with a Dutch feature film. Between shots she worked out a simple solution to the problem of making him look older. The top of his head should be shaved, leaving a rim of hair at the sides and back which could, if necessary, be made grey with stage make-up. Winnie would make a toupee to fit over his bald crown for the times he might need to return to his own hairstyle. It wouldn't take her long to knot up his toupee while she hung around during filming. His full beard would also have to go, she thought, and she suggested darkening his skin. She taught him how to apply the high-quality and heat-resistant film make-up with a damp sponge.

To me this was still not enough – balding, beardless and with darker skin. He should have spectacles as well; they were always effective.

Floris helped us find a pair of small horn-rims. He had the idea of substantially thickening the ends of the arms to push out Sabata's ears, which normally lay flat against his head. When everything was ready, Sabata was not merely bald, clean-shaven and darker, but he also had impressively protruding ears. I hoped that these would not become painful, but Sabata at least was more than satisfied.

His natural mild-mannered bearing meant that he only had to let his shoulders droop a little, keep a friendly smile on his face, and there stood a pleasant, rather dreamy clergyman; certainly not the well-trained guerrilla fighter he was in reality.

But I still wanted something more, something to create a man to whom one would spontaneously want to offer help ... a hearing aid! That was the extra touch: an old-fashioned version, where you still had to use the knobs to adjust the volume for the sounds around you. At the optician's shop round the corner I unearthed one from a box under the counter, and it even still worked. I was welcome to it – no charge. It was a fine, ingenious apparatus, exactly the same as the one my grandfather had used: a small round box with a shell which clipped behind the ear. I put it on, and gave

Sabata my impression of my grandfather as I remembered him, always fidgeting with the box. He would turn his bad ear towards you, the volume level was always either too high or too low, and sometimes the machine would emit a shrill whine. Like many elderly men with poor hearing, my grandfather used his deafness to attract plenty of attention and sympathy.

Now we were both happy. I was convinced that if the South African police ever circulated a description of Sabata in disguise, it would read something like: "African, age about fifty, very dark skin colouring, ecclesiastic, balding, ears stick out conspicuously, hearing aid."

Together we bought a drab dark suit, and a shirt to match. He already had drab enough shoes and he would be able to find the dog collar himself. I knew nothing about priests' clothing. Perhaps clergymen in South Africa dressed completely differently from their fellows in Europe.

Once more it was clear to me how inconvenient it was that I had never been to South Africa, and had no real feel for how people dressed there. I decided that from then on I would take every opportunity to get hold of South African magazines, with photographs of everyday men and women, both black and white. City people and country folk, old and young, fashion magazines with stylish young people, well-dressed ladies and businessmen. I cut out everything I thought might be useful, sorted it into categories and pasted it in books. I added photographs of large groups of people on the street, waiting in stations or at bus stops, of university students in denims – everything I could gather to develop a better picture of how I could help someone blend into a group of people and disappear.

I was to use those scrapbooks many times to find the right type, or to stimulate my ideas. Sometimes my visitors just searched through the books until they at last came across a photograph which exactly fitted the impression they wanted to create.

When Sabata left, he carried in his luggage a false beard and moustache, the toupee and spectacles, the hearing aid, make-up, the false teeth Diederik had made for him, and a whole stack of swing and bebop cassettes. With Diederik he had filled tape after tape with Charlie Parker, Dizzy Gillespie and Coleman Hawkins – music which would help shorten the long hours of waiting, waiting and more waiting.

One morning at the end of January there was an airmail letter in my postbox. I could see it through the slot, lying diagonally on the bottom. I recognised the handwriting, and had to sit down quickly on the stairs. A letter from Chota. I pulled the envelope from the box. The date and place of the postmark were clear, December 19th, 1986, posted in Gweru, Zimbabwe. He must have entrusted the letter to someone just before he was kidnapped. Inside was a card:

"My dearest Conny, Love and Greetings. I am well."

He wrote that he still had high hopes that we would see each other before the end of the year, or otherwise for sure early in the new year. "I'll write you a long letter soon. With love, Eb."

Not long after that, he got a message smuggled out of the prison. Wolfie sent me part of the text. Chota wrote how he was being tortured, in an isolation cell. He was bombarded with high, piercing sounds, and was afraid of losing his reason. The sound made any thought impossible. The cell had no windows, and he was becoming disorientated.

"By the fourth day I was broken. I felt I was going mad. I do not think I shall be able to mentally survive this torture, and what is still to come. I can feel my spirit breaking. Do something!"

Angry and grieving, I sat with my colleagues in the AABN office trying to work out what more we could do. An urgent call had already gone to the Dutch government, through a member of Parliament, to put pressure on Pretoria. Chota had been kidnapped, after all, and illegally taken over the border; international law had been violated. We had called lawyers and judges, and asked the European Council of Ministers to take action. But I had gradually come to realise how it would be: The Hague would make enquiries of the Dutch embassy in Pretoria; the Dutch ambassador would make enquiries of the relevant South African authorities, and the latter would deny everything. They would do nothing, then, except make routine enquiries and be satisfied with a denial.

I telephoned colleagues in the anti-apartheid organisations in England, Germany and the United States. They had all by this time been called on by the ANC to get their governments to act, but they too were up against a wall of disinterest. An international tribunal must be set up to look into the kidnapping practices – on that we were all agreed.

I hung around the office, discouraged. It would be a long time before something like that could be organised and financed. I went home and tried to concentrate on other work. There was nothing to do but wait until he was formally charged; then I would be able to try and get a letter through to him.

Meanwhile, Mac had recruited someone else in the search for a solution to the communications problem: Tim Jenkin. I only knew of him by reputation. Together with two others he had escaped from Pretoria's heavily guarded prison in 1979. The escape had been very unorthodox; with great patience and perseverance he had worked in his cell at reproducing ten different keys for ten different doors. After a great deal of careful surreptitious testing he and two companions had one day virtually strolled out of the prison and escaped to Swaziland. The authorities had then completely closed down the prison wing from which they had made their escape.

Tim was my age, born in Cape Town into a typical white family, and grew up to be a typical young white man. During a vacation in London he joined the ANC, which made him less typical, to say the least. He returned to Cape Town to join the underground resistance. In 1975 he and his comrades had brought about a veritable chain reaction of letter bombs in several cities. Inexperience, recklessness and poor guidance had, in 1978, led to his arrest and to a sentence of twelve years. He told me that he had planned to escape right from the moment he walked into the prison.

Tim, like most of the others, bore no resemblance to a storybook hero. He was a very thin young man who walked with a stoop, and had sharp features behind very thick glasses. He always looked very pale, was usually very serious, and sometimes rather severe, almost inflexible. He was still recognisable as the cleverest boy in the class. It took me some time to get accustomed to him, and this was mutual. Once we discovered a common line of humour, however, and he got used to my changing moods, no longer being put off by my extremes of exuberance or deep dejection, a strong friendship developed between us which was later to help us through difficult times. However, at first communication between us was awkward. We kept strictly to our tasks, and discussed only the subject which had brought us together: communications.

Floris had indeed managed to get hold of several examples of the old-model communications apparatus. Tim was to test them. He had examined the device with suspicion. You could indeed type a message on to it, make corrections, code it and send it by telephone. But he couldn't see how the coding system worked.

His experience was extensive, mainly based on what he had learned when he himself was on the other end of the communications line in Cape Town, and he was almost fanatical about good communications systems for resistance people. He could recall with some bitterness how things had been done and how frustrating it had been.

"All those invisible inks," he growled, "the recipe had to be changed every month. And every time something was intercepted in the mail, or whenever someone was arrested, it meant another change, another mix."

They had used book codes too, but those had the same disadvantages; they were time-consuming and only allowed brief messages. He gave as an example the instructions for setting off a pamphlet bomb.

The message might be sent from London, for example, and be more than a week in the mail. It often had to be picked up at another address, sometimes miles away. Then the invisible ink would have to be developed, and the message decoded. All this would use up half a day, just for a few lines. The result was: "letter bomb, time, date." And that was it – you were on your own. There was no other way, but they were stuck with it – the only kind of message that could be sent. You couldn't discuss the problems involved, and there were always plenty. But the worst of all to him was the fact that there was no way of explaining, if things went wrong, and no way of venting your frustration. From his end, the complicated contact line was only used to ask for money or chemicals.

"In underground work above all, it is so important that you don't come to see yourself as a machine," he said gravely. "And you don't want others to see you like that either. You want them to understand you. Misunderstandings can happen so easily. And the people outside, over the border, should really know what state you're in mentally, how your morale is holding up. So much depends on that. When you're underground you've no-one to talk to, absolutely no-one. So those messages from outside are very important to you. They're your lifeline."

Later, stationed in London, he had had to train the people who were to return to South Africa for undergound work, teaching them the same traditional methods; still the invisible inks, the book codes. Ten years after he had been trained he was teaching others exactly the same techniques.

"Every time I had to say goodbye to them it gave me a bad feeling. They were being sent back into the jaws of the lion, with oh, so little to keep them going. How would they be looked after, and how would they survive? Would they manage to maintain contact with the outside?" His experiences had taught him that in every operation communications should be absolutely central. It should no longer be treated as just one aspect among many. The quality and frequency of contact between the resistance inside and outside was of vital importance.

AMSTERDAM – SPRING 1987

SOME MONTHS BEFORE, MAC HAD ASKED ME TO TRY AND FIND someone to set up a safe house inside South Africa. I responded with a worried look. Inside South Africa itself – that was a very different matter from the front-line states, which were free African nations, even if they were often put under heavy pressure. You could still find a safe haven there, get across a border quickly, or ask an international aid organisation for help. But right under the enemy's nose, close to the source of the threat – that would be more difficult, and very much more dangerous.

On top of this, the situation in South Africa was now becoming much grimmer. Under pressure from the country's business community, which felt more and more keenly the effects of the unworkable system, President PW Botha had come up with some reforms. But without success. International sanctions were starting to bite, and South Africa was finding herself severely isolated.

Organised resistance among the black population was taking stronger and stronger forms. Rent and consumer boycotts were making the whites very nervous, and powerful anti-apartheid organisations openly supported the ANC's demands for freedom and democracy. Reaction to this resistance was characteristic: under the state of emergency, still in force, more than 25 000 people had by now been detained. Imperceptibly, unnoticed, true power in the country had shifted to the armed forces. The generals were steadily gaining influence, and labelled every form of protest as a security problem. Even the most insignificant forms of resistance had to be handled within the framework of the "total strategy against the Communist threat". All branches of South African society were controlled by the military. In secret, they made all the decisions on strategies and policy lines, which were only implemented by government in name. South Africa had become a society under siege.

I would have to find a man or a woman with plenty of courage, strong natural survival instincts and a capacity for hard work. Someone deeply committed to the struggle against apartheid; and, most importantly, someone capable of finding a job.

After a long search along roundabout carefully negotiated paths, I found someone who seemed suitable through a friend who had first made exhaustive enquiries. A meeting was arranged, during which I cautiously kept things fairly superficial. My confidence in this candidate grew quickly, however.

I was now seeing him, Henk Oostveen, regularly, usually early in the morning in a coffee shop. He would arrive looking untidy, with rumpled hair, after working until the early hours as a cook in a small restaurant beside one of the canals. Henk was a trained chef, and this seemed ideal to me. A chef can find work anywhere, certainly in South Africa. Surely his experience in French cuisine would easily land him a job in a first class hotel.

He came from a thoroughly Red nest. During the war his parents had worked in the underground. Clandestine work, resistance, it had all been stuffed into him with his baby food, as he put it. Although he came over as a calm and collected young man, who had taken this decision after some time for consideration, he had, in fact, years before, taken part in wild demonstrations outside the South African embassy, during which it was not unknown for a rock or a pot of paint to fly through the air. Such events were always filmed and photographed, and this was the only thing that worried me about him.

I had consulted Lusaka, his whole past had been examined again, and we still hesitated. It was agreed that he should stay well away from anything at all connected with South Africa for the time being.

Now I had been given word that we could embark on the next stage. He was to make an exploratory trip to South Africa. Mac ideally wanted to see him based in Cape Town, where he could function as a front for one of the people involved in the project.

Henk was given a couple of weeks to find out whether he would be able to find work as a chef, and whether he would be able to find a suitable house. We made up a story for him to tell his friends at this early stage, so his eventual departure would not come as a surprise. Botswana seemed the best choice for the story, because working in South Africa was out of the question – amongst his circle of friends it was somewhere you simply didn't go.

In Botswana he would be working as cook for a refugee project, initially for a month, with the possibility of going back there for a longer period if it all suited him.

To his parents, he had confided the truth. I had not really been in favour of this, feeling that he would just be saddling them with unnecessary tension and worry. If the plan went ahead it would last several years, and that was a long time to wait in uncertainty; to watch the news on television every evening and wonder if your own son has been caught up in the violence, or is among those who have been arrested. There was a danger of panic if there was no letter for a long time.

But he thought his parents were used to this kind of thing. Nevertheless, unexpectedly, his mother expressed serious doubts. Did he really know with whom he was working? Was it really the ANC? Before you know it you can easily be used for purposes you don't agree with, she had warned him. I asked him if he did indeed know with whom he was getting involved, and he looked at me in surprise.

"Of course," he replied. "Why do you ask that?"

"Because I think it's a sensible question. Your mother's right to be concerned."

He reacted with irritation: "Nonsense. I know what I'm doing. I know who I'm dealing with. It's not as if you're a bunch of strangers turning up out of the blue. The only thing that's getting to me is that I'm going to have to go to that bloody embassy to ask for a visa, and to South African Airways for a ticket. In the old days I spent nights spraying slogans on that place."

It was springtime before I again stood in front of the glass in the arrivals hall at Schiphol, waiting for Gebuza, one of the ANC's most important military commanders. I had met him before, in Lusaka, and recognised him immediately he joined the end of the long queue at passport control. Although we were several hundred metres apart, his great height made him easy to follow as he moved forward step by step until he reached the immigration counter. A few words were exchanged, and then I saw him retreat. Damn! They were sending him back. I could see him pacing up and down beyond the immigration desk, chin held high. I pushed my way through the other people waiting, trying to keep him in sight, and found myself squeezed between two large men and the glass, which was smeared by greasy fingers and children's runny noses. What had gone wrong? He had a visa, after all. I forced my way through to the information desk and asked to be let in to the immigration office, with no success. Whether or not one was admitted depended entirely on who was on duty that day, and what they'd had for breakfast.

Time dragged on and on. Gebuza had taken off his pullover; now I had a yellow T-shirt to keep in sight. Finally, an hour and a half later, after I had long given up hope, he came through the glass doors. His mood was all too easy to read from his face.

He greeted me with a brief glare, and I asked what had gone wrong. He answered by thrusting his passport at me as if I were an extension of the Dutch Immigration Service – a Ghanaian passport, the worst of all. Ghanaians always had problems getting into the Netherlands, as I knew from a friend who regularly met them at the airport. I would have to let Lusaka know quickly: no more passports from Ghana. ANC people, often stateless, were allocated travel documents offered to them by sympathetic governments. But even a South African passport would give you easier entry to the Netherlands than virtually any other African passport, even if you were non-white.

In the taxi I tried to cheer Gebuza up with stories of everything that had happened to me while I waited for him. I had received three invitations from unsavoury-looking gentlemen to come and have 'something to drink'; an over-dressed lady had told me the story of her life, and I had followed the course of a marital row. He did not react, just looked out of the window. I asked if this was his first time in Europe, but his answer was an unintelligible growl.

That evening during dinner, after he had settled into his lodgings, I tried to establish better contact between us. I had to get to know him better if we were going to be able to discuss a disguise. The agreement with Winnie was that he and I would come up with a proposal together, but first I had somehow to win his confidence. He watched me coldly, without the least attempt to hide his distrust. He was at least giving me plenty of time to size him up, and I did so just as openly; his indifference did not waver. Opposite me sat a tall, strongly built and well-proportioned man, with broad shoulders, fairly light colouring, large but rather cold eyes and a hard face, sometimes almost cruel. His hands were long and elegant. All in all a distinctively handsome man who was probably very successful with women. I was worried, however, by the arrogant and inflexible air that he so openly presented to the world. What a very different character from mild-mannered Sabata.

This superficial first impression fitted fairly well with what I already knew of the man. His name had appeared with increasing frequency over recent years in the South African newspapers, always linked to guerrilla attacks. Between the lines one could read their irritation at never being able to get their hands on him. Within the ANC he had the reputation of being utterly fearless. He had gone many times into South Africa for all sorts of military missions and had been involved in armed skirmishes with the police and army. His stubbornness and courage were familiar to many, but little was known about his private life, except that he had been dealt some heavy blows. His brother Zwelakhe, also active in the resistance, had been brutally murdered in Swaziland by a South African hit squad. His wife Sheila had only a few weeks before been kidnapped from Swaziland by the South Africans. She had been the next after Chota to be seized from her own house. As yet no-one knew where she was being held. When I asked him if he had heard anything he rubbed his hands over his face, but would not talk about it.

The next day dawned fine, and I suggested a long walk. Perhaps that would help to break the ice. I had come to think that Gebuza was in unfamiliar territory, and perhaps just needed more time to acclimatise.

We took the train to Castricum and walked into the dunes. I had a hiking map with me and searched out a route to the sea. The dunes were familiar ground for me; throughout my childhood I had spent my summers exploring them with my grandfather, fascinated by his stories of my great-grandfather, a dune warden and beachcomber. My grandfather found the fantasy world of his fading memories much more worthwhile than reality.

Gebuza walked beside me, a spring in his step, radiating health and power. I broached the subject of disguises, and suggested a few possibilities. It had to be something simple, something he could immediately visualise. I dared not be over-adventurous – I was too fearful of immediate rejection.

A black businessman, I suggested – not very original, but his reserve was not exactly stimulating my powers of imagination. He would be one of the up-and-coming young men, like those I knew from magazine pictures and had seen at airports and in the hotels of Harare. Ambitious, sporting Western dress, a member of the international corps of well-dressed men in a suit and tie, unobtrusive, never loud; differing not at all from other business people, apart from in the darkness of their skin. Men epitomising money, profit and adaptability. Many hotels in South Africa had now opened their doors to them. Their credit cards and expensive automobiles assured them of a welcome; they were accepted because they followed the rules. I sketched out the type for him, and he nodded. He knew of course that he would have no trouble playing that kind of role.

Somewhat encouraged, I embarked on another proposal. The strict orders from Lusaka were that he should have at least two disguises. This time I tried a young man: snazzy jacket, wet-look hairstyle, a regular at the disco. I snapped my fingers, swung my hips, pouted my lips, and saw from the corner of my eye that he was watching me with a mocking smile, a little girl engrossed in her imaginary theatre piece.

"Not the disco – the shebeen," I said quickly, to show my knowledge of township life. Now he was laughing out loud.

"The type that's not interested in politics, a trendy kid who's good with the girls, with his Walkman headphones ..."

"Walkman headphones." He repeated slowly, shaking his head.

It struck me suddenly that in Soweto you probably can't walk around for long and keep a Walkman on, and very few young men would be able to afford one anyway. I felt myself flushing in embarrassment.

I must have looked crestfallen, because he came closer as we walked and gave me a slap on the shoulder, saying that it really wasn't such a bad idea at all.

We reached the shore at about midday, in hot, muggy weather. We drank coffee outside a beach café, and I turned my face upwards to catch the sun. We couldn't talk freely anyway, amongst the other people on the terrace. I could feel him watching me with curiosity. Then he too turned up his face, as if teasing me. Our chairs, with armrests, were side-by-side. He had rolled up his sleeves, and our arms now lay close together. I saw him look at his own, and at mine. My skin was well-tanned; his was very pale. We had exactly the same colouring.

As we walked back into the dunes the rain clouds were gathering. Gebuza had pulled on a plastic raincoat I had brought along in my knapsack. "What does the name 'Gebuza' mean?" I asked. It was certainly not his own, and often an MK name had a whole story behind it.

"It was given me by Moses Mabhida. " he replied.

"Why?" I insisted, although I could see he didn't really feel like talking about it. After some pressure, he related how Mabhida, Secretary General of the South African Communist Party until his death a year earlier, had given him the name on his return from a clandestine mission in February 1977. Gebuza had been one of Shaka's generals, famous according to tradition as the man who could fight with his spear in either hand. If one arm became tired he would throw the weapon to the other.

Gebuza stood still and demonstrated. Slowly he raised his arm, his fist closed. Laughing, his shoulders turning in slow motion, he thrust with an imaginary spear then tossed it across to the other hand; again and again so I would see the movement clearly, as supple as a tiger. Finally, he told me, no-one was left to oppose the general; all his enemies were either dead or had run away. So then the general speared the sky. That was the meaning of the name – to spear the sky: "The man who speared the sky."

Winnie and the whole team worked at full speed. Louis made a cast of Gebuza's head. For now, a grey wig was to be made for the businessman, and one with dark curls for the trendy guy character. Beards and moustaches were added for variety. Yan Tax, the costumer, gave us advice on clothes. Together we chose a selection of spectacles, but everything seemed to lead to misunderstanding and differences of opinion. I generally gave way, for I knew that in the end, whichever style of frame he chose, the greatest problem with Gebuza was his posture. I knew no-one who walked as he did – not merely bolt upright, but with shoulders held back and chin raised high: an officer of the Imperial Guard. Winnie had already commented on it, Louis looked worried, and Yan had offered to sew lead into the hem of his jacket. This man could be recognised half a mile away just by his gait, whatever we hung on him or took away.

Gebuza worked with the actor Han Romer, who had also joined the team. Han drilled him in dropping his chin and walking less upright. He tried hard, but did not succeed for long, however often I kept reminding him. This was his way of looking out at the world, his attitude, proud and invulnerable. His physical carriage had probably been established for his entire adult life; it couldn't be changed this quickly, within just a few weeks.

The spectacles, however, or rather our arguments about them, gave me an idea. Floris had once pointed out to me the great importance of having properly ground lenses in false spectacles. On stage and in films, flat lenses are often used, which give a mirror effect. Any trained police officer would spot them immediately. To do things properly, some focus effect must be ground in, he said. Perhaps this could provide our solution: bifocal spectacles, with the lower sections differently ground for reading, forcing Gebuza to look over them – preferably strong bifocals, with the lower section impossible to see through. He would then be forced to drop his chin closer to his chest.

We had the glasses made, and the effect was very rewarding. I wondered if he would ever take the trouble to put the things on his nose. When I voiced my fears he looked very pleased, amused at my perception.

We spent weeks building up both the businessman and the young guy. In the shops he showed knowledge and taste in his choice of expensive suits and carefully selected silk neckties to go with them. He loved good clothes.

I wanted to do something special for his last evening, after all our hard work together. Now I felt like rewarding both of us, and looked through the paper for what the city had to offer. Film was no good, no companionship. Not theatre – language would be a problem. Music, jazz – we both enjoyed that. I looked through the listings for the jazz clubs, the Bimhuis and the Kroeg.

"Do you like Archie Shepp?" I asked, casually. His head turned sharply. Bulls-eye! I laughed in surprise at the sudden excitement on his face. He sprang out of his chair, pulled the paper from my hands and I pointed out the announcement of an Archie Shepp concert in the Kroeg. "Shit!" he exclaimed, and fell back into his chair with a boyish, almost shy smile on his face.

We took a taxi into the city centre. Along the canal outside the Kroeg there was already a crowd waiting, pushing to get inside. We were soon swept into the smoke-hung bar, scented with hash, marijuana, warm bodies and spilled beer. Gebuza was lively and talkative, even giving me a playful shove. He was still very excited. We'd agreed to make a real night of it, and we ordered whiskeys.

The bar was packed full – faces from every corner of the earth, and the barman knew his drinks in any language. I saw a beautiful black woman give Gebuza an over-the-shoulder look. He stood tall, in full glory, chin high.

The elated expression on his face made him especially attractive. I moved a little closer to him. My job was to protect him from dangerous influences, and I had the immediate feeling that this lady belonged in that category.

There was a stir near the entrance, as a rather stooped figure pushed through the crowd. Archie Shepp was arriving, through the front entrance just like the rest of us. The master with his horn in its case. Gebuza stared, his glass held against his teeth. He took me by the arm and we pushed our way through behind Shepp to the edge of the stage. Gebuza stayed there, and I quickly found a bar stool in a corner which raised me high enough to see over the heads of the audience.

Shepp stood for a long time by the microphone, hunched over his huge tenor sax. We waited. Then he played his first notes, slow, sad, almost tired. But so very fine.

I could see Gebuza standing motionless amongst the swaying crowd.

"Have you always been this angry?" I had asked him the evening before.

"Gradually. I got angry very gradually," he had answered. "It was always there, everywhere: no chances, just humiliation. There was no possible escape. That is my first memory, and my last, until I went over the border. Then the fighting and the pain came too."

"Is that why you've grown so hard?"

He replied gravely: "I can still sing like a schoolboy."

I was finding the small space suffocatingly hot, almost unbearably so. At the bar people were crammed in.

During a short interval Gebuza came to stand beside me, no drop of sweat on his forehead. With an air of complete fulfilment, he ordered two more whiskeys.

It was close to dawn before we again walked along the canal, looking for a taxi. His springy walk now seemed more like a dance.

"I shall never forget that," was all he said.

A few hours later I brought him to Schiphol, he had an early flight. I hugged him, standing on my toes to do so; he didn't bend down as much as an inch. He mumbled something I couldn't make out and he turned quickly away, Ghanaian passport in hand. Once he was safely through passport control he didn't look back.

AMSTERDAM – SUMMER 1987

HENK OOSTVEEN RETURNED FROM SOUTH AFRICA AFTER EXACTLY four weeks. He had searched for a job and for a house, and sized up the unfamiliar territory to facilitate his final move there. I had been too busy to think of him much. In fact I could form no real picture of Cape Town, or how it might be to wander the streets there.

My limited idea of the city had been gleaned from a mixture of nostalgic stories, photographs and film images of government buildings and of sandy flatlands on the outskirts, where the people lived in corrugated iron slums. Most of my knowledge of Cape Town was of what was no longer there: District Six, Abdullah Ibrahim and my friend Wolfie.

In New York, where he lived, I had once heard Ibrahim evoke Cape Town on the piano. With his music he had led me by the hand round the foot of the mountain, its summit hidden in white cloud, all the way to Manenberg.

Wolfie always made me laugh when he described how huge the pumpkins grew in Cape Town, for I knew that in reality the place was buffeted by a fierce south-east wind.

A city only really exists when you have walked its streets, been lost in it, bought bread, been given a parking ticket and grown to hate the local police; when you've been in love, and written letters with the city's name, in flowing letters, on the envelope.

Before he left, Henk and I pored over the city map together, and I now knew the map of Cape Town as well as I did that of my own city, knew districts and street names by heart: Oranjezicht, Paardeneiland, Vredehoek, Zonnebloem, Voortrekkersweg, De Buitengracht, De Heerengracht.

When Henk came through the door of the house where I'd arranged our meeting, so we would be able to talk undisturbed, he looked tired and confused. There were dark circles under his eyes.

"I've got a job," he said, without enthusiasm.

"For God's sake, what happened?" I stroked his head in concern. What on earth could have made him so despondent?

"Well, I suppose I've been lucky. Although ... actually I'm not so sure," he began hesitantly.

"From the beginning, Henk," I urged.

"The beginning and the end are a bit the same. Maybe because I just stayed in the one place. A hotel in Greenpoint, near the harbour. It's winter there. Stupid, isn't it – we never talked about that at all. About the weather. Now and again the sun did shine, but it was always spoiled by that rotten cold wind. I had to wear a coat every day.

"There was a bar in the hotel, and I had a beer there now and then. Pretty quickly, around the second day I think, I was approached by a regular customer there, a property dealer. Actually he didn't have much to do except find someone to talk to now and then, and drink too much. An ugly old man, short and fat, soft belly hanging over his belt. About fifty, I suppose, incredibly big-headed. He introduced me to the hotel manager, Manfred Klipper, well-dressed and also in his fifties. Even uglier, if anything, and very chummy with John Sailor – that's the property dealer. They were both very interested in me."

I looked at Henk's tired young face with its full mouth and understood very well.

"I told them that I'd quit my job as a chef in Amsterdam, because I'd had enough of it, and because I'd broken up with my girlfriend – she'd gone off with someone else. I hoped to find work in Cape Town, even if it was only for a while. Right away they offered to help me any way they could, and I started to hope that Klipper might even offer me a job in the hotel. Anyway, they both wanted me to stay much longer.

"John Sailor drove me round in his car and showed me Cape Town and the country around it. That was fine with me – that way I could check out the city safely, and get experience of how that kind of white man thinks. He was a real racist. Not militantly so, more sort of: "Aah, those blacks, it's best just to have as little as possible

91

to do with them. If they're not under your feet you don't have to use your boot on them."

"That Mr Sailor was just bored stiff. Lots of mornings he'd already be standing there just waiting for me, asking: 'What are we going to do today, then?'

"Then he'd take me along, and on each of our drives I'd get to hear yet another chunk of white history. Everywhere we went he'd know of a hill with some memorial, or another leftover from the past. He was umpteenth generation, on the English side. Proud of his history. He tried to use it to make himself worth something. He lived mostly in the past, just like some other whites I met through him.

"And then in between I had to go along to gay bars, I think it was very important to him to be seen with a young man. I didn't know that there was such a strong taboo on homosexuality in South Africa. Everything goes on in secret. The hotel manager had to hide it completely, or it would cost him his job. Nobody could know.

"But I couldn't feel much sympathy for them, even though they certainly belong to a more or less repressed group. The gays I met were all very rich and very frustrated. And in those bars, the Wine Barrel, for instance, a gay bar – they amount they drank! Everywhere I went, in fact. Endless drinking, even during the day!

"In the mornings I went round hotel agencies, employment agencies for the catering trade. It was harder than I'd expected. The tourist industry has collapsed there and there's a lot of unemployment, even among the chefs. I tried to get some idea of South African cooking, as well. Now that was a shock, really. Cooking a meal, I mean a well-prepared meal, put together with some care and attention – they've got no idea! I can't judge how far that comes from the political and social set-up. But it's a tragedy what you get on your plate. Western cooking everywhere, American style – big slabs of meat. Gorging yourself to show you've got plenty of money. It's not about taste, or any refinement in the way it's prepared. It's just all about how much you can afford to cram on to your plate. If you can pay for it you can eat lobster every day, but what they do to lobster in Cape Town… I can't even describe it to you. There's plenty of staff everywhere, but nobody seems to have any motivation at all. And you're just going to be stuck working under a chef who's been reduced to being a slave driver, just giving you orders and pushing you to go faster. I didn't see or taste anything of the creative side of the profession. Now me, I'm nuts about my job. You put me in a kitchen and all my troubles float away – I just get to work."

"So how did things work out with Mr Sailor?" I asked, seeing that the talk about food was making him miserable.

"He just made me more and more sick of him. He kept saying: "I couldn't care less ..." That was his signature tune, he just couldn't care less about anything. He was just so rude to people, and he'd just sit there trying to get his hand up my crotch. One evening he took me to the German club, and that was the limit! There I sat, surrounded by ex-Nazis, crowing over their beer. Sailor was well-known in that club, everyone said hello. I just thought: 'Once I've got a job I'll find my own bloody way around.'

"The thing was, it was getting more and more obvious that my chances of finding something in a month weren't good. I was going to have to use him to find work quickly. And sometimes I was very suspicious. He kept coming up with just what I needed at the time I needed it. I even thought, maybe he's working for the security police.

He was so vague about his work and his income, and he had time for me any time of the day. I was never in his house; our appointments were always at a bar. But once he had to pick something up at home. We stopped outside a a villa with a huge garden. There were shutters down over all the windows, with locks. I had to wait in the car and he quickly went in and fetched something. Sometimes he made telephone calls, too, to someone who took care of business for him. I found it all very strange, and got very cagey.

"On the other hand he was definitely a regular at the hotel, everyone knew him, it was his special drinking hole. I'd found the hotel by chance, that wasn't planned before. His homosexuality was genuine, and so was his interest in me, too, which went with it. But maybe it had been used against him for a long time. In a society like that, his type is easy to blackmail, of course. But he never asked many questions, it was all just empty chat. Now and then he'd ask my opinion of the political situation, and I just kept it superficial: 'Oh, you read so much in the Netherlands, you've got to be there yourself ...' That was enough for him.

"After two weeks I bought a motorbike, to get a bit more freedom and also to be able to look for work outside the city. Every time I went to apply for a job I got roped in for a whole afternoon. It all looks like hospitality, but there's another side to it. Those whites are so bored, they've got nothing to do, there are others to do the work for them. If a stranger turns up, like me, then right away the wine bottles pop open, the lobster's on the table.

I never had any chance to talk to black people about food. I wanted to, and tried to as well when I was in a kitchen, but it was just made impossible. 'You don't talk about cooking with them, you just tell them what to do,' they told me."

He was smiling now, his eyes red with fatigue and emotion.

"Okay, I've got all that off my chest. The good news, still, is that I've as good as got a job, as under-chef in Klipper's hotel. Now I've got to get hold of a work permit, and I can start in a couple of months. They're waiting for me there. But first I want a couple of days' sleep. Oh, yes, and a house won't be a problem. I can sort that out all right from here. But I'm afraid I'm going to have to put up with help from Sailor and Klipper again."

Tim Jenkin was visiting Amsterdam regularly, still busy trying out Floris's wonder-gadget. He'd sent coded messages to his house in London from several different countries to test them for reception quality and then he would decode them. From Europe it worked fine, but from Africa there were problems. The telephone links via satellite gave time-delays of fractions of seconds, and the sound quality was often poor. He was becoming unsure of the reliability of the device. It might be worthwhile for communication within South Africa, but there were questions about its international usefulness, as a lifeline to the outside.

He was experimenting with all sorts of computer systems. There was one computer that could take care of the encoding so that much longer messages could be sent. But sending them was still a problem.

Tim struggled on, searching in electronics stores, talking to Floris, trying out different telephones, and walking around with a permanently wrinkled forehead.

He had asked me to find someone at short notice to make a quick trip to South Africa, someone with good technical insight. I had found Hugo – a real loner, very suitable for this kind of task. Once already I had tried to interest him in the idea of living in South Africa for a longer period, but he had refused.

"I'd never be able to keep it up, in the middle of all those racists, that kind of double life. But I'll always be willing to make short trips."

The three of us drove to Durgerdam and sat on the dike looking out over the water. Tim sketched out the situation for Hugo. He was researching a communications system for which public telephones were to be used. Hugo was given detailed instructions on what he had to do. I just counted the ships sailing out over the IJsselmeer; I wanted to know no more than absolutely necessary.

Three weeks later Hugo was back, and he told me about his travels as we sat in a motorway car park. I would later be able to use both his experiences and those of Henk for preparing others. Besides, I was also simply curious.

"I was soon out of that expensive hotel you arranged for me," he laughed. "I found something myself in a nice district in Johannesburg. Hillbrow. Laid back, just like Amsterdam. Tim had told me that he wanted to know everything about how the public call boxes were wired. I was to try and take as many photos of them as possible, because I can't describe the colours to him – I'm colour blind. I strolled about Johannesburg endlessly, day after day, with my camera bag. I photographed an unbelievable number of public phones, showing their locations. Before going out I found all the districts and suburbs he'd mentioned, on the map. It was a big area to cover – I had to rent a car. I went everywhere: Germiston, Boksburg, Brakpan, Springs, Benoni, Krugersdorp, Randfontein,

Roodepoort. I marked each public phone on the map and then took a picture. I noted down if it was on the left or right of the road, and how many phones there were at each site. Sometimes two beside each other, sometimes as many as ten. Direct dialling, or not. In the end I'd made a complete inventory of all the public phones in and around Johannesburg.

"I had a bit of luck and found a row of phones right in the city centre which had just been repaired. The fronts had been taken off, and they were just hanging open. So it was a cinch to take a shot of their insides. I just stood across the street with my telephoto lens, pretended to shoot the building behind them, and got their inside secrets full-frame! That way Tim got exactly what he wants, and I didn't have to stand there unscrewing the thing myself.

"Then the headsets. I just sliced the cable with a knife and took them back to my hotel room. There I could take my time dismantling them, the speaking and the hearing parts. Later I scattered the headsets in small pieces, in rubbish bins, and out of my car window on an empty stretch of road. So there was no trace that could lead to me.

"After that I went to Durban to do the same thing, list all the public telephones on the street, plus the ones in public buildings. Stations, airports, city offices, post offices. I saw hundreds of public phones there as well, marked them on maps and photographed them. Then on to Pretoria, the same again. And there I went to see the building where Klaas de Jonge's cooped up. Just for a minute, I couldn't resist it.

"During the last week I sent off all my material safely. After that I had time left over, and I was just wandering around feeling dissatisfied, as if I hadn't done enough. The whole business of public telephones had set me thinking. I started to wonder about portable phones – car phones. At one post office where I enquired they referred me to someone who dealt in telephone set-ups which didn't fall directly under the existing system, but which weren't completely illegal. That man turned out to just build phones into cars, but he did put me on to a dealer in real portable phones, who came to my hotel with a demonstration case, with no secrecy at all.

He showed me how it worked, sitting in the lobby, with everyone walking to and fro all around us. A genuine travelling salesman, not a shady character. I just sat looking at that case. So it was that simple, you could buy it just like that.

"In fact it was just a portable phone in a case. You opened it up and the aerial appeared, and everything you needed to transmit was there inside. He could call anywhere, just sitting in the lobby. That was the first time I'd ever seen anything like it. I've brought all the information on it for Tim; maybe he'll find it interesting."

"That's great." I said. It looked as if he'd done some outstanding work.

"How was it, travelling around there?" I asked curiously.

"I love travelling round a country I don't know. And not meeting anybody. I keep to myself on that kind of trip. As soon as I arrive at a hotel I go straight to my room and stay there. I'm very cautious with people, I don't want to run into the wrong ones. In those three weeks I didn't make contact with anyone I didn't need for the job.

"I did drive along the coast a bit near Durban, though. An uncle of mine lives near there with his daughter. I had half a mind to pay him a visit. The crazy thing is that he could actually have told me everything I wanted to know. He's an ex-post office man. He worked all his life for the South African telephone service."

In the spring – in fact, autumn in Zambia – I was introduced to Ivan Pillay by Joe Slovo, Chief of Staff of Umkhonto weSizwe. The three of us met on a covered restaurant terrace in Lusaka. It took me a little while to realise that I had come across Ivan before, in 1983 during a visit to Swaziland. We had only spoken briefly, and no names had been mentioned. I had known Joe Slovo since the early seventies, in London, by which time he already had the reputation of being one of Pretoria's most hated enemies: born in Lithuania, a Jew, a communist, lawyer and member of the ANC – the epitome of all the things most loathed by the establishment. Slovo had already paid a heavy price for his work. In 1982 his wife, Ruth First, had been killed by a letter bomb in Maputo.

I never ceased to be surprised by Joe's habit of driving round with no bodyguard, and the fact that he would sit openly in a public restaurant. "Otherwise I just wouldn't have a life any more," he would say, waving away any concern. Where he lived, however, remained a closely-guarded secret. The other tables were all occupied by whites: expatriates, development workers and foreign business people, the occasional South African.

But no-one seemed remotely interested in the rather elderly grizzled figure at our table. I also knew that he carried a revolver strapped to his calf.

Mac had told me that Joe Slovo, ANC President Oliver Tambo and himself were directing the project we were working on in the name of the National Executive Committee, and Slovo now explained that preparations were so far advanced that it had become necessary to bring in Ivan as organising secretary. This meant that he would be taking care of a large part of the practical side, and Joe urged us to work together closely. "I have complete confidence in him," he said, at which point Ivan took out a small notebook and laid it beside his plate.

That evening Ivan drove me back to my hotel, and up in my room sat on the chair at the dressing table, knees together and feet slightly turned in. His long, slender hands lay over the open notebook. "We meet every day," he said, so softly that I had to close the window against noise of the trucks thundering by outside before I could hear him. "The leaders of Operation Vula get together every day," he repeated.

"Operation Vula?" I asked.

"Yes, that's what the operation has been called. In full, 'Vulindlela'. That means: 'open the path, open the door' in several African languages. It's an everyday expression." He watched me gravely in case I had further questions, and when I remained silent he continued: "I'll make notes at the meetings and discuss with you the aspects with which you can help us." The point of his pen hovered over: "A. Transport": the first item he wanted to talk about.

There would be a regular need for various things to be carried into South Africa: money, travel documents, everything that could not be transferred in words over the communication lines. It looked as if computers would be chosen as the communications system, so floppy disks with the new codes would also have to be taken in.

"And people. We'll have to smuggle them in too," he added.

Once I understood what was needed, we grouped everything into three categories. Firstly we needed something in which small and mainly flat items such as money, passports and computer disks could be carried. It ought to be possible to find a simple solution for this, as long as it was effectively and professionally made – books, or boxes; something that could be used again and again.

Secondly we needed someone to actually carry the stuff into the country. This would have to happen on a very regular basis. Our person would have to travel to South Africa from Europe every month at least, without attracting attention.

Finally, transport of people. We decided to go further with the idea I had already discussed with Mac and Floris: a car with a secret compartment to carry a person. I had already set the preliminary work for this in motion. Just as with Mac previously, I was given a deadline to get everything ready, and then Ivan would come to Amsterdam to check what I had accomplished.

And so it went. In August Ivan arrived, and I introduced him to Elizabeth. She restored old books and prints for museums and collectors. She knew everything there was to know about Japanese rice paper, various kinds of cardboard and types of glue.

When Ivan and I visited her at the workshop between the Singel and the Herengracht, she had a couple of prototype versions ready for us, hard-cover books on nature and art history. She let us examine and handle the books, challenging us to find where her own passport was hidden inside. We had a suspicion where it could be, but couldn't make it out, and certainly couldn't work out how to get at it. She showed us. The cardboard of the back cover was split, and partly hollowed out. A sort of envelope was the result, just big enough to hold a passport. The endpaper, or pastedown, one piece with the final page, covered the space. It was held by a rim of double-sided tape, which could be opened and closed a number of times. It was fine work, and very simple. We took the whole pile of prototypes away with us, for there was no reason they should not be used. Ivan was to take them with him to London, where he had to visit Tim, who was in charge of sending materials from Europe.

I had a lot more trouble finding a carrier, someone who could regularly transport Elizabeth's loaded books to South Africa. I was losing sleep over the problem. It was going to be impossibly expensive anyway, even if I found someone who regularly went there on business, or for another logical reason. The task seemed impossible – until I realised that the only person who could solve the two problems all at once would be an airline stewardess, regularly working on the Amsterdam to Johannesburg route. Her flights would cost nothing, she would not need a visa, and her frequent appearances at the airport would arouse no suspicion or comment. But how was I ever going to find a trustworthy stewardess prepared to take that kind of risk?

During one of many nights of brooding over endless cups of coffee I suddenly remembered a friend who had a somewhat unclear relationship with a stewardess, in which a deep friendship underlay the love. The bond between them seemed to me strong enough for her to feel able to refuse if she found the idea too dangerous, but also to be able to say yes, in the knowledge that he would never lead her into a trap. He sounded her out carefully, and when we finally met I understood at once why he was so crazy about her. Elise was vivacious, vital; her speech flowed over one like a waterfall!

When I described what would be expected of her, she became very quiet, nervous; but almost immediately seemed to gain strength of purpose. She was willing to do it, but when I started to talk about the situation in South Africa, to try and strengthen her resolve, she quickly stopped me. "I understand what has to be done, and I'll try to do it as well as I can. But please don't tell me any more about the awful state of things there. It makes me sick, and I get very angry. That way I can lose my cool."

Floris had made working sketches of some ideas for a secret compartment in a car. They were just rough drawings, and everything would still have to be talked out in detail. However, we already had a type of vehicle in mind, a bakkie, like the thousands running around in South Africa, especially outside the towns.

During his telephone research in South Africa Hugo had also photographed bakkies. He had recorded all sorts of details: how many lights and where they were placed, and all sorts of visible features that make a vehicle typically South African.

The truck would be purchased in Europe – we wanted to do the work on it in the Netherlands – and then it would be shipped to Africa. It was somewhat more difficult than I had hoped. I consulted Hans Dulfer, a musician who often performed at solidarity concerts but was also a car dealer. He immediately pointed out that in South Africa the steering wheel is on the other side. You wouldn't find that kind of pickup truck so easily in the Netherlands; it would be much easier to look in England. Ivan and I decided that for the moment I would work with Tim to take the car plan further.

Shortly before Ivan was to leave for London I had a frantic telephone call from Elizabeth. She asked if the books had already been sent off. She was just about to leave on holiday and we had all forgotten to remove her passport from its hiding place in the book!

Chota's trial opened on August third. The papers reported that he was the most important ANC person to be tried since Nelson Mandela. He was described as one of Umkhonto's chief organisers, and as chairman of the regional political and military committee responsible for the ANC infrastructure in both the Transvaal and Natal. He was accused, along with two others, of high treason and terrorism, attempted murder and, of course, membership of the ANC.

I was shocked when I heard that the trial was being held in Piet Retief, a small town close to the border with Swaziland, far from the great cities in a farming area populated by Afrikaners who were fanatical supporters of the ruling National Party. Family and friends visiting him or attending the trial would have a long journey. His lawyers had to find accommodation at least fifty kilometres away, as none of the hotels in Piet Retief would admit "non-Europeans".

A week before the trial began I received a letter from him. "I've been through a traumatic time, but I've survived it. My fellow

defendants underwent very severe torture, with electric shocks.'"
He was very disappointed that the international protests had had no
effect, and he wrote at length about the legal aspects of the case. He
wanted to prosecute the state for kidnapping and torture.

"It is such a pity you can't come to my trial," he wrote. "Then
at least we would be able to see each other now and then. But once
I'm back on Robben Island it will be easier to correspond. I have the
right to a certain number of letters a month there. Find out how
many words you're allowed to write per letter."

On September the fifth, out of the blue, came the news that
Klaas de Jonge was to be released in an exchange of prisoners. It
was his birthday and we sat, his son and a group of friends, waiting
to call him in his little room in the Dutch embassy in Pretoria,
where he had been confined for twenty-six months now,
surrounded by soldiers.

Then the news came over the radio. We called quickly, and Klaas
himself answered the phone. He had just that moment seen the
news of his release himself, on the television in his room. We
shouted and laughed and cried over the telephone, seizing the
receiver from each other's hands, with a dumbfounded Klaas on the
other end of the line. His lawyer had just brought him two kittens
as a birthday present. In both places champagne corks were
popping, and a month later I was reminded of the party by an
impressive telephone bill.

We only had one and a half days to prepare for his arrival in the
Netherlands, but crowds of enthusiastic people ready to welcome
him home streamed into Schiphol airport – people I'd never seen
before carrying banners reading "Klaas – Freedom Hero!" An
entire choir sang freedom songs in Zulu with an Amsterdam accent.
In The Hague a right-wing member of Parliament was asking the
Minister for Foreign Affairs if De Jonge could serve his sentence in
a Dutch jail, but we were all far too happy and proud to get angry.

Then he appeared, surrounded by police, photographers,
camera crews and great bunches of flowers. We cheered ourselves
hoarse; Klaas was back home. A group of amazed Japanese
tourists who had just arrived asked me who this man was. "That's

Klaas. That's our hero," I cried to them. They laughed, and bowed and waved to Klaas, who was being carried shoulder-high across the hall.

In the press room he spoke to the journalists and, very much aware of the cameras, he called on everyone to demand the immediate release of Helene Passtoors and all other political prisoners.

HARARE – AUTUMN 1987

IF THERE'S ONE THING I HAD COME TO DETEST IN ALL MY YEARS OF anti-apartheid work it was The Conference. I have sat through dozens. Bored and half-asleep I've listened to endless addresses mumbled by uninspired government representatives and professional conference-participants – almost all of them grey-suited men trotting out the same speech as last time. I knew almost every one of these inflated bullfrogs and their boring speeches, which were almost indistinguishable from each other. There must be one, at least one, who had been reading out the same speech for years, without anyone noticing.

However, the conference in Harare in September 1987, about violence against children in South Africa, was to turn out very differently. It could hardly be otherwise, because for the first time the organisers had succeeded in bringing a big delegation straight from South Africa over the border to Zimbabwe, a couple of hundred in all. Apart from the exiles, I had never seen so many South Africans together.

After a visit to Lusaka to meet briefly with Mac, Gebuza and Ivan, I went on to Harare to join the Dutch delegation. My feeling that this conference was to be something out of the ordinary was shared by my colleagues at the AABN office, and we had carefully put together a group to represent the Netherlands, including a juvenile court judge, a lawyer, and a police commissioner.

I checked into the Sheraton Hotel just outside Harare, a flashy golden box stood up on end, completely out of place in that landscape, but large enough and safe enough to house the conference and the South African delegation. The hotel, normally just for rich tourists and journalists, buzzed with activity. The huge ground-floor lobby looked like a village square during an annual market. Excited people rushed to and fro, friends rediscovered each other and walked around arm-in-arm. Exiles, years away from home, no longer recognised little cousins, now grown. Old friends introduced me to strangers who without hesitation took me in their arms – chairperson of an anti-apartheid organisation, that was enough for them.

The "comrades from home", as they became known, were easy to pick out amongst the crowds. They looked awed. At home, inside South Africa, this just wasn't possible. So many small gatherings took place to the accompaniment of police sirens, and eventually truncheons and bullets. And all those well-known names: Nkobi, Alfred Nzo, Joe Slovo, Thabo Mbeki, whose faces they had never seen, voices never heard. If you were caught in possession of a pamphlet containing one of these people's speeches it could mean prison.

The ANC had come out in strength. The "chiefs" joined in the celebrations just like all the rest, and some became again the boy or girl next door they had once been, shouting and laughing as I had never before seen them do.

The exiles were on home ground, in a strange sort of "home match". Harare was theirs, they were the hosts. They carried themselves with self-assurance and tried not to show the burden of life "outside". The longing to get to know each other was mutual, however. The South Africans from the townships brought thousands of personal messages from those who could not come themselves. The exiles wanted to know how things were at home. Are you from Orlando? Do you know this or that family? Aren't you a cousin of my former cellmate?

But there were the hesitant questions too, someone from home asking: "Perhaps you can tell me, comrade, if Solly .... his mother lives across the street from me ... I know I shouldn't ask really, but she's so worried, do you know if Solly has joined MK? It's so long since we heard anything from him ..."

Commitment was high; the conference was important to everyone. Typists and secretaries rushed about with notes and documents. People were dragged away in annoyance into a corner to quickly sort out problems if possible before they occurred. The young men of the security team stood at strategic points, watching, their eyes everywhere.

The six hundred participants, from forty-five countries, gathered in the huge auditorium. The delegation from home, grouped together with an exile amongst them here and there, radiated excitement and impatience. And they sang, sang music which thrilled to the bone. New songs that I had never heard. The emotion in the voices grew as more people appeared on the stage, and suddenly erupted into yells and screams of joy. President Tambo had entered the hall. Everyone stood up, clenched fists were raised. Women ululated their traditional African cry of joy and excitement, tears pouring down their faces.

Tambo, the personification of the long, long struggle, of the dignity of the African. A man who had never betrayed them, a father with whom their ideals were safe, who at this moment was also Nelson Mandela and Walter Sisulu, Shaka and Makanda too, Moshoeshoe and Mzilikazi, Gandhi and Sol Plaatje, Albert Luthuli, Yusef Dadoo and Bram Fischer. Fighter for freedom and justice.

The song of the ANC, their song, the new national anthem, arose from the crowd.

Nkosi Sikelel'iAfrika!

The conference got under way. The children told how they had been tortured or incarcerated, or fell silent, unable to speak of their experiences. That silence hurt my ears. Experts explained the consequences that would later follow this cruelty. Politicians promised to place the issue of the children high on the international political agenda. Outside the auditorium plans were laid, promises and agreements made, and hope started to grow once more that perhaps things could be different; if we would just be determined enough, and cry out loud enough to be heard across the world.

I was standing in a corridor talking with a few others when I saw a short, stocky figure approach us. He had a slight limp. He stopped beside me, shook my arm, and spoke my name twice. I nodded, and he introduced himself as Chris Watters, one of Chota's lawyers. I felt my stomach contract. He said he had been looking for me for

106

days. Everywhere he came, I had just left. Such a search could take a long time in this huge hotel.

Chota had told him there was a good chance I might attend this conference. He was to search until he found me, and ask why I had sent no letters. Since he had been charged, way back in May, he had received nothing from me. I stared at him in disbelief. I had written eight letters, all addressed to the lawyers' office in Johannesburg. "What about the box of clothes?" I asked. "Didn't that arrive either?"

"I haven't seen any box," answered Watters.

A woollen pullover, socks, warm underwear, I had sent it all in May, securely parcelled, to Priscilla Jana's office. Winter was coming in South Africa and those cells were cold, Wolfie had told me.

"A dark blue pullover, pure wool, with a woven pattern." I tried to refresh his memory.

"It must have been confiscated," said Watters, not at all surprised. A very unpleasant feeling crept over me. Where was that pullover now? Had the police opened the box, pulled the clothing out and thrown it away? Or kept it themselves? Had they read my letters? My carefully considered words with which I had tried to say everything possible that might comfort him? Read them and defiled them! I became sick and angry.

"You can give me a letter now," Watters said quickly. "And you know ..." he hesitated a moment, "just possibly I may be able to arrange for you to speak to him, on the phone." I caught my breath.

"During the coffee breaks we always go outside with the defendants. If we agree a date and time I can make sure he's standing beside me by a telephone."

"You mean I could call from home, in Amsterdam?"

"Yes, why not?" He found a number in his diary and wrote it on a piece of paper with a date: October sixth, and a time: one o'clock in the afternoon. I looked at the slip of paper. The telephone number of the court building in Piet Retief.

The conference closed the next day and I moved to another, less expensive hotel. Leave-takings were thorough, especially for those who were returning to South Africa and were anxious, uncertain whether they would be welcomed by their families or by the police.

I still had several days in Harare, and had booked a room well in advance to be on the safe side. The receptionist greeted me as if he recognised me from the last time, and handed over my key. Then I emptied the suitcase I had only just packed, to furnish my new room; toilet bag in the bathroom, books by the bed, underwear in a drawer.

I don't mind hotel rooms. It isn't your own home, you don't have to look after it yourself. The door can be locked, and that gives temporary privacy. I always swiftly make my peace with the "artwork" hanging on the walls. There's nothing to be done about it anyway, and the only thing that really matters is the bed, which must be soft, with enough blankets, freshly ironed sheets, and must be placed so you can see out of the window from the pillow.

I opened the cupboard to hang up my clothes, but the hangers were already in use. Two women's jackets, obviously left behind. One was a beautiful black woollen garment, and the other was blue with an Oriental pattern. I took them out, and saw immediately that they were my size, and that I'd have bought them myself if I had that kind of money. I held them against me in front of the mirror, and then tried them on. They gave off a musty smell, not someone's body smell, but something stuffy, like stale perfume. I quickly hung them back in the cupboard, keeping them away from my own clothes, which were all light summer wear. It was very hot, although still only early spring. Then I fell asleep.

After an hour I woke with a dry mouth and slight headache, took a quick shower, ordered coffee and revived sufficiently to go through my papers to check what I had to do over the next few days. It was dark outside, growing quickly cooler. I closed the door to the gardens and sat down shivering to work at the table. I'd never felt so cold in the evening. There was nothing among my clothes to keep me warm enough, so I took out one of the jackets, the black one. I shook some air into it outside; perhaps the mustiness would fade more quickly. I lit a cigarette, and that didn't smell so fresh either. After about two hours I had finished, and went to bed feeling dead tired.

It must have been about four when I was awakened by someone screaming. It was a while before I realised that it had been me. I was soaked with perspiration, and every few seconds my whole body was gripped by cramps, as agonising as labour pains. I held on tight to the bedclothes and tried to regulate my breathing to control the cramps. What was happening to me? The pain was unbearable. I tried hard not to scream, and to understand what could be causing this. The pain would fade, would seem for a moment to have disappeared, then I would be swept by another attack. My stomach and intestines contracted into one hard knot. My arms and legs seemed paralysed and my breathing was shallow. What was wrong? Why was there no-one with me?

I pulled the telephone towards me and called Jan de Graaff, there with a Dutch camera crew who had rooms nearby. He came at once, banged on the door and shouted for me to open it. With difficulty I lowered myself from the bed and dragged myself across the floor. Jan gripped me under the arms and laid me back on the bed. A new wave of cramps came over me, and after one look Jan raced off to reception. Soon afterwards a doctor arrived.

A big white man was leaning over me, pressing here and there on my stomach and belly. I could hear him talking, and asking questions in a heavy South African accent. In God's name where was I? He pressed my flesh some more, and then said decisively:

"Gastric ulcer."

I looked at Jan. This man had to go, just get out, this South African. The doctor put a jar of pills beside my bed. When he left, after less than ten minutes, I just wanted to be alone. I crawled to the bathroom and stuck a finger down my throat. There was something rotten inside my body, and it had to come out. I took laxative tablets, which brought on such bad cramps that I could no longer even stand. They brought no relief, however. The awful pain stayed, and I faded in and out of an exhausted sleep. Half awake, half asleep, my uneasiness grew; there was something in the back of my mind I didn't want to think about, something very alarming, unexplained, which had happened in Lusaka. I was almost too frightened to let it into my mind. How could I have been so stupid?

For the two nights I had spent in Lusaka, on my way to the conference, I had booked a room at the Ridgeway Hotel, which had become my usual base. I had got through my appointments quickly. Ivan had come, and Joe Slovo, and in the evening I had seen Gebuza. All the equipment for his disguise had been in my case: wigs, moustaches and make-up. We had practised together in front of the mirror. I had pulled the tight wig over his thick hair, and stuck on his sideburns. He had been pleased with the effect.

Very early the next morning Ivan had picked me up again. There were some urgent matters which would be better discussed in a car. After an hour he dropped me off again at the hotel, a little after eight in the morning. It was still too early for my room to have been cleaned. My bed was unmade; everything was as I had left it. On the bedside table stood a brown glass jar with a label. Not mine. I examined it more closely. The label described the contents as "all-vitamin pills", and on the lid was a Zambian price sticker.

I had found the chambermaid at work on the floor below, and asked her if she had been into my room yet. The apology in her eyes said enough.

"Could anyone else have been in there?" I asked.

No, she was sure of that. There were only two keys; she pointed to her huge bunch, and at the one in my hand. Downstairs at reception I enquired if anyone had asked for me, and told the receptionist that there was something in my room that was not mine. He looked at me in disbelief. Things might sometimes be removed from the rooms, but he had never heard of anything being put into one.

"Possibly you have forgotten that you had it with you," he had called after me.

Back in my room, I sat on the bed by the night table and tried to think of a logical explanation. If the jar had been set down there, it could also be moved, so I carefully turned it, and saw that the label did not quite fit at the back. There was a gap of half a centimetre. The sunlight was shining through the window, and if I held the jar slanted, the light flooded through the gap. The contents moved. It was filled with something fluid, a thick syrupy mass, and on top of it something which looked like pills.

What should I do? My first impulse was to call Ivan. But how? I had no number for him; he always made contact with me. There was no further appointment arranged, because I was due to leave for Harare the next morning, and that afternoon was scheduled to meet someone from the cultural department.

There was not much time to think of something. I was picked up for my appointment and not brought back to the hotel until late. The meeting had run over time and after that we had all eaten together. I had not thought any further about the jar. Not until I was brushing my teeth did I again notice it standing in the corner of the bathroom where I had put it down before leaving. I suddenly knew for certain that if I opened it, it would explode. And in the morning, in just a couple of hours, I was leaving. Maybe the jar was dangerous, maybe not. If I just left it standing there, the maid might open it to see if there was anything left inside; everyone in Lusaka could use a few extra vitamins. It was the middle of the night; I couldn't go outside to bury the thing. Anyway, how long before someone just dug it up again?

Then the doubts came – it couldn't be true – was I just falling victim to the local paranoia? There were so many stories going round. But there that thing stood, in the corner, and a million dollars wouldn't tempt me into opening it to find out what was really inside. There was only one answer: I would just have to dispose of it, as safely as I could. I wrapped the jar in toilet paper, and put it very gently in the rubbish bin. Plenty of rubbish had to go on top – cotton wool pads with lipstick and rouge stains, damped down with some of the contents of the toilet. It already looked suitably unattractive. I added cigarette stubs and ashes – all the rubbish I could manage to produce in one night.

Hopefully the maid would empty the contents straight into the big plastic bag on the side of her trolley; then it would be carried off to the rubbish dump.

Uneasy, I caught my flight to Harare. During the conference it suddenly occurred to me that perhaps in poverty-stricken Lusaka it was not unusual for people to scavenge on the dump. During one lunch break I overheard that a bomb had again exploded in Lusaka, close to the railway station. I frantically searched out people I knew from Lusaka to ask as innocently as possible if they knew where the Lusaka rubbish dump was located. No-one had any idea.

"Isn't it close to the station?" I tried again.

"I wouldn't know, really."

AMSTERDAM

THE JACKETS HUNG IN MY CUPBOARD AT HOME. I FOUND NO LABELS or tabs on them to show their provenance. Before leaving Harare I examined them again, closely, inside and out, even picking loose a few seams. Something wasn't right about those jackets. I had been unable to find anything unusual, and I had packed them in my suitcase, carefully wrapped up in plastic; not in order to have them checked out in the Netherlands, but rather because I somehow preferred to keep that nightmare close by me; perhaps it would help me to overcome my vague anxieties. Among the rest of my wardrobe they would gradually become just more ordinary clothes, and then my memories of their history would fade. I had to go on with my work, after all. To prove to myself that I attached no importance to the events in Harare I had the jackets dry-cleaned. I had to send them back twice; that strange smell turned out to be stubborn.

My doctor could find no trace of a gastric ulcer, and as I told him nothing of my suspicions he just advised me to take things easier for a while. I recovered quickly, however, and was soon hard at work.

When I told Ivan about the jackets a few months later, and somewhat hesitantly added the story of the jar of pills in Lusaka, he was furious – not so much at what had happened as at my naivete and stupidity. I defended myself, saying I wouldn't be able to work if I let myself be intimidated. Angrily he recited me a list of examples of people being poisoned through clothing. Hundreds of people had been murdered that way. The South African security apparatus was known for the technique. They used various unidentified poisonous compositions that entered the bloodstream through the skin.[1]

On October the sixth I sat ready at my desk, the telephone in front of me, with fifteen minutes to go. I had twice checked the precise time difference between South Africa and the Netherlands, and the evening before I had written down what I wanted to say. Every second would count; the conversation might be broken off at any moment. As much warmth as possible must come over in everything I said. He must realise that he was in our thoughts, that he was not forgotten. My hands were trembling, and I scribbled down a few last key words, sure that I wouldn't be able to think of anything to say, or only trivial nonsense, or precisely those things better left unsaid.

I dialled the number, twelve digits. After some international silence the phone started to ring faintly. So that was the courthouse in Piet Retief. I held my breath — who would answer? I had written down a different name for myself, on a scrap of paper I now held in my hand. The phone rang at the other end, five times, ten times, twelve times. No answer. I dialled again, and still there was no reply. Again, and again. I checked the number, in the lawyer's handwriting, then banged down the receiver, ripped all the bits of paper to shreds and kicked at the desk. I pulled out the map of South Africa, and searched along the Swazi border with my finger. There it was, Piet Retief, less than a centimetre from the border line. So it existed all right, but they just weren't answering the telephone.

---

[1] In January 1992 I learned from Nico Basson, a former captain with Military Intelligence, that this was indeed an attempted poisoning, which was carried out on the orders of the Civil Cooperation Bureau (CCB). The latter organisation was set up by the South African security apparatus and is responsible, among other things, for "the removal from society" of political opponents.
In April 1988 Klaas de Jonge visited a friend in Nijmegen, in the East of the Netherlands. He left his luggage, a weekend bag of clothes, in a luggage locker at Nijmegen railway station. When he returned a few hours later he found the locker open, with the entire door missing and the bag gone. He recovered the bag at the left-luggage office. A man had handed it in, he was told. The staff on duty had no idea why or by whom the locker had been opened. Klaas de Jonge had them check the contents, and at first sight everything seemed normal. The next day, after wearing clothes from the bag, he experienced severe pain and swelling of his right eye. He was treated for an eye infection at the Free University Hospital. Within a few weeks, however, Klaas was blind in that eye, and there were fears that he would also lose the sight of his other eye. Examination at several hospitals by a number of specialists failed to establish the cause of the infection.

Winter 1987

By pressing a couple of keys I could now enjoy direct contact with London and Lusaka. Tim had brought me a small portable computer which was connected to my telephone. I had to dial a number, tap some keys, and then the computer recorded the incoming message. A disk did the decoding, and then I had only to find the code word, through a number cipher, in a book that Tim had given me: *Buckingham Palace, District Six* by Richard Rive, which stood amongst my travel guides. After that – I could scarcely believe it at first – the text appeared on my screen; with no delay, at any time of the day, and secure because it could not be decoded without the disk and Richard Rive.

Tim regularly sent me reports to convince me that it worked, but in the early days I always called him afterwards to hear a human voice confirm that my answer had been received. One day he proudly demonstrated how we could actually converse through the equipment. He typed a question and I could reply immediately. Ivan, who had a computer in Lusaka, also sent reports, in telegram style, set out point-by-point, information arranged in a clear, logical sequence. My method was to carefully write out everything in advance, as concisely as possible, until Tim one day described the weather in London, and asked if it was hailing in Amsterdam too. After that we just wrote each other letters by telephone, and I understood that this form of communication was not only extremely convenient, but was also strengthening the bond among the three of us.

One of the first serious messages concerned the imminent arrival of a woman who needed a disguise, merely informing me that I could expect another visitor – no other information, no name. She would report at an agreed location in Amsterdam, so was obviously someone used to travelling in Europe. When we met I realised that I had seen her before, in London and in Lusaka, but retained no more than a vague memory. Then it came back to me: her name was Janet Love, and I remembered seeing her at a party in London years before. She had been in animated conversation, interrupting herself frequently with loud laughter, and I had been struck by her skill with words. She had wiped the floor with one opponent in a way that had thoroughly appealed to me. She had an attractive, forceful face, strong bones, and an athletic way of moving, but above all simply a powerful presence that made her hard to forget.

In preparation for her disguise Janet had herself picked out some clothes, but she had no definite ideas. She wanted to appear smart and independent, a woman with style, because she was going to be operating on her own inside South Africa. She already fitted this description, however, so we searched through piles of women's magazines from a newstand for the stereotype of the young independent woman. The only one who caught our attention and attracted our comments was Princess Diana. We compared the photographs and read out the captions to each other. So why not? In Janet's disguise we would try to approach Di's image as closely as we could without producing a ridiculous imitation.

Louis made up a fine blonde wig, Diederik made a new set of teeth, and Janet tried out a set of tinted contact lenses over her brown eyes. It took a little while before she could see anything through the tears, but then I heard a squeal of surprise as she saw a pair of huge soft-blue eyes staring back at her from the mirror.

We would certainly have to make changes, too, in the way she walked. Even on high heels she still moved like a well-trained guerrilla choosing her path through the jungle.

In the evenings we talked; not of the future or what was to come, we avoided that. I was more curious about her background, her parents and their influence on her.

They had come from Europe, she told me, after the war. Janet was a first-generation South African. Her mother had been born in Lithuania, and at sixteen was carried off to a German concentration camp, Stutthof in Poland. When she was set free after the defeat of the Nazis she had spent in total seven years in ghettos or camps – her entire girlhood.

Janet's father was English, and had fought the Nazis with the British army. He had been wounded, but had reported back fit as soon as he could. As a soldier in a Canadian detachment he was among the liberators of Stutthof camp, and there he got to know Janet's mother, where she lay in hospital with cholera. When she recovered, she joined the British troops as a translator, and with her new husband stayed in Germany with a repatriation team, helping people through the chaos that followed the end of the war. When she could no longer stand it, they moved to England, where Janet's father was given a job by a company that sent him out to South Africa. This had been during the 1950s. The company soon ran into trouble and could no longer honour his contract, and the family had to choose between staying, or returning to England and starting again. They stayed, and Janet was born in 1957.

"It's still hard for my mother to talk about the war. Very hard. As I got older that sometimes annoyed me; she was always so afraid. But of course she has horrible memories. Her mother and her sister both died in her arms. One of her brothers was executed before her eyes. When she does talk about it you can see how it hurts her."

"Wasn't it very hard for her that you became active in politics?" I asked. "My mother never really understood how I could voluntarily put myself into dangerous situations in Africa."

"Yes of course. They were both very concerned. They had already seen as much as they wanted of what went on in South Africa. Lots of their friends and acquaintances had been arrested early in the 1960s. But they had brought me up with the idea that there was no other solution but mass resistance. The only thing they were genuinely frightened of was that I'd get involved in the real underground."

"And that's just what happened."

"Yes. I think they understood that my choice for that was unavoidable. One advantage was that we were always very open with each other at home. It was normal for us to discuss everything very frankly. Really debating. If there was a point of disagreement my father would bring out the encyclopaedias and dictionaries. It was a very healthy atmosphere, which allowed you to say what you thought."

"So they didn't try to dissuade you?"

"No. They respected my choice; but the fear stayed, and will for some time, I think."

After Janet had left I had to concentrate on the bakkie. Floris had worked out a design on paper. The fuel tank would be reduced to half its size. This would greatly reduce the range of the vehicle, but eighty kilometres or so should be more than enough to cross a border. A reserve tank could be mounted on the load bed. This type of tank was common in South Africa, where there are long distances to cover. Between the reserve tank above and the half tank suspended under the bakkie, an opening would be cut out to create a space big enough to carry a curled-up human being. It would not be pleasant, but it ought to be possible to survive it for about three hours, we thought.

Right up until the last moment several questions remained unanswered. How would the passenger get enough fresh air? Wouldn't too much dust get in on dirt roads? The space obviously couldn't be made completely airtight. Would petrol fumes be a problem?

Tim and I found a suitable vehicle in North London. It had all gone easily. A dealer had a reasonably new light blue bakkie on his lot. We had walked round it, and then looked under the bonnet. Tim suddenly nudged me hard and pointed to a small plate on the side of the engine: "Made in South Africa". We looked at each other in triumph. This was the vehicle we'd been looking for, and we decided to call her Clara. We would then be able to refer to her in our communications, and also in our contacts with Ivan, without it being obvious what we were talking about.

We were extremely careful in our messages, even within Europe. Code names were thought up for everyone and everything, and in a secret place I kept a list of them, which was also coded. My memory is not bad, but the sheer number of names for people and things would sometimes dizzy me – and every month they were all changed. If someone called out a name on the street – any name – I always looked around.

In December a major cultural event opened in Amsterdam: CASA, a conference for South African artists. We had been preparing for it for more than a year. Hundreds of Dutch people had been recruited in order to bring hundreds of South Africans to the Netherlands and find them places to stay. Amsterdam was to become a great meeting place. The theatres, music venues, jazz cafés were all ready for performances by South African actors, musicians, poets and writers. Musicians from inside and outside South Africa, who had often not played together for years, sometimes not at all, were rehearsing all over the city, and gradually their notes came to harmonise. Actors built their stage sets, and dancers and singers wandered along the canals in the icy winter air, amazed at the relaxed atmosphere in the city. The organisers handed out woolly hats. This was the greatest harnessing of forces that the AABN had ever undertaken. With relatively little money we had to house and feed everyone, and make their stays pleasant and worthwhile.

It was a time of great expectations. The ANC was breaking down barriers. More and more groups from South African civil society sent representatives out, with or without an invitation, to meet the ANC; not just students and trade unionists, but also church representatives and business people. They were getting around the table together, and talking. Pretoria seemed to be losing its iron grip. Newspapers loyal to the government railed at the ANC's visitors as traitors when they returned home. But the process could not be halted. A new road was open: in the direction of Lusaka, Harare, London and New York – everywhere the ANC had offices, away from propaganda, press censorship and repression.

International sanctions had transformed South Africa into a beseiged fortress. But the ANC was breaking down that isolation, for all those who were prepared to discuss a new future. That included the artists.

The people of Amsterdam appreciated this culture, wholly new to them, and came in their thousands to listen to poetry and music.

The theatres were all sold out. The official opening of the conference took place in the Stadsschouwburg, the City Theatre. The mayor welcomed the South Africans to Amsterdam, the anti-apartheid city. Barbara Masekela of the ANC called on her fellow countrymen and women to seize the opportunity offered and bring something good into being; and I addressed those present in the name of the organisation.

The evening before this I had set aside time to work on my speech. It had not been easy to concentrate. Tim had brought the bakkie over from London, and it was now garaged in Durgerdam. That afternoon I had taken out the petrol tank, with a welder and another mechanic, and my nails were still black. Ivan had sent me several urgent messages on the computer, and I was preparing a number of people to leave for southern Africa. Immediately after CASA two of them were to fly to Botswana to take care of arms transport, and in early January two more would go to Swaziland to set up safe houses.

I was tired, and the presence of so many South Africans drained me emotionally. I wanted to say something in my speech, to find a form to give words to the special link between the peoples of the Netherlands and South Africa.

My story opened by recalling how one Jan van Riebeeck, from our city, had long ago voyaged to the Cape, and how after him the Boers had pushed further and further inland, driving the Africans from their own territories. How there had always been resistance – resistance by artists. I drew parallels that cut across modern history, from the Dutch writer Multatuli who had composed a bitter assault on Dutch colonialism, to Sol Plaatje, the South African poet who had found words to describe the oppression.

My words came out stilted, in a heavy accent. I so much wanted to get more feeling into them, but what I really wanted to say was taboo, and I felt disillusioned and confused.

I stood alone on the stage, behind the lectern, and passed my fingers over the cloth of my jacket, the black jacket from the hotel room in Harare. Obeying a sudden impulse, I had pulled it on just before leaving the house to come to the theatre to draw strength from it, and the certainty that I was not going to buckle under the pressure.

120

Spring 1988

The search for new people suitable for underground work began to take up a lot of my time. Everywhere I went, as I met new people, I was on the lookout. I even looked at old friends in a different way. Sometimes I would go to a birthday party with no other aim than to check someone out: "What are you doing these days? You've just left your job? Really? How are things with your girlfriend, what's her name again? Oh, so you just want to get away and travel for a while..?"

I generally moved in circles of politically kindred spirits, so I concentrated on practical aspects. If someone had just got the promotion they'd had their eye on for years, I crossed them off my list. Setting up house with a woman and her three children also meant elimination. But mild jealousy of my work at the AABN, or a spontaneous outburst like: "It's about time those Boers were dealt with properly!" or even: "My brother's just finished his degree; he's thinking of getting a teaching job abroad for a while ..." were enough to make me prick up my ears. After that there was still a long and tricky road ahead of me. Each potential candidate had to be subtly but thoroughly screened. Success was rare.

Once we reached the stage of open discussion, there was never much time to really get to know the new people. I questioned them about their youth, school days and everything that had followed. While they talked I scrutinised them from top to toe, and listened for hidden messages in every voice inflection or broken sentence.

I tried to understand something of their dreams and ambitions. It was always a relief if the person opposite me was not a real idealist. I had long ceased to believe in the idea of sacrifice; I much preferred it if they were looking for a good opportunity for self-development, or an adventurous way of doing work for which they had always admired others.

Robert and Tina had left for Botswana at the end of December. I hesitated to send them because of their youth; they were both in their early twenties, but I had allowed myself to be persuaded by their youthful courage and earnestness. They belonged to a generation of young radicals that I did not know well, and therefore found difficult to assess. However, they would be together, and were apprehensive enough to be careful. They were to travel to Gaborone, and later would be deployed in South Africa to set up arms caches and transport.

Mirjam left early in January. A short, strongly built woman in her early thirties with seemingly boundless energy, she thrived on the idea of entering unknown territory and refused to be intimidated by the slightest thought of danger. Lucia would take care of her initially, and then as soon as possible she would set up a safe house on her own.

Andre, who had originally put me on to Joop, had left for Swaziland a few days after Mirjam, by a different route. Swaziland was where the most people were still needed. They knew nothing about each other, because I wanted to avoid the possibility of the Dutch gravitating towards each other for security if danger threatened. Andre had been picked for a special task within Operation Vula. He knew what to expect because for some time he had kept in touch with Joop, who complained so much in his letters that it impressed me that Andre still wanted to go.

When they left, there was no way I could really assess how much any of them would be worth once they were in place. I did not yet have the experience to make a reliable judgement. I had no idea, and never would have any idea, how someone who gave the impression of strength and stability here would react once they were in danger over there.

I wanted to end the exchanges of letters, and now avoided promises to correspond. The box of unanswered letters in the bottom of the cupboard bothered me too much. Now and then I pulled one out and tried to put some words on paper in reply, but without success. And then I'd just feel guiltier. In fact I preferred not to think about them too much. It was just wasted energy; if something went wrong I'd hear about it soon enough.

And then came the first setbacks. The hotel manager in Cape Town was calling and writing letters continually: when was Henk Oostveen coming? But his application for a work permit was stuck somewhere in the South African embassy in The Hague. We had decided to go through official channels. Was his application being held up by Pretoria's notorious bureaucracy, or was there some more sinister factor involved? The hotel manager sent a letter of reference to the embassy, along with some advertisements from Cape Town newspapers to show that he was unable to find a chef locally. Everything had now been dragging on for months, and Henk was becoming very restless. Finally the letter from the embassy arrived, just one sentence: "I have to inform you that the relevant authorities in South Africa, after careful consideration of your application, are not prepared to grant your request."

After all our efforts, a rejection. Henk was bewildered, and very disappointed. We discussed the possibility of sending him out there anyway, and letting him sort out a work permit on the spot. This seemed foolhardy, however, as long as we did not know the reason his application had been refused. We decided to let things lie for a while.

So I had to start all over again. Someone still had to go to Cape Town, and soon.

Near the Albert Cuyp market, on a corner, stands a dark, rather shabby Indian shop. The steel-mesh shutters protecting the windows make it seem that something is being hidden inside. In the window there stands a dummy wearing a gold-embroidered sari, surrounded by trays of cheap jewellery and embroidered linen slippers. Overhead on plastic hangers hangs children's clothing covered in frills and flounces. I had cycled past this place for years.

For some time I had been tempted to go inside, but had not dared to without a good reason. I now finally had an excuse: Rita.

She had just arrived in Amsterdam to be fitted out with a disguise, and had spent the first few days looking through my photo albums and switching television channels. This gave me the chance to look her over thoroughly. She was short, black, with big eyes and fine features. I was surprised when she told me that in South Africa she was registered as coloured. She had a white ancestor, whose influence on her appearance had been lost over the generations. The only reminder of him was her classification. This gave me an idea. Race, colour and appearance, after all, were one's most important distinguishing features in South African society. If I could help Rita through a colour barrier I would be giving her extra security. I examined her again, closely. I would indeed be able to turn her into an Indian with good make-up and the right clothing. If she had a second disguise and learned to swiftly change her appearance – from one skin to the other, as it were – then her chances of evading the long arm of the law would not be bad at all. Together, we looked at her face in the mirror. With my finger I sketched in imaginary eyeliner, a mark on her forehead, and long straight hair. Now she could see it as well.

A man in a turban waved us towards the back of the shop, where two women were vaguely busy amongst the racks of clothes. They retreated in confusion and watched us in amazement from a safe distance – a black and a white woman looking for sari material. I draped a length of cloth round Rita's shoulders, and one of the women rushed forward. She giggled shyly, unable to understand why we favoured a discreet brown material instead of the red, glittering with silver thread, which she held up for us. However, she was more than willing to make a brown sari for us, and took Rita's measurements while explaining that she would make an under-garment and a short blouse, a choli, over which the outer sari was worn with its end fastened either across the shoulder or over the head. The manner of draping the garment showed a woman's social status; I could not ask her more about this because status was determined by husband or family – that much I knew. Perhaps this disguise was less simple than I had thought.

Back at home I made up Rita's eyes with eyeliner and kohl. We lightened her complexion, and fitted the half-length wig Louis had lent us for practice. Winnie was out of town, but she had arranged for her colleague Arjen van der Grijn to visit with useful advice. Arjen examined our progress with interest, and cautioned us about the way of draping the sari and using the forehead mark. He had once narrowly avoided equipping an actor with an incorrect Turkish moustache – points downwards was wrong, or was it the other way round? He had forgotten, and looked rather worried. The idea that this young woman, made up and in costume, was not going on stage but out into the real world made him almost physically ill.

We searched through library books for information on the Indian woman's way of life. What we read under the heading of Hinduism was indeed very useful for our disguise, but did not make us particularly cheerful, and led to long talks until late in the night about women in politics, about marriage and men. Rita became thoroughly worked up, her voice now and then rising high in indignation. She had little good to say about South African men – only her father came out of it well. Things were not easy for a black woman in the liberation movement, in spite of pretty theories about women's rights. Without fierce ambition and plenty of endurance it was difficult to avoid ending up stuck in a creche or sitting at a typewriter. "You just have to do everything better – ten times better – than your male comrade," she cried angrily, for the umpteenth time, and we both burst out laughing. "And you mustn't have a big mouth – at all costs keep your mouth shut!" she added angrily.

Together we finished a bottle of wine, then became dejected, and very tired. Rita looked so small sitting there on the sofa with her legs tucked up beneath her. I decided I would send an extra-enthusiastic report on her to Lusaka.

Two months later I looked her up in London. She had been told to wait there for further orders. I assumed this was to avoid her being seen too much in Lusaka before she made her illegal border crossing into South Africa. Fewer questions were likely to be asked if it was generally believed that she was studying abroad for a time.

Before leaving for London I had collected the sari, and tried it on at home; Rita and I were the same size. I made up my eyes with kohl, darkened my skin, put on the wig and stuck the little spot on my forehead; a couple of steps backward, eyes closed, then a quick glance in the mirror. There stood an Indian woman. What would it be like to have to go outside in such a disguise, in Durban for example? I half covered my face with the end of the cloth – I had been stopped by the police and they were asking for my identity papers. My false papers. Above all keep your eyes down and your voice soft! If the policeman was white I might get away with it, but what if he was an Indian and asked if I was perhaps related to so-and-so?

That night I dreamed of arrest, of the humiliation of being stripped. Strangely, in my dream I was dressed as myself. Nobody would recognise me, I'd thought. Nobody would expect me to just be myself. But I was picked up nevertheless – suddenly gripped by my upper arm, and my hair was being pulled – insanity. I awoke upset and breathless, with no feeling in my arm.

In London, Rita tried on the sari; but I didn't feel at ease until she had on her second disguise: as an African woman in a smart suit and a wig of fashionable curls.

We spent the afternoon together; that evening I was due to leave for Lusaka. She was annoyed to be still stuck in London.

"It's taking much longer than it was supposed to," she complained. "I don't understand why there's such a delay. I'm all ready. Will you tell Ivan that?"

I promised her I would, and before I got into the taxi she gave me a letter and a present for her boyfriend, for his birthday.

LUSAKA

IVAN PICKED ME UP AT THE AIRPORT. HE WAS STANDING inconspicuously in the background, then came forward to greet me briefly and dive into the chaos where the luggage was being unloaded. He threw my cases onto a trolley which squeaked loudly as he conducted me swiftly past Customs and security checkpoints, ANC card held high.

After I had caught up on a few hours' lost sleep, Mac arrived. He was in a hurry, and got straight down to business: "Gebuza needs an extra wig," he said.

I was surprised, to say the least. "But he's got three different ones, plus moustaches and beards!"

But Mac was adamant. I would have to get it to Lusaka as soon as possible, within a couple of weeks at the latest. When I protested further, a wide smile flashed briefly over his face. He knew he had given me the feeling that I hadn't done my job properly.

"Just one more wig, and he'll have enough." There was a determined undertone in his voice. "You'll be getting a lot more people," he added quickly.

We went on to discuss the setback with Henk Oostveen. I was already working up someone else for Cape Town. This time we were going outside legal channels – it was safer that way.

Before he left Mac once more went over with me who was where in the front-line states, and he stressed that I should continue to co-operate closely with Ivan. He stayed for a moment more, hesitating, already half out of his chair, and lit another cigarette. He looked as if he wanted to say something more, but then stood abruptly and moved to the door. I had the feeling that I should quickly ask him all sorts of questions, but he was already in the doorway. He turned once more, put a hand on my shoulder, and said: "Thanks."

It was to be a long time before I saw him again.

To Ivan's great satisfaction we had managed to ship Clara, the bakkie, to Dar-es-Salaam. From there she would be driven to Lusaka, and then further southwards. The secret compartment had been beautifully finished off with foam rubber and chamois leather, to make lying in the small space more bearable during journeys over rough roads. The welds under the truck were hidden by a thick layer of underseal. From the outside it was impossible to see that the vehicle only had half a petrol tank.

Ivan was radiating the same kind of tension as Mac, even as he sat with his notebook on his knee, composed as ever. In everything we discussed he was giving me the feeling that time was pressing. We took stock of how far we had come, where new people were needed and what technical equipment had to be supplied. There was an urgent need for cases with false bottoms, and handbags with small, secret compartments.

Then he asked after Rita. I passed on her complaint, and gave him the letter and the gift. He interrupted me as I pleaded her case: "Before I forget ... Gebuza needs a new wig."

"I know. Mac's already told me."

"Just the one more. Then he's ready to go."

AMSTERDAM – SUMMER 1988

ONE EVENING IN JULY, THE TELEPHONE RANG. IT WAS HOT AND muggy, and I had opened the windows. The sudden loud ringing cutting through the peace sent the birds clattering as one into the air from the tree outside the window. Reluctantly I picked up the receiver.

"Hello ... it's me," said a familiar voice, which I couldn't place immediately – familiar, yes; but somehow out of place.

"A bit unexpected, right?" said the woman's voice, with a brief nervous giggle.

"Luce? Is that you?" I asked, hesitantly, "Where are you?"

"Here. I'm back."

Another whole day passed before we saw each other. Lucia could only laugh at first; her hands were shaking. We hugged each other.

"It was all over, just like that," she whispered into my neck. "They just put me straight on a plane."

I held her away from me and looked into her eyes. She was ready to burst into tears at any moment. "There were just so many signs that they were on to me."

She took off her glasses and rubbed a hand over her face – her contact lenses were just for Swaziland, of course.

I made tea, to give us a moment to calm down. Then I wanted to hear everything, from the beginning.

"The beginning of what?" she asked, wearily.

"Start where you and I left off."

"Then I've got to go back to the beginning of last year, just after Chota was kidnapped. I wrote you then that I'd found a house and quickly been given a housemate."

"Yes. Up to then I know what happened."

"Well, in the beginning there we were, my housemate and me, sitting sizing each other up in that empty house with no electricity. It felt strange to be living with someone I didn't know. Mostly he sat in the living room with piles of paper, reading and writing. I saw him always making lots of notes on little pieces of paper, but I didn't ask about them. It was all fine with me, and I didn't want to see too much. We had to find out together what worked and what didn't, because he had to stay hidden from the neighbours. We were surrounded by other houses.

"I made double curtains, so that nobody outside could see shadows, and after a while he started to move around a bit more freely. At first he never left anything lying around. Everything was neatly hidden away in his room. Later on he got a bit less careful, maybe because he knew I'd clear up anyway.

"He had a strict routine. During the day he never went out; only in the evening when it was really dark, then he'd be away until well after midnight."

Lucia was talking fast, her hands waving. "I found a job quite soon. An office job with an awful man. He'd spent his whole life in Africa, but he still considered himself a German. He was in road construction, and the only reason he was in Swaziland was that in South Africa he'd lose all sorts of contracts because of the boycott.

"I was working in a little office, with a Swazi woman and a South African Indian man. The woman had been working there for ages and did her job very well, I thought. She knew the company inside out. But in spite of that I was given twice her salary, and made senior to her. She's black. The boss could hardly hide his contempt for her, and bawled her out for any little thing. The weird thing was that his wife was South African coloured.

"I only lasted three months there. He offered me a long contract, but I couldn't face it. He drove me up the wall. Not long after I left he was shot dead, in his own house. There was a rumour that his wife had organised it."

Lucia stood up, and wandered round the room. The heat wasn't bothering her; my blouse was sticking to my back.

"Where was I? Oh yes, my housemate." She was silent for a moment.

"We were so careful together. If I had to drop him off somewhere in the car, all the windows had to stay closed, all the doors locked. And we never drove home by a direct route; we parked round the corner to check we weren't being followed. It's funny – now I'm telling you about it, it all seems so strange and over-dramatic – but we were very close to the border with South Africa. Sometimes we'd see South African police helicopters by the Swazi police headquarters. But we didn't have much in the way of weapons in the house. He had a pistol, and later they gave us an AK-47 and a few hand grenades.

"I gradually began to do more and more for him. I bought components for radios and photographic equipment; a white woman doesn't get asked so many questions. I always cooked, which I enjoy anyway, did the washing and the shopping. Sometimes I'd buy candy for him, for his trips. I think I fell in love with him during that time." She smiled briefly.

"Didn't that make it difficult?"

"Well ... No. It was great. Without that it would really have been heavy. He was away a lot, and then it was very lonely. I couldn't have visitors - not even Mirjam, who lived close by. But when he was there I could share my feelings with him, and he with me.

"He helped me, too. While I was still working for my first boss I came home miserable every day. 'Resign,' he'd say. I'd yell back angrily: 'We need the money!' But he stuck to his guns, even though it didn't make things any easier.

"At night, in bed, he'd sometimes tell me about when he was young. How he lived as a child, in the country. How he went fishing secretly with a friend. His little friend was so scared – he thought that only whites were allowed to fish in the river. Or he'd sing songs from his schooldays, and I'd sing any Dutch songs I remembered. And there was lots of laughter; and silly little incidents, like when we saw a comrade driving around with his car number plates upside down. He'd usually come home in the middle of the night, wake me up, and sit on the bed with a plateful of food, and then he'd want to talk. It turned into a kind of ritual.

"Then everything went wrong."

She stood up again, and closed all the windows.

"Damn! Then it all went wrong."

She went to sit on a chair by the table, further away from me, smoothing her skirt down over her knees.

"Exactly what did go wrong, Luce?"

"It began with a telephone call for me at work. The shop was very busy, and so I wasn't really thinking very clearly when I answered it. Do you remember that resistance cell being rolled up a few weeks ago in South Africa? Near Broederstroom? Well, I'd never actually been in contact with anyone from that group, but for a while I did drive around in a car belonging to one of them. I was really mad when the comrade who'd lent it to me said it had belonged to Susan Wescott, who was one of the people arrested. But anyway, these things happen.

"So I was at work as usual, picked up the receiver and a woman's voice asked for me – which was strange. Nobody ever called to speak to me, except the owner. The caller asked again, checking my name, and then: 'Did you ever work for ...' And she named my old boss's company. And I said yes, again. Then she began: 'I know Susan's parents, you know, the one who's been arrested, and I'd really like to help. I've been told that maybe you can arrange something for me ... that maybe you can put me in touch with someone who would know what I can do.'

"I hesitated. I can't remember exactly what I said. I think I said yes again. Probably. I could still kick myself so hard when I think of it.

"And then she asked me if she could get in touch with me somewhere else, and that made me very suspicious – at last! I said no, very firmly. Then she said 'I'll call you again' and hung up.

"I was thinking 'Oh, you stupid cow, it's a trap!' even before I'd put the phone down. I was so nervous I couldn't do a thing, so I went home. Luckily my housemate was there. If only he'd yelled at me ... but he just said very calmly: 'They've just been trying it on.' Neither of us could think how they'd got hold of my name and number.

'You've only, given them confirmation of something they already suspected,' he said. Then he started to pack his things.

'You'll just have to go on working as usual at the shop,' was his advice. 'Keep a close eye on everything that goes on around you.'

But he had to leave. It was too dangerous. That was so hard for me! Awful! Everyone who knew me, like Mirjam and Joop, were warned straight away. There could be no contact with me at all. It was as if I had the plague. I was completely isolated."

"So then you left, I hope?"

"Well, no. I went on working in the shop for another week. Every day I'd see Mirjam walk across the square. She was checking to see if I was still there behind the counter. But the nights were the worst. I was completely alone then. I stayed awake for hours, listening to every little noise. That last house, my third by then, was very secluded, but all the advantages of that were gone now. Every night I just listened for them to come.

"One day after a week, a woman came by. I knew her by sight. She worked in another shop on the same square. She walked straight up to me, said my name, and whispered: 'Are you involved in the work too?' I wasn't going to be caught a second time. I didn't react.

'Oh well, leave it,' she said. 'I was just asked to warn you.'

'What do you mean? What about?' I managed to say.

'That's all I wanted to tell you.' And she was gone.

"After that little visit my housemate decided I should leave the country. But I didn't want to. I thought I'd just stay where I was and see what happened. I went on working as usual. Around midday I went to my regular café for lunch. There was a woman who worked there – Rose, a super person. I often chatted with her. But that day she stood by me for a bit longer than usual, leant over, and said: 'See the men at that table?' I hadn't noticed them. 'I reckon they're ANC people.'

"I felt my heart turn over. Now I was really getting the feeling that there was a conspiracy against me. Rose! Even dear Rose! I would never have taken her into my confidence, but her working for the enemy? Never! I didn't trust anyone any more. Perhaps it was better to get out, even if it was just for a little while.

"So I left. A rotten way to go. I saw my housemate just once more, just for a moment, and very rushed, in a car park on the way to the airport."

Lucia sat staring in front of her, tired out. No tears. Just an apologetic smile. "When I'm together again, I want to go back as soon as it's possible. Will you fix it?"

The summer slipped by with no holiday, or even plans for one. On sunny free afternoons I would take my daughter Tessel to relax in the swimming pool, or to the zoo. She was six years old, still always holding tight to my hand as we walked down the street.

She was accustomed now to having people about the house who she could not understand. It's because they come from England, I'd told her. That seemed to me safer, because little girls shouldn't have to keep big secrets. Oh, those angels from their angel-land, she would sigh. But presents arrived for her with the South Africans, who hugged and petted her, missing their own children. In bed she sometimes sang a little Zulu song that Gebuza had taught her.

Tessel was already back at school when Ivan next came. He was in a remarkably good mood, cheerful, even frivolous – not the Ivan I had known until then. Finally, after Tessel was tucked up in bed and we'd settled down with his duty-free whisky and a pack of cigarettes, I realised why he was so happy. "Has it happened?" I asked in excitement.

He laughed, his face radiant, and raised his glass to me: "They're inside. It all came off fine. Operation Vula is underway."

Mac and Gebuza had been infiltrated into South Africa on August 1, a fortnight earlier, and about the only thing I could remember about the day was that I had called my younger brother for his birthday.

"My God!" Ivan burst out, "We took so, so long to make the decision to go! Every possibility was considered, everything was checked out. In the end the only question left was where and when to get them over the border into South Africa. In the end we chose our old familiar patch: Swaziland."

They hadn't been able to do a thing for the whole of June, because of the 16th and 25th, important days for the ANC.[2]

[2] June 16th, Soweto Day and June 25th, anniversary of the Congress of the People, Kliptown.

There was always far more political activity in South Africa around that time, so the police were extra-alert, especially in the border areas where the guerrillas entered the country on sabotage missions. But early in July they had been able to move.

There were still things to be taken care of before they could go. They both had to have good cover stories to explain their being away from Lusaka for so long. For Mac the solution had been easy. His health had not been good for some time, and this was widely known. He had already been to the Soviet Union once for treatment on his knees. Now he had to go back for longer-term treatment. The news was already going round. Gebuza was going on an officer's training course. No-one would think that at all unusual. Many ANC commanders went away for training. And the advantage of the Soviet Union was that is not the kind of place where you just pop in to see someone because you happen to be in the area.

Mac and Gebuza had left Lusaka at the beginning of July, very visibly, and in a northerly direction. They were to travel many miles, along circuitous routes, before finally arriving in Swaziland, in disguise and ready to go.

Ivan poured more whisky and rolled his glass backwards and forwards in his long fingers. "By then I'd found someone to help me with all the preparations – Totsi. You'll meet her soon, because she's next on the list to come here for a disguise. I've known Totsi for a long time. We've worked together a lot. In '86 she helped me get into South Africa illegally. That's her speciality – border crossings; she's bloody good at it. It was us who got Chota safely out, after Helene Passtoors had been arrested. And that wasn't easy, I can assure you, the whole police force was hot on his trail. I've got a lot of confidence in her. She knows the border area well, speaks the local language, and passes easily for a Swazi.

"But she was working with another group, and when I went to ask if they could release her for a special job it turned out there was a problem. There's a big investigation going on into a whole lot of comrades; there've been unexplained arrests. Someone's gone missing. It's also connected with Chota's kidnapping, and missing papers which have fallen into enemy hands. And Totsi was named by someone. I won't say any more about it, because I think there's something personal behind it. Luckily it was soon clear that there was no serious problem. Nothing more than a jealous outburst from another woman."

After a few days Mac and Gebuza had arrived. They were travelling in the same aircraft, but separately and well disguised. They were housed in different places. Nobody knew how long it would be before they could cross the border. It was a time of discussion and consideration, waiting and worry. "Gebuza was tense and wound up, complaining about his disguise. He hated having that false moustache stuck on his face, and was still practising putting on the make-up. When I visited him in his safe house in the Smokey Mountains there'd often be make-up showing on his shirt, or he'd angrily tear off his wig because it was too hot. And then we had to sort out our new South African travel documents. Mac knows how to forge stamps, and Mirjam, your Mirjam, helped him gather together all the bits and pieces he needed. She was working in a printer's and turned out to be really good at 'liberating' all sorts of things.

"Mac was staying with Andre, who was great. He changed large amounts of currency, drove me around all over the place and took care of that safe house for Mac, for weeks, keeping the atmosphere really relaxed." Ivan laughed, and fell silent.

Much later, Andre told me: "Ivan hadn't said what it was all about. Just that someone was coming. It was only when Mac had arrived, and took time to explain everything, that I understood what was going on. That knocked me back on my heels a bit, I can tell you.

"He was going to be there for at least three weeks, and we made up a story that he was just a friend of mine coming to stay while he recovered from a knee operation. He usually went for a bit of a stroll very early in the morning. To stretch his legs, he said. I reckon there's really something wrong with that knee, anyway.

"When he wasn't off meeting Ivan or the other one, he'd sit reading, or rather dissecting, the South African newspapers. I've never seen anyone use his time so efficiently. Nothing he did was without a purpose. Then came the point when I realised that the time to go was getting close. I had to pick up a handgun and an AK-47 at Joop's place; I was amazed. I'd no idea he was storing that kind of thing. Joop had given them a good extra oiling. Back home Mac checked them out very well before I hid them away. Gloves on – he didn't take any risks, not with anything.

"Things were getting more tense and restless. They were having maybe three meetings a day, sometimes more. I was sent off to the library to find out the exact times of moonrise. It was coming up to full moon.

"One of those last evenings there was a nasty incident, which I felt bad about for a long time. Mirjam had come round. I hadn't met her before. Mac's hair had been bleached, and she was going to make it dark grey with charcoal – quite a job. Joop had brought her over, and because we were all together so unexpectedly I cooked up a whole meal. It was a real good evening, with Mac telling stories. He had all three of us spellbound. God, the way he can spin a yarn! All about Robben Island, and the other prisoners.

"It was stuffy inside, but I didn't dare open any windows in the room where we were sitting. So I just opened them a bit in the kitchen and the bedrooms. Halfway through the evening Mac went to fetch something from his room and came back asking if I knew where his jacket had got to. I went to look. The jacket was gone, and his money and diary with it. The money didn't bother Mac so much, but his diary was all prepared for the trip. Someone must have climbed in through the window; probably just an ordinary thief, because there was some small change gone from the table as well. I took a look around outside with a torch, but not for long. I didn't want to attract attention to the house.

"The next day I was so pissed off I went out and had another look. I don't know what for – footprints, I think. And I found the diary, just thrown down in the grass, everything still inside."

Back to Ivan: "We were all nervous and edgy from the waiting. There'd be complaints about the most trivial stuff."

Totsi and he were checking the border area every day by then. The exact place for the crossing wasn't going to be fixed until the very last moment. They checked the terrain with binoculars and kept an eye on the army units. Ivan made a map of the area, showing any nearby houses, the best places to climb the fence, where the paths led and any good cover to hide them if anything went wrong.

"The Swazi soldiers remained the main problem. They bivouacked in tents along the border, and Totsi kept a record of how often, at what times and in what numbers they patrolled the no-man's-land on each side of the border which had been stripped of trees and undergrowth. On the Swazi side there were a few houses and a shebeen where the soldiers bought food and drink.

"In the evening we could hear them talking loudly and laughing in their tents. We had to find out the times when they were less on the alert. They could be deadly dangerous, them and the Boers on the other side. In June last year, a bit further along the border near Piet Retief, ten of our people were shot dead on one day. And that wasn't exceptional."

They found out that at the end of each month the soldiers would go to the city to cash their cheques at the bank, and to send money home. It was a crazy system, because they all went at once and the Swazi side of the border was sometimes virtually unguarded for more than twenty-four hours.

Once Ivan and Totsi were certain when payday would be, they could give the "all clear". Mac became absolutely single-minded. Between midnight and six-thirty in the morning they all went over everything again, and even worked out an alternative plan. Very early the next morning they were ready to leave.

"Gebuza was in his element. As soon as an operation is underway he's fine. Waiting, that's the problem for him. We walked cautiously to the border fence. Totsi was going to lead them inside, scouting ahead. It was still wintry that early in the morning, and there was a stiff breeze. Even so, I was feeling hot and out of breath when Mac said goodbye. He was very calm. But Gebuza hugged me. He held me tight for a moment. It surprised me. I don't know him as an emotional person at all. 'We're relying on you,' he said quickly, and then they climbed over the wire. I saw them cross through no-man's-land, quickly, bent low, and then disappear into South Africa.

138

"There was nothing left for me to do but wait for Totsi to come back. She may have been a half-hour, or several hours, I've no idea. I just remember the surprise on her face when she found me waiting there in exactly the same place by the fence. Not so very clever, maybe, but I just couldn't move another yard ..."

Ernest had come up from Drente on his motorbike to meet Ivan. He was due to leave for Cape Town soon. He carefully extricated a Walkman from his helmet, pulled off his thick leather biker's gear, dropped his gloves on the table and his heavy boots in the corner of the room; and there stood a pleasant, blonde young man. Briefly and formally he introduced himself to Ivan, and they sat down at the table. I kept my distance.

Ernest was in his mid-thirties, and had grown up on a farm. He was a technical engineer, and his chances of finding work in Cape Town looked very good. I was convinced he was capable of swiftly setting up a safe house. Ernest was to fill the gap left now that Henk couldn't go.

As this was someone who would be operating in South Africa itself, Ivan wanted to check for himself that I had made the right choice. I felt as if I was sitting an exam. Ernest didn't disappoint me, giving concise and pithy answers to the questions.

"So, what have you told your friends?" asked Ivan finally.

"That I want to see some more of the world before I settle down," was the simple answer. "They think it's crazy that I'm doing it in South Africa, I reckon."

"And your parents?"

"I didn't tell them until last weekend. I wasn't looking forward to it. My mother started crying, I knew she would. We were sitting in the kitchen, at home on the farm. My father was doing the milking. I think he came in because he heard my mother. So then I told him too. First he didn't say anything, for a long time, then he looked at me angrily: "So you're going to work for Botha" was all he said. He turned away and didn't speak to me again. My brothers told me that they won't take me to the airport, but that they'll meet me when I come back."

Ivan was just staring at him, perplexed.

"I've written a letter – for my parents. In case anything goes wrong. It explains the whole thing."

In two days Ivan taught Ernest to send short messages, coded and in invisible ink. He worked out a simple system so that Ernest would be able to keep in touch with me during the first phase. For this we each used a copy of the same book, a thriller. A message consisted of a sequence of numbers, one of which gave the page, the others lines and letters. He was to write the numbers on a card with a salt solution, and by heating it I would be able to decipher the figures. It was not too time-consuming, and would enable him to let me know when everything was ready – job and house – and of course if anything went wrong.

After the two days he once more pulled on his leathers and roared away on his bike. He was ready to go. His friends were to drive him to Schiphol.

Now that Mac and Gebuza were undergound inside South Africa, the communication lines were in intensive use. There was almost daily contact between South Africa and London, London and Lusaka, London and Amsterdam. In London Tim was on call 24 hours a day receiving and relaying messages. I had my computer always within reach, and if there was a message for me I'd get a signal on my answering machine.

But Ivan and his comrades in Lusaka were quickly overloaded. His job involved not only getting all the reports to President Tambo and Joe Slovo, but also sending their replies out quickly. He was worried, because soon he was due out in the field again to prepare new infiltrations, and what would happen then? I thought of Lucia, who was still waiting to hear if she could go back. She'd be perfectly suited for this job.

Ivan talked with her at length. He wanted to know every detail of what had happened in Swaziland, in order to be able to estimate how much was known about her. But Lucia and I found an answer to everything. She would get a divorce, and take back her own name. Temporarily she could work in Lusaka under an alias. I would again completely change her appearance, and we invented another cover story to tell her family.

Lucia was thrilled at the prospect. I had to warn her about Lusaka. Swaziland had been lonely maybe, but was nothing compared to what was now in store for her. Apart from contact with a small number of Vula colleagues, she would be completely isolated. There would be no relief or recreation, and mountains of problems. In Swaziland everything was still available, imported directly from South Africa, but in Lusaka there were just shortages, and a black market in things like soap, oil and bread. But Lucia was undaunted.

"If I'm going to be working for Vula, then great! Better than sitting in a safe house and holding down a full-time job."

Tim was to teach her the ropes, so she flew on to Lusaka from London, to embark on her voluntary incarceration with the computer.

In a very short time Ivan and I were getting through a great deal of work. He fitted himself into my daily routine, and we muddled through the household chores together. We drank tea all day, because his stomach wouldn't take coffee, and occasionally he would tell me something of his past. I showed him photos from my school days, and from the early period of the AABN. We cooked, or fetched food from a Jewish restaurant round the corner, and in the evening he would dictate messages for Tim which I sent off straight away.

One afternoon we decided to go shopping. On the street he took my arm and stopped me.

"There's something I have to tell you ... it's about Rita."

"Ah!" I replied with enthusiasm. "Have you seen her disguise?

His face was very sombre: "She's in trouble."

I said nothing. This felt very ominous indeed.

"Her boyfriend is suspected of working for the enemy."

"The one I brought the present for?"

"He's the one. Frankly, he never received it. He couldn't. He was already inside."

"What do you mean, 'inside'?"

"Well, ANC security had a fair amount of evidence that he was working for Pretoria. So they decided to interrogate him. Now the whole case has turned into a real mess. Apparently he's committed suicide; at least that's what we've heard. Meanwhile Rita has gone back to Lusaka from London."

"My God! How awful for her!" was all I could manage to say.

"There's worse," he went on, gripping my arm tighter. "It seems that during the questioning he said that she's working for South African security too." I was speechless. "But our people aren't convinced. Now they're checking into everything. The indications against her don't seem to be very strong. But there's nothing we can do for her."

It was as if I was struggling through a thick fog. This couldn't be true. It didn't make sense.

"So now they're holding her, too, for questioning," said Ivan gravely.

"Oh, My God ..." I hardly knew where I was any more. I couldn't believe it. I was beside myself with fury.

"You're lying!" I screamed. "This is not true!"

He walked beside me, staring straight ahead. I could see her, in the sari, in that curly wig. Together on the sofa. All our talks about men. The bottle of wine. "She never asked me anything at all. Damn it, she never ever talked about anything with me which could be any use at all to those bastards," I shouted, tears beginning to flow. "That idiotic paranoia! It gets everyone in the end. Can't you see that's exactly what they want? They send a couple of idiots to spy on you, knowing full well they'll be caught, and that just from fear they'll point the finger at the first person to hand. So then everyone's suspicious of everybody else. Destruction from inside out."

I was stumbling over my words. Ivan had long let go of my arm; he looked as if he was afraid of my anger. We were way past the shops by now, and I had no idea where we were going. "That's the perfect way to lose good people. It's because she's a woman, of course! Good looking and clever and ambitious, and that just had to be punished ... "

Ivan tried to break into my tirade: "It looks as if there really is plenty of evidence against her friend. You really shouldn't worry too much about Rita. It's not as if she were in prison or something. She's just got to stay available for questioning."

I shouted at him: "How can you say that? 'Really shouldn't worry too much ... ' She's finished. She can forget it. Once you've been under suspicion and your lover's been branded as a spy, you carry it around forever. Even if your innocence is absolutely proved, the gossip club will make very sure it's never forgotten."

Ivan looked at me sideways, and patted my shoulder clumsily.

During the days that followed I was depressed, with a sort of grief I had not known before. Now and then the fury would flare up again, and sometimes I felt betrayed – especially if I tried to imagine that perhaps it was true. That was the worst – very nearly impossible to live with.

I slept badly, and one thought kept going round and round in my mind: such a great fear of betrayal had grown up within the ANC that it must be a tremendous relief every time someone was accused of treachery; because then answers could be found or created for all the questions around unexplained problems. Then there could be relief for a while. The invisible monster gnawing away at the organisation had been partially exposed. After a little while the anxiety grew again of its own accord. The spies were there, all right. But where? And who?

The terrible truth was of course that the ANC had indeed been infiltrated, probably on a large scale. This was known. So everybody was preoccupied by the question of who could be trusted, and who were the villains.

But in that very complex situation who could prove they could be trusted when the worst came to the worst? And who could claim the right to throw the first stone?

Amsterdam – Autumn 1988

IVAN INSPECTED MY FLAT CLOSELY, INSIDE AND OUT, WHILE TRYING to convince me that the suspicions about Rita could also have consequences for me. He examined the dark "dead spaces" in the entrance stairs, and said with some irritation that I might do better to allow for the possibility that the suspicion was justified.

"She knows your name, your address ..." and he tested the locks on my front door. Looking out of the windows, he analysed the area, out loud, and made notes. I lived on a corner, on the second floor, next door to a tram depot that was guarded twenty-four hours a day. From five o'clock until late at night tram drivers and inspectors walked continually up and down my street.

"If anyone does force their way into your flat, scream out the window for help," said Ivan. I found the idea ridiculous.

He made me describe how, if I'd been out visiting someone in the evening, I locked up my bicycle on my return. "Chain around it, search your bag for keys, walk to the front door ..." he repeated. "That's plenty of time, if they're waiting for you, to drag you into a car. They don't need much time at all to get information out of you."

I protested, but he went on:

"They have access to all sorts of drugs. Once they've finished with you they'll just chuck you out on the street. And you can try taking that story to the Dutch police."

"I can't do without my bike," I objected.

"Don't be so stubborn. You know the names of all the people involved in the operation. If Rita passed on information to them then they'll draw their own conclusions. You've also got a responsibility in this. Think of Mac and Gebuza, of the Dutch people out there on the line – and think of your daughter."

We agreed that I would use taxis, at least in the evenings. Then I would ask the driver to wait until my babysitter opened the door.

144

That meant I would always be in sight of someone.

After Ivan left I followed his instructions religiously. But it soon became too much for me. I couldn't see it as anything but an unfair intrusion on my life, and I missed my bike rides. But I did become far more careful. Gradually I began to dig myself in, inside my home. Extra locks were installed on the door, and secret compartments were constructed all over the living room and bedroom for the papers I needed often. The rest went into safe-deposit boxes in the bank. The only place where I had nothing hidden was Tessel's room. I drew the line firmly at that.

I also got into the habit of looking outside regularly, at cars parked in front of the building. Ivan had warned me to be especially on my guard if I saw one with two men inside. But there were often cars parked there with two men inside. When they got out, and I saw their tram company uniforms, I would again feel ridiculous.

The few friends who still occasionally visited had to telephone in advance, and call their names from the outside door downstairs. After a while I could recognise them all by the distinctive sound of their footsteps on the stairs. My house fell silent; I no longer played music on the stereo because then I couldn't hear other noises in the house: the door being tried, sounds on the balcony, movement on the stairs. I listened to my upstairs neighbour, and became annoyed if his music was too loud.

I was still busy strengthening my fortress when Totsi arrived. I resolved to keep our contacts as businesslike as possible, and to avoid being drawn into friendship. She would be able to stay at an address I had not used before, and for the first few days I just left her alone with the photo albums. After that we sat for many hours together working out a plan.

It was not easy to stay distant. Totsi was the warmest and most cheerful South African woman I had yet encountered. She chatted companionably and without restraint, as if I were a sister. She was so overflowing with energy that at the house where she was staying she had asked to do the ironing just to keep herself busy. In contrast to the other guests, who never went out unaccompanied, she had already explored the city, knew where the shops were, and had figured out Amsterdam's confusing ring of canals. She was not the least bit intimidated by this strange new environment, and her cries of amazement echoed round the room as she described the people she saw on the streets, and laughed aloud at the bicycles, the houseboats, the red light district and the narrow houses.

"What a crazy city!" she cried. "And so friendly!"

Three days with her and I was seduced. Arm-in-arm we sallied forth to the shops, Totsi pointing out the shoes or dresses that I absolutely had to buy. Sometimes as I looked at her broad, dark face I tried to picture her as the same woman who had climbed the border wire with Mac and Gebuza. I longed to ask her about it. But her openness did not go so far as to let fall one word about her work or her experiences. She never used names, except that of Ivan because she was aware that we both knew him.

In July 1990, however, as we sat grimly together in a house in Harare after a catastrophe, unable to go outside because of the danger, we had lots of time on our hands. Deeply affected by the events of those days, I decided that our shared experiences should not be lost, should be written down. The only thing I could find in the house for recording sound was an old portable radio-cassette player. On some old tapes, over music which no-one wanted to listen to any more, I recorded Totsi's story.

She first asked if it was all right for her to begin with 1977.

"Before that I was just a child," she said. "But when I turned nineteen I wanted to get out of Soweto and I took the bus to Swaziland, to find a better education.

"I didn't understand what was going on in my country, so it was a big relief when I met a South African there who explained things to me. Then I understood why I felt so much anger about everything, and I wanted to join the struggle right away. He'd admitted to me that he was an ANC member and had promised to get me work as a courier." But the man was arrested. She waited week after week for him to be set free, until she read in a newspaper that he had died in a police cell. It was months before she again met someone from the ANC.

"He spoke to me in Zulu, and I plucked up enough courage to

146

ask him if he was an ANC member. He listened to me for a long time, and taught me a lot, and in the end arranged for me to become a courier. Not long after that he and his wife were killed by a car bomb. That hit me very hard."

When Ivan asked for Totsi's help in getting Mac and Gebuza into South Africa, she had just returned from military training in Angola. He told her right away that there was a problem, that there was an investigation going on, into all sorts of people. It was all about papers which had gone missing between Swaziland and Maputo, after Chota was kidnapped – precisely the area where she'd been working as a courier. "Apparently Maud, who was working for us in Maputo, thought that I was the leak. She'd warned Ivan against me. 'She isn't clean,' she'd said. I was really shocked. I'd thought we were friends. There had been one problem between us, but it was a personal thing; we'd both had the same boyfriend, without knowing about each other. Maud was out of her mind when she found out. Hey, I was really disappointed, too. But I couldn't understand how she could let that business have any effect on the work; that hurt me a lot. It made me so unsure ... Luckily she was the only person with any suspicions, so I was cleared for this job. I was really happy because I could feel that it was something special. I decided that whatever they asked me, I'd make a success of it. But it was hard to put what Maud had said behind me. Do you understand?"

I nodded.

"Well, then. In July I left for Swaziland with Ivan. I still didn't know what it was all about, but that didn't matter. I just gave all my attention to the journey, and arriving there safely. I was very frightened of going back to that place where so much had gone wrong, where I was wanted by the police, and where lots of my friends had been arrested and murdered. But it was strange – I felt at home again very quickly. Then Ivan finally told me that the job was to infiltrate two important people into South Africa. We had to maintain absolute secrecy, and make the preparations very carefully indeed.

"We reconnoitred the border area for weeks. I checked out all

147

the places we'd used before to climb over the fence, and searched out new ones. My first choice was for places where the local people cross over now and then, visiting family or going to a clinic. I've never prepared so intensively for an infiltration before. If I thought we'd done enough Ivan would want to go on, and if he wanted to stop then I'd think of something else to check. Then the two comrades arrived.

"Then, one evening – I can still feel it in my belly – Ivan picked me up in the car. We drove for a while, and stopped by a gate. A stranger came up to us out of the darkness. Before he even got in I recognised his voice – Mac Maharaj! I was so shocked that I didn't dare look round once he was in the car. 'Please don't let it be him,' I thought. 'He's only here to organise something ...' I was praying that it wasn't going to be him. That responsibility was just far too much for me. While we drove he kept stressing how important it was for me not to talk about this with anyone, even if I got arrested. Even with Ivan I was only to refer to him by his code name – Ben.

"And that evening Ivan told me that the other one was going to be Gebuza, whom I knew from my time in Swaziland. I always had the feeling that Gebuza saw me as a bit of a chatterbox. Maybe that's why Mac told me not to talk to anyone. I lay in bed, shaking with nerves. I couldn't sleep at all, and just kept thinking: 'What if it goes wrong? God, what if it goes wrong? Then all those fingers will be pointed at me. Please God, let it all go well.'

"The next day I went back to the border alone. The others stayed in town. By now I had back-up from Swazi people I'd known for years; old people, who lived close to the fence. We kept an eye on a huge area, between Pongola and Amsterdam. That's the Amsterdam just over the border in South Africa. We knew that the soldiers would leave their tents at the end of the month to go to town and cash their pay cheques. We had to find out the exact day it would happen, and somehow work out which bit of the border would be temporarily unguarded. I dressed as a Swazi woman and hung around near the houses and the shebeen, gossiping here and there, and trying to keep a good view of the tents and the soldiers.

"On the last day of July I saw they were gone. I'd warned Ivan the day before that it could be any moment now, and he was waiting in a house close to the border, where I'd been for days. We drove fast, back to town where Mac was staying at Andre's place. They fetched Gebuza, and then they decided that the next day was it.

"The three of them spent the whole night talking through the plan. I managed to get a couple of hours' rest, because I'd finished everything I had to do – sketch-maps of the border area, with all the details worked out on paper. At five in the morning we all washed, and got going.

"I left first, took a taxi to the border to check that nothing had changed, and then waited in the old woman's house where I'd been spending the last few days. I called her Mama. She knew all about me, that I was with the ANC, and that I was going to be doing something important that day. We sat together at her kitchen table. She hated the Boers so much that she'd do anything to help us, and she suggested taking me along to an sangoma. He could give me a charm to make me invisible to the Boers. Then I'd be able to cross borders and go through roadblocks without being seen. She's a simple woman – really believes in it. I managed to refuse politely. I said there was no time left for that. Then she brewed up some herb tea – she saw I was nervous.

"The others arrived an hour later. It still wasn't quite light. In the house they quickly pulled on the overalls we'd bought. The high grass we had to walk through is still wet in the mornings, and if you get caught with wet trouser legs it's obvious right away that you've come out of the bush. Besides, they were wearing their smart suits, for later when they arrived in Durban, but those would be a bit conspicuous in an area where the only people around are poor. Now any passers-by would just think they were labourers from one of the farms nearby. Mac had a hat to wear, there aren't many Indians in that area. They weren't taking any heavy weapons with them, just their handguns. I wasn't given anything – it was better that way. If I was caught I'd have a chance of talking my way out of it. That's a bit trickier with a pistol in your pocket.

"Mama sent a little boy who lives with her out ahead of us to make a final check that there wasn't a single soldier around. When he came back it was my turn to go, ahead of the others, through the scrub and past some trees – it's not very far. The bit that crosses no-man's-land is the most dangerous, because you can so easily be seen from the South African side. But there wasn't a soul in sight and I quickly climbed over the border fence. It's about three metres high, but I've done it so often now, it only takes me a moment. On the other side I quickly walked to the clumps of trees there which give a good view of the road which runs parallel to the border.

"Andre had already crossed the border near Amsterdam some time before, with his car and Dutch passport, and he was checking the stretch of road they'd have to use to get deeper into South Africa. We had to know if there were checkpoints set up. The South Africans did that when there were so few Swazi troops on duty. I waited in the bushes until I saw his car coming, then walked out on the road. He stuck up his thumb as he passed by – all clear. He was supposed to turn round further up and come back. It was all timed so Mac and Gebuza would arrive in the meantime, and he would pick them up. I stayed by the road, because there was something strange: lots of women kept walking by. It took me a few minutes to realise what was going on; there was a Catholic church nearby, and at the end of the month the priest sometimes sold old clothes. He must have decided on just that day to get rid of the stuff.

"I saw Mac and Gebuza appear from the woods in their overalls, looked at their obviously expensive shoes, and then at the women. But they were much too busy chattering to take any notice of two ordinary farm workers. Mac pulled his cap further down over his eyes, and Gebuza came up to me with a huge grin on his face. He said: 'Good morning South Africa!' I wondered what he was feeling inside. Mac looked tense, he was already taking off his overalls. Andre pulled up in the car and they quickly gave me their pistols, got in and drove away.

"I didn't dare stand looking after them too long, and I walked away with all their stuff under my arm. Ivan was still standing there, just where we'd left him. I didn't realise how tense he was until I'd climbed back over the fence and we'd gone back to the car. Then we found that Ivan had been so nervous he'd locked the keys inside. It took all the energy we had left to smash in a window with a pistol butt. So we drove back to the city, with three AK–47s and the pistols in the boot. All we had to do then was wait for the message that they'd reached their first stopping place safely. Then we'd be able to just leave Swaziland as fast as we could.

"There was nothing more to do. Ivan had dropped me off and gone on to his own place. I was alone, waiting and waiting. We didn't hear anything that evening. No sign of Andre. I was up before five the next morning, starting a really thorough spring-clean. I dusted and scrubbed, and washed all the windows. Ivan arrived late morning. Still no news. He sat in the living room smoking, and I took a bath.

"Such a wave of panic came over me, lying there in the water. 'Oh my God, what's happened? What's gone wrong? And if it's gone wrong, what will they say? They'll say I'm not clean.' I cried so much in that bath...

"That afternoon Ivan decided we'd leave the next morning, message or no message. We didn't dare put it off any longer. Andre still wasn't back. For a last check, we drove to a friend's place. We'd agreed with Mac that he could always call this person and leave a message, but the man had no idea what was going on, and when we rang the bell and asked if there was by any chance a phone message for us, he had to think for a minute. Then he casually said: 'Oh yes. Yesterday evening. Somebody just said that everything was OK.'

"We left the next morning. We were taking the same flight, but we didn't want to be seen together. So we were standing in separate queues with our tickets when I just started shaking. I couldn't control my body anymore; my passport fell out of my hand. I was shivering out all those six weeks of tension. Ivan came over to me quickly, took everything out of my hands and helped me through Customs and with my luggage. Our bags were checked, and then one of the policemen put his hand on Ivan's shoulder. I froze.

'We're going to have to arrest you,' he said.

Ivan looked at him, cool as ice, and asked why.

'Because you're taking our beautiful sister away without our permission!' And he burst out laughing. There were more of them standing around, all sniggering.

"Once we were in the air, we finished a whole bottle of wine together, and in Harare we just wobbled off the plane. We were both tipsy, and we'd got the giggles."

On Totsi's last evening in Amsterdam everything was ready for her disguise. Suits and dresses were hanging up all over Winnie's living room. Wigs and makeup were laid out on the table. Yan Tax walked around with his mouth full of pins and a tape measure round his neck. Totsi changed in the next room, and Winnie made her up.

After about fifteen minutes I heard a loud scream followed by cries of amazement. "I'm Diana Ross!" Totsi screamed and rushed over to me wearing a huge curly wig, false eyelashes and high heels.

An hour later she'd been helped into her second disguise. Yan had made her a new body, from soft materials. Everything seemed very quiet, so I went to investigate. She stood still before the full-length mirror, staring at herself. She was strangely fat, with drooping breasts and high shoulders. She was wearing an old woman's dress. Her face looked old and weary. She looked at me, very serious, spread her arms and said: "My mother".

WINTER 1988

THE FLOOR OF MY WARDROBE HAD BEEN INCONSPICUOUSLY RAISED. The board lifted out easily to reveal my computer's little hiding place. I no longer dared keep it in the living room cupboard; if my home were to be burgled the computer would be the first thing stolen, and besides, no-one should know I had anything like it in my house. My friends and colleagues would be very surprised, for they knew that I always wrote by hand or with a typewriter. I'd always been contemptuous of computers; mainly because I just couldn't get the hang of them.

Ivan sent me regular reports, telling me that Ben and Carl, alias Mac and Gebuza, were doing fine. He said they were making excellent progress in establishing contact with various resistance groups, but gave no details. In autumn Carl had sent an urgent request for the AABN to support an international campaign against the white elections in South Africa, and had asked if Ernest was making progress in Cape Town. Communication with Ernest was still through birthday cards, on which he had reported in invisible ink that he had a job and a house in Rondebosch. A courier had been sent to him to find out more details. We had to know exactly what his position was before sending someone from Sabata's group to stay in his house. There was also a top priority request for another person in Cape Town. It looked as if the work there was gaining momentum.

I was reporting through Ivan on the new people I was preparing for departure. There were a fair number at that time: three married couples, a nurse, and two women friends. My preference for couples or pairs had grown from the stories reaching me of the loneliness of the work. Mirjam's early return especially had set me thinking.

I had been worried about her for some time. Lucia had said

when she came home that Mirjam's life in Swaziland was no more than a hard, endless succession of lonely days. I had been surprised; she had been so full of optimism and expectation when she left.

In November she came home. She was suffering from arthritis and an eye infection, and was very disappointed that she had had to give up, especially as everything had gone so well in the beginning. Within two weeks she had found a job at a small print shop and soon afterwards a house and a car. The problems had started with her first housemate, a young African woman who had made it clear right away that she would rather be with her friends than with Mirjam. The ANC, however, had decided that because of the work she was doing she had better stay in a safe house. There was friction between them from the start. They had rows about broken appointments and about endangering each other's safety. The young woman was regularly called to order by her ANC chief, but she became more and more depressed, finally spending whole days in bed.

"Are you ill?" Mirjam asked her.

"Mind your own business. Piss off!" was the reply.

Sometimes she said nothing for days, just shutting herself away.

"Things were really tense in Swaziland," said Mirjam. "We lived in constant fear of raids by the South Africans, who regularly attacked houses belonging to ANC people, and both of us were living on the edge of our nerves. What made it all worse was the woman living in a cottage behind the house. She was completely round the bend. I couldn't ask her to leave because she was the land lady's sister from Cape Town. But her carryings-on weren't exactly healthy for my housemate, or for me. Sometimes this woman would walk round and round the house screaming at me: "Revenge, revenge! You will be punished!" Once she shouted that she had dreamt that I would soon be murdered. I tried to calm her down, but my housemate had already got out of bed, in a complete panic.

'Oohh!' she bawled. 'I dream that too, all the time.' I think she really did have trouble with nightmares. Before she shut herself away like that she'd told me a little about herself, that her sister had got her involved in the resistance, and that was how she met her boyfriend. She'd fled the country with them. But once they were out of South Africa they were split up by the ANC, and sent to work in different places. 'He'll come soon,' she'd say sometimes. 'Then he'll marry me.'

"After six weeks they took her away. I found that very painful, as if I'd blown it."

Soon afterwards another woman was brought to live with her. Mirjam described her as friendly and amusing, but also level-headed, with nerves of steel. She worked as a courier for the ANC and was away a lot, often all night and sometimes for days at a time. Mirjam was almost always alone, and saw almost no-one except for her colleagues at work. She would be in bed by nine-thirty, as she couldn't go out anyway. She had no television, and the diary she had started finished up as little more than a record of what she ate each evening. The weekends were sheer disaster. Only when her housemate came home from a mission was there any relief:

"Then we'd both just blow off steam. Her from the tension – I think she transported weapons – and me from sheer loneliness. So we'd put the stereo on, turn it up as loud as it would go and dance around the room yelling out the songs, for hours and hours."

Mirjam did small jobs for the ANC. She had not only helped Mac to forge official stamps, but had photographed sites that interested the ANC. "I had no idea why they were so keen on having snapshots of some house front, or a path in the mountains. I just did it – saw it as a chance for a day out." But almost everything they asked she could do at home. A copy machine was installed in her house, and at night she turned out pamphlets that would be smuggled into South Africa the next morning. Her training at the journalism school was coming in handy. "The problem was that it had to happen at night when everyone was asleep. Every time the machine made a copy it gave out a flash of light. You've no idea how bright that seems after dark, it was like living with a lighthouse. So I'd run backwards and forwards between the machine and the window to listen in case anyone came. But it was a great thought that the stuff would be going into South Africa the next day. That made up for a lot of things.

"The hardest thing of all was the kind of shadow life you have to lead. You can never even have a good moan. Lucia is different. She likes to keep plugging on. I need to be able to get out of the house, take a walk, go to a bar and really talk to someone. It didn't work out. I just ended up sick."

Wilma came back home after two years for a short family visit, and we agreed to meet in the same cafe where we'd said goodbye. I'd finished three glasses of juice by the time she finally came in – very pregnant indeed! She manoeuvred herself through the tables, kissed me, and pulled out a chair so far that the people beside us had to move their table. Wilma patted her belly in triumph. "Not bad, eh?" She laughed and leant forward slightly. "We'll talk in a minute. First I want you to meet him. He's waiting outside." A tall, strongly-built African entered swiftly, shook my hand hard and long, and I immediately knew just what Wilma must have told him. She still had a contented look in her eye, but there was a touch of defiance in the way she laid a hand on his shoulder. "We're here to get married," she announced loudly. The elderly couple at the next table turned their heads. Disconcerted for a moment, I stumbled out my congratulations. Wilma ordered rolls, and we relaxed into talk of anything and everything – Amsterdam, Gaborone, marriage, children and parents. Nothing about the work. She steered the conversation skilfully so that he never felt excluded. After half an hour he rose, and again shook my hand thoroughly.

"My God, Wilma, what happened?" I asked, before he had even reached the door.

"Oh, it's a real, beautiful love story, and so strong! I met him very soon after I got there. It took me by surprise too, and I told my ANC contact man about it straight away. He was against it. He advised me not to get into a relationship. In this work, he said, you mustn't fall in love. You get tied to someone and then that gets more important than the work. If you're under pressure you'll make bad decisions. Well, I didn't agree with that at all. Life goes on. Falling in love as well. Anyway, it was already too late by then."

"Does your boyfriend know why you're in Gaborone?"

"Yes and no. When we were first together and I was regularly going into South Africa transporting stuff, he got very suspicious. Actually he thought I was working for the Boers. So then I was forced to tell him that I was connected with the ANC. But he came back hard as nails: 'It's easy for you to say that but how do I know you're not lying?' I said 'Well, that's your problem. I'm not going to start proving everything to you.' He stayed suspicious for a while, but that's over now. Exactly what I do stays my business. He just has to trust me."

"Isn't it horribly complicated? You're not exactly leading a quiet life right now."

"No. That's another reason I need him. Look – in the first year I moved house fourteen times, and I always had guns and explosives stored at my place, or there were cars being worked on in the garage. That all stopped, thank God, because the comrades decided that safe houses and arms smuggling don't go together. And it was really getting too dodgy. Like the time they brought round a carload of grenades and Makarov pistols at ten in the evening. A comrade and I lugged it all inside, while a night watchman stood looking from across the road. I pulled a case out of the boot. The comrade said 'Look out!' but the thing was already falling apart and the detonators all just rolled over the ground. The night watchman saw it all right, but he just walked away. It could just as easily have all gone very wrong. We just shoved everything in my wardrobe. The next day I stood out in front of the class in a dress that stunk of dynamite."

"When did you start transporting arms?"

"Almost right away. First I made some scouting trips to get to know the terrain a bit. I'd told my contact that I'd rather not do the digging myself, to get the weapons underground. I'm no heroine at night – imagine if you hit some hard ground, and I'm so jumpy at night my heart's in my mouth if a rabbit runs across the road. Frankly, I'm scared of the dark.

"I usually begin a weapons run on a Friday. During the day I teach class as usual, then hit the road straight away. That way I'm in Johannesburg the same evening. The car, or usually a van, is loaded up beforehand with guns and explosives, in special compartments.

I'm always a bit tense when I leave. They'll let me through all right at the border – I just assume that. But even so I'm relieved once it's behind me. Then I buy some crisps and raisins as a reward.

"Over the border you drive for hours over a bare, flat landscape. The Western Transvaal, very dry. People generally look down their noses at it – a backward and isolated area, with peasant farmers fighting drought and lions. Lonely farms and tiny villages. Africans walking along the road or over the fields. You can't see any houses or huts, but there must be a settlement somewhere behind some trees. Just as you think you've left a village you come into a shopping street all lit up. That's where the Indians live. You just drive from village to village along an endless strip of asphalt. I do it in seven hours, because you can't go fast with a van that heavily loaded. Every little hill knocks you back to second gear, and even then you're struggling. Long drives wear me out when it's so hot and so boring. But when I feel I'm about to end up in a ditch, I pull over and sleep behind the wheel for fifteen minutes. Then I'm all right again. I've never managed that trip without stopping to sleep.

"The worst part is the suburbs: Krugersdorp and Roodepoort, traffic light after traffic light – that takes forever. In Johannesburg I look for a hotel, then call Gaborone to tell them where I am, all in code of course. The next day I drop the van at the agreed place, usually a corner on the outskirts of town. Whoever picks it up has their own set of keys. They drive it away, unload it and bury the stuff.

"Meanwhile I go shopping. On those days, Johannesburg's a sort of London or Paris for me. A big cosmopolitan city where you can get anything. It's great to shop there, and then I always enjoy the evening, just relaxing in bed and watching television. We don't have it in Gaborone. I order up food and a glass of wine, and always sleep like a log. It feels safer inside a hotel than on the street.

"Sundays I wait for the phone call from Gaborone to tell me everything's safe, then I pick up the van again. It's parked as close as possible to where I left it. When I've found it I call them again to say that everything's all right; at least, if I can find a phone that works. They're always broken; sometimes the whole receiver's just been cut off. By that time I'm glad to be driving away from Johannesburg – great big ugly concrete city. Suddenly I want to be back home, in Gaborone, in the village. I've got to cross the border again, but by then even the white South African border guards seem comfortably familiar, somehow. I've got to know some of them quite well now – I sometimes bring them beer or chocolate. They work long hours and their pay's rotten.

"There was one Friday, my van was so overloaded, with rocket launchers I think, it wouldn't move again after my passport was checked at the border. They were all standing around watching, and I shouted out the window at them: 'Hey listen, this is your fault – if I hadn't had to stop here there'd be no problem.' So then they all got behind and pushed the van over the border into South Africa. They even waved as I drove away."

Wilma leant back. She looked tired.

"Will you stop now that you're pregnant?"

"Are you nuts? Why? I can keep going fine until the baby's born."

"And your fiancé?"

"What he doesn't know won't hurt him. Oh yes, before I forget. We're going to have a traditional wedding, in his home village. Will you come?"

"Not a hope. But I'll visit you when I can."

"Well, that'll be a long wait," said Wilma.

On November 21st Chota was sentenced to twenty years for high treason and terrorism. In December I received a letter from him. He was once again on Robben Island. It had now been two years since his kidnapping, and his judges, determined to convict him, had brushed aside all the protests from home and abroad over the violations of international law. Twenty years. He would be seventy-one years old when he again left the Island. Last time, he had served out every day of his fifteen-year sentence.

The mood of his letter was different from those written during his trial. The defiance was subdued now. He had once more become a prisoner and must have resumed an old, familiar routine. He wrote that the newspapers he received were snipped to shreds. All political news was removed.

"We have complained to the prison authorities," he wrote. "The newspapers are already censored anyway under the state of emergency. They have also confiscated my copy of War and Peace. It was a gift to me during my trial. They must have mixed Tolstoy up with Trotsky.

"Sometimes I imagine that you're here with me in my cell. It would certainly give you claustrophobia. It's very cramped, with a tiny window. Everything is small, even my bed. But I have a chair, a wash basin and a toilet. I would make tea for you. I have lots of tea."

SPRING 1989

MAC AND GEBUZA'S REPORTS FROM THEIR CLANDESTINE BASES IN South Africa were getting steadily longer. Tim was by now only leaving his room full of computers for quick essential shopping, and Lucia had shut herself away in a small well-barricaded house in a Lusaka township. She received and decoded the reports, which arrived in Lusaka via London, and Ivan delivered them to President Tambo. Tambo's replies and comments, even longer, were sent back by the same route. The codes were changed every couple of weeks because we had to allow for the possibility of the enemy managing to intercept our messages. It would take security police experts weeks in any case, if not months, to break the code that Tim had developed with a Dutch computer expert.

The disks with each new code could not be sent by post, so for months they had now been brought through South African customs in Elise's handbag. As an air hostess she had little trouble with the tight security checks at Jan Smuts Airport, and the fact that she came to Johannesburg every two weeks raised no eyebrows.

In the past she had frequently worked the Asian and North American routes, and she and Tim had therefore been obliged to find a clever reason for her suddenly to want to fly regularly to South Africa. In Nairobi, where the Boeing 747 made a two-day stop-over on its way south, Elise wanted to use the free time to take private flying lessons, at a bargain price. This was not unusual for flight crews and made her flights to Johannesburg seem a secondary decision. Before she left, Tim would bring her one of the books which Elizabeth had doctored so that disks could be concealed in the cover.

When Elise returned after her "active" flights she would come straight from Schiphol to my flat, usually very early in the morning. The doorbell would get me out of bed, and Elise would come bounding up the stairs, with a box of chocolates and greetings from Mac, usually looking tired and wound up, especially after the first time.

"I was nervous as hell!" She ran a hand through her short blonde hair, fidgeted with her uniform, but stayed in the corridor. She wanted to get home as soon as possible, but also to tell me everything.

"When the plane landed I had to work really hard to get my nerves under control, concentrate and above all keep my eyes open. I made sure I was with the first group of crew to leave the plane. There were seventeen of us. My identity badge was properly visible, and we went through customs and security with no problems, just as usual really, and through the arrivals hall to the mini-buses that take us to the Holiday Inn. The flight arrives at one o'clock in the afternoon, and it's at least half-past before we're in the hotel. We have to be back on board by quarter to five, so ready to leave the hotel at four o'clock. So I only had a couple of hours. The rest of the crew use the time to have some lunch, but I'd already told them in the air that I wanted to meet some friends from Johannesburg.

"Tim and I had agreed that I'd hang around by the shops in the hotel lobby, where someone would approach me. Tim had sent photos and a description of me, and just before I left also told them I've got three assistant-purser stripes on my uniform. I'd thought three stripes would be a clearer identification than just my blonde hair.

"I was standing looking into the hairdresser's shop when a young woman came past me slowly – Indian, I think. Dark, anyway. She glanced at me, turned round and quickly recited a room number. That was what we'd arranged. I looked at my watch as if she'd asked me the time. She repeated the number, then disappeared."

Elise decided she had time for a quick coffee after all. The tension was leaving her face as she came with me to the kitchen, still talking.

"The other crew members had already taken the lift to their rooms. I followed them and changed, as quickly as I could. I'd taken extra clothes because I didn't want to be seen around the hotel in that conspicuous uniform. I didn't set off until all the others had left for lunch – they couldn't see me go off to another room. Oh, you wouldn't believe how I crept along the corridors. I don't know why I was being so cautious – it was ridiculous, but I really tiptoed along until I found the right room number.

"The curtains were closed. The man was sitting in the dark, and the girl was there too. He was in a big armchair, and looked rather short. Luckily he broke the tension first by pleasantly asking how my flight had been. I was supposed to call him Ben. He asked after you, and I gave him the book. I was there for about half an hour, chatting about this and that. He seemed really concerned about how I was doing. Just as I was about to leave he gave me the box of chocolates, and it was only then that I saw what a cheerful face he's got."

From then on Elise made it a habit to come by for coffee when she got back from Johannesburg, and we usually had chocolates with our coffee. Now and then she'd relate incidents from her trip, snippets of information.

"He's always very smart, a businessman in a dark suit, with graying hair. Sometimes a moustache, sometimes not. Actually I can never remember afterwards if he's been wearing a moustache or not, or even glasses or no glasses. I always look at his eyes." Or:

"I've got the feeling that my visits are a relief to him, little relaxed interludes. He knows he can rely on me. I'm always right on time." This was clearly a rewarding thought for Elise, especially when he complained of the heavy workload. He had told her how he had to work through the nights, then come to her straight from Durban. He had driven non-stop to arrive on time and had to go back immediately. "But he's never depressed. However tired he is he always radiates energy – how can I describe it? Something optimistic."

After one trip she was very worried. "I'm not sure, but I've got the idea he's having to keep his head down more than usual. There's something about him, like a refugee, someone who's staying on the move. Not that he said anything about it, you know, but with that restless look in his eyes and a kind of tension I could feel just under the surface – as if he's living under a lot of pressure. He'd slept for a couple of hours before I came. He seemed pretty exhausted, and he was smoking an awful lot."

One time in early January she was very excited indeed. "At long last I've got hold of that radio–telephone. It's taken me two months. Tim gave me the name of someone in Johannesburg, and I had to make an appointment with him from Amsterdam. I did it without letting slip where I was calling from. This man was sitting watching the tennis on TV, and assumed I was watching as well.

"I saw Ben briefly when I got to Johannesburg, then grabbed a taxi to the place we were to meet. Twice it fell through – the man just didn't turn up. I was mad as hell – it meant I'd have to wait two more weeks until my next flight. But in the end it worked out.

"The thing was a sort of mobile phone in a little case, very expensive. The salesman wanted to give me detailed instructions on how it worked. I couldn't tell him I had a plane to catch. The thing was really heavy, more than twenty kilos. But I lugged it into the Holiday Inn and up to Ben's room. He could have hugged me, I think; the phone was very important to him.

"I changed in seconds flat and only just made it to the airport on time. I'm always so relieved when it's all over. Each time I go I have to pass Security twice, Customs twice, and all the police and those strict checks. When the plane pulls its wheels up I heave a huge sigh of relief. It's hours after that before I can eat anything, even though I always miss lunch."

She had brought gifts for me, a Monopoly game in Afrikaans and a big bunch of *suikerbossies*. Those I had to throw away. Who on earth would be likely to bring me *suikerbossies*?

I was aware that the ANC people selected to go into South Africa for Operation Vula were given an exhaustive course in security. Now that more and more Dutch were becoming involved I felt that they too had the right to be prepared for the possible dangers. Ivan had made sure that I received instruction material, and I built up a whole collection of books on CIA and KGB methods, of leaked reports describing the investigation techniques used by the South African police, and others. So many organisations were part of the South African security apparatus. They included not only the Security Police and its clandestine arm, the Civil Co-operation Bureau, but also the Bureau for State Security. There was Military Intelligence, of course, but also a clandestine organisation set up by the military, the Directorate of Covert Collections. And there were even more shadowy groups working for the apartheid government.

I devoured everything I could get my hands on about former agents, or agents who had defected from various security operations: for us it was essential first of all to know the enemy, his strengths and weaknesses. At least the most obvious mistakes could thus be avoided.

The short course I put together consisted largely of warnings such as: avoid casual chatter with strangers or conspicuous behaviour. Don't work too fast or carelessly. Get to each rendezvous on time. Beware of over-friendly strangers and anyone unknown to you talking too militantly. Each action must be carefully planned, but avoid falling into repetitive patterns. Do not try and get to know anything about ANC people you work with. Unnecessary knowledge is just extra baggage. Be cautious on the telephone. Keep your voice down in public places; someone could listen in, especially if you get angry or agitated. Avoid leaving signs of your presence, such as fingerprints on typewriters. Never write down names or addresses; try and learn everything by heart. Make sure all your papers – driving licence, passport and so on – are completely in order. Avoid unnecessary complications.

But there were also instructions such as: get to know the village or town where you live like the back of your hand; that facilitates finding agreed meeting places. I invented possible scenarios where trainees would have to get themselves out of trouble with a good, plausible story. Some elements of the course involved practical learning-situations, such as how to lose people who are following you. The South African Police were well trained in shadowing suspects. Very broadly speaking, they might use two techniques to follow you: tail you on foot, or keep your house under observation.

They would often use informers to find out who you're in contact with. I always added, however, that things have to go very wrong before they'd decide to have you watched – it cost them too much in money and manpower.

I tried to sketch out a typical situation for them: your "tails" are usually in very ordinary clothes – forget raincoats or trilby hats. They work in teams of at least three or four. As far as we know they follow a fairly definite pattern. In busy streets they come closer, pulling back if there are few people around.

We practised typical situations in the city. The trainee had to follow his or her own chosen route, and would be shadowed by strangers, usually members of our technical group, or two friends of mine who had become very skilful. The assignment, of course, was to shake off the tails. Afterwards we used maps to discuss what had gone well or badly.

They also learned to follow a check–route, designed to expose any shadowers. It was very important to use this kind of check–route before any rendezvous with a contact person or visit to any house used by the liberation movements. You had to be sure you were clean of any "tail". This term and others had to become familiar as part of the underground vocabulary. The check–route had to be three or four kilometres long, and lead through busy areas of the city and quiet districts. It had to include some distance by bus and a stop somewhere to drink something. It involved watching continuously for a tail, but without looking over your shoulder. Shop windows or display cases can be used as mirrors, and a wide area of a street can be checked from inside a shop. Crossing the road gives the opportunity to have a good look around.

We also practised shaking off a tail: changing clothes en route, unexpectedly getting on or off a bus, using the last cab on a taxi rank, fading into a crowd.

All this took a great deal of practice, and not everyone became good at it. And however seriously we took the work, farcical situations would always arise to give us a chance to laugh at ourselves. Attempts to set up dead-letterboxes, or DLBs, were a case in point. This is the term for a place somewhere out of doors where messages or other material can be left for another to pick up, avoiding any necessity for direct contact. ANC people also used the term for small arms caches.

It was important to learn how to select good places, secure and accessible for people of any skin colour. We always practised first in a candidate's home town, and then again in Amsterdam, which was unfamiliar territory. Once a suitable spot was found – a plant tub in the public gardens, for example, or a loose brick in a wall – then it was essential to make sure that it couldn't be affected by changing weather; rain can loosen things and wash them away. Dogs can dig things up, children at play can move stones around.

Once the message was in place, wrapped in plastic, a map had to be drawn showing its location very accurately. It sounded easy, but every one of the trainees made unforeseen mistakes. A nurse, due to leave very soon, hid her message under a loose paving stone very early one morning, in front of an old disused building on a deserted street. That evening, around six, I went to pick up the message, but the long-unpainted door turned out to conceal a bar, overflowing with uproarious beer drinkers. A vague acquaintance amongst them saw me standing there hesitantly, and called me inside for a beer.

The DLBs were very important, as they minimised unnecessary contacts. We wanted our people to know as few others as possible by sight or name; that way they would actually have very little to reveal if they were arrested.

The possibility of arrest was something which had to be discussed. From one angle there was plenty to say about it, from another almost nothing – no more than a few tips on how to get through the first few days, and a tactfully couched request to hold out as long as possible before revealing names or addresses. That would give colleagues a chance to reach safety. "If someone from your group is picked up," I would say, "your contact person, for example, then assume that black comrades will be tortured straight away, so it's much more difficult for them to avoid talking. Make sure you get out fast, and get your housemate and all your material to safety. Make sure you always have an escape route planned and ready."

And there was one final warning I had to give: "If there are serious indications that you're being watched, your contact person may decide to put you on ice for a while, which means that no-one will have any contact with you at all until the situation improves. That can take months, and it's a very, very tough time and you just have to grit your teeth and get through somehow, very much on your own. You must not try to contact anyone. Not even me."

At the beginning of March, Ivan sent a short message announcing the arrival of "Christopher". He gave the date and time this visitor would arrive, and added a few vague allusions to problems. "There are difficulties with his wife. He's not in good shape. Maybe something can be done? His leg is giving him trouble too."

I was surprised that Ivan would communicate this kind of thing, and was slightly amused by the tentative words. It was not customary in the ANC to engage in real discussion of psychological problems. Naturally, everyone had headaches or digestion problems; they were all suffering the consequences of stress. But talk about the possible underlying causes was avoided. "If we start on all that, we'll never get anything done anymore," was the general opinion. "We're all the products of misery – that's where our motivation comes from."

There was a lot of truth in this approach, but for those who really became trapped by their traumas and fears it gave little support. A large number of ANC people, especially those who had seen active service, thus paid a double price in their own lives. Not only had their ruined youth left them no choice but to take up arms, the struggle itself had also marked them deeply.

Ivan was willing to talk about it, albeit with fitting scepticism and levity, and always in a somewhat dismissive tone of voice. He was, however, well aware that nervous, damaged people are quicker to make mistakes, and can behave unpredictably.

No-one in Lusaka had the time or the expertise to tackle these problems effectively. But for some time I had been in touch with a psychiatrist who had treated freedom fighters in west Africa for the effects of their traumatic experiences. Ivan had met him several times, and now seemed to be suggesting that I should enlist his aid.

168

The young man whom I picked up at Schiphol looked like a ballet dancer. Christoper was tall and slender with a pale face and a deer's sad eyes. He was to be deployed with Sabata's group in the Cape. As he came towards me with his luggage I was already trying to imagine him in the environment of an ANC military camp. There must be something strong and steadfast concealed by the frail exterior.

During those early months of 1989 I had to provide disguises for three Vula people in quick succession; before one had left the next was already arriving at Schiphol. There was less and less time to consider each disguise. More and more I was going ahead with my first impulses, and searching for ideas in each person's specific appearance. Christopher's fine-boned figure immediately brought to mind the image of a really boorish type, not least because he was to travel to South Africa from Zimbabwe with false papers. This was the key: Zimbabwe, a Rhodie, one of those whites still reminiscing sentimentally about old Rhodesia. Rough and racist, and with a completely unfounded conviction of his own superiority which by comparison made all Africans seem the epitome of culture and refinement.

Yan had made him a jacket with plenty of shoulder padding, and Winnie had clipped back his long eyelashes. Christopher sat for days on end watching rented videos – *Rambo* One and Two, *First Blood*. Sitting on the edge of his chair, he struggled to assimilate the essentials of macho–aggressive behaviour. He made notes on a small pad, shoulders pulled high and legs crossed. In the evenings Han Romer, the actor, trained him in crude habits. I had to leave the room: Romer's personification of the Rhodie had me laughing so much that my presence was a distraction. After a week Christopher was drinking beer from a can, sitting sprawled back with legs wide, and managing a steady insolent stare. But as soon as he could, he would again set his legs close together and drink elegantly from a glass.

His second disguise would allow him to feel more comfortable – a type which took advantage of his own social graces: a successful young businessman, a yuppie. He gleaned ideas from the film Wall

Street, and made a date with Marieke van der Poll in an Amsterdam yuppie bar, to learn behaviour patterns. Help from an actress seemed preferable to me for this disguise.

Christopher worked hard, with concentration, practising endlessly. We filmed him on video and examined the results until we were convinced that he would be able to maintain his yuppie character in Cape Town – in white Cape Town, needless to say. But what if he needed to visit someone in a mixed area, or a district where only coloured people lived?

"Shall we make a coloured man of you?" I asked. He looked at me in dismay.

"If you can turn into a Rhodie, surely you can manage a coloured?"

A week later he sat staring at his darkened face and curly black wig in the mirror.

"Shall we give him his eyelashes back? False ones?" asked Winnie.

As Ivan had warned us, Christopher was very tense indeed. He complained of the pain in his leg, and the sessions with the psychiatrist only partially calmed him. One evening he began to talk to me about his wife.

"She lives in Cape Town. Can you imagine? I'm going to be living underground just a few miles from her. She'll have no idea I'm so close."

I found it painful to watch him. His whole demeanour betrayed an intense longing for her.

"And isn't there any way you can think of to get a chance to see her sometimes?"

"No. I'd be putting her in danger, as well as me and other people. Everyone has the same kind of problems," he said with resignation, glancing around him restlessly as if looking for a way to shake off the feelings oppressing him.

"It'll be very strange to be going home in disguise and in hiding. As if I can see the city but they can't see me."

"Do your parents live in Cape Town as well?"

"Yes."

170

"Do they support what you're doing?"

"I don't know. Maybe. My father's always tried to stay well out of politics. Because of his background, I think."

As a child, Christopher's father had come to South Africa from Lithuania with his parents, fleeing from anti-Semitism. Christopher's mother was from a conservative Afrikaner family. There had been strong resistance to their marriage. The Afrikaner family did not want her to marry a Jew, and his parents disapproved of a non-Jewish wife. He qualified as a doctor, but even in his work could not escape politics. He did research for the first heart transplant carried out by Christiaan Barnard. When the extent of the international interest became clear, the South African government sent out Barnard and Christopher's father to improve the country's image abroad. Barnard had enjoyed it all immensely, accepting the praise and fame like a prima donna; but Christopher's father had hated it. They had parted as bitter enemies.

"When did you get interested in politics?"

"In 1976, I think, at the time of the student protests. I was thirteen, and never saw black or coloured children. I was just very curious. When we heard at school that six black schoolchildren had been shot dead at Elsie's River, a group of us wanted to go to a coloured school to show our support. We set out, but close to the school the police blocked the road and sent us back. We made our first pamphlets then, from anger and disappointment.

"But we quickly reverted back to just being typical white kids. We hung around on the street, drank a lot, and smoked dagga now and then. Sometimes I'd read a poem by Breyten Breytenbach; his language was very strange and intriguing. Through the dope I got to know some coloured kids, members of a gang. I always hung around as long as I could to talk with them. But it wasn't until I was at university that I first went into a township, for a political meeting.

"The first time I was arrested was three months after I started university. I was taken to a security police office. I couldn't believe my eyes. There were confiscated ANC posters all over the walls, and photos of weapons. They started screaming at us: 'You fucking communists!' and 'All you want is the chance to fuck a black woman!' I couldn't believe I was hearing that kind of language from policemen. We were prosecuted for organising a demonstration, and the case dragged on for three years."

"How did your parents react?"

"For my father it was the last straw. He gave me a choice. Either I stayed out of politics or he'd stop paying my tuition. So then I left home and went to live with friends. From then on I got more and more involved in illegal work, like printing pamphlets on paper we stole from the university at night. The people I was staying with were in touch with the ANC. I didn't know how, or to what extent, but sometimes someone would just disappear. You wouldn't see them again, and you weren't allowed to ask questions.

"In 1986 they arrested my girlfriend, who's now my wife, and six weeks later they let her out of prison, broken. Something snapped inside me while she was in detention. That was the first time someone close to me had been picked up. The fury was growing in me by the day. I wondered more and more if perhaps armed struggle wasn't the only answer.

"By the end of 86, inevitably, I was completely involved in clandestine military work, smuggling in weapons from Botswana. Sixteen hundred kilometres in the car every weekend. The work got so heavy that everything suffered, and in the stress I lost my girlfriend. She wouldn't and couldn't see me any more. She'd never got over the effects of her arrest. That was awful for me – she was my last remaining contact who wasn't underground.

"After that my life was completely undercover, until everything went wrong. I was working with Jenny Schreiner, and one day Tony Yengeni, our commander, told us to sort out passports for ourselves so we could leave the country and go to Lusaka. Then one day Jenny didn't turn up at a meeting; twelve hours later I read in the paper that she'd been arrested.

"I was on the run for three months, from hiding place to hiding place. And then on top of everything I broke my leg in a motorbike accident. That cut out my freedom of movement entirely. The police were getting steadily closer on my trail. Then one day my last two contacts were arrested. The police were on the way to the house where I was sitting with my leg in the air. I was warned, and got away right at the last minute. I knew I just had to leave the country as soon as I possibly could, so my girlfriend and I went straight to Johannesburg – we'd been together again for a while. That's where we got married. The next day, December 30th 1987, I left the country and reported to the ANC in Botswana."

"Have you seen your wife since then?"

"Yes, a few weeks ago in Zimbabwe, very briefly. They let me see her because I was going to be going underground for so long in Vula. But I wasn't allowed to tell her I'd be going back to South Africa. I said that I was going to the Soviet Union for two or three years of military training. That was a horrible feeling, lying to her. I talked round and round the subject, because I really wanted to give her a hint, but I didn't in the end. She was determined to record part of our conversation on cassette, so that she'd be able to listen to my voice now and then. And when I think of all the things I've said to her on that tape, how I've lied to her ..."

Christopher was slumped forward, rubbing his neck. I could feel my own neck muscles tighten in sympathy, so tense it seemed as if they were holding a painful sort of helmet in place inside my skull.

"Shall I call a friend of mine to give you a massage? She always helps me."

Marloes was a physiotherapist, and quite prepared to jump on her bicycle even in the middle of the night if my headaches became unbearable. Almost before she was inside the house she would have the oil on her hands and be busy working my whole back over, with a continuous commentary. "You're breathing all wrong as well," she said once. "That short panting – no wonder you're so tired. Pull some more air deep into your belly now and then. You'll be calmer and your whole body will function better."

She demonstrated, and I learned to breathe all over again.

Marloes gave Christopher a massage and some tips on ways to reduce the pain in his leg, and checked his breathing. It gave him a lot of relief, and he became just as addicted to her as I was. While he told me how pleasantly relaxed he always felt after the massage, and how she'd taught him to rub his own neck, it occurred to me that this should become a regular part of the preparation of all the South Africans who visited, and of the Dutch people going south.

After Christopher left a small group gathered together to discuss the idea: Marloes, a colleague of hers who was a psychologist, and the psychiatrist. They realised that there would never be enough time for the people who came through to learn the relaxation exercises fully, and decided to make a cassette tape. Against a background of soft music, the psychologist's warm voice talked them through the exercises they would have learned in Amsterdam.

Two months earlier, Marloes had been to Cape Town as a courier. She met Ernest in a park. He had everything ready, a house and a job. Marloes brought him his final instructions, because soon a housemate would join him in his safe house. At that stage I had no idea that the housemate would be Christopher.

Summer 1989

He had a distinctive face, with pockmarked skin, a great broad forehead, virtually no eyebrows and small lively eyes. He was very short, and slightly built. His movements were swift, with much gesticulation, and he had the physical presence of someone three times his size: Little John, or LJ. I had been warned – "You're getting the most difficult one of all to disguise".

Sabata's group in the Cape was being expanded with all possible speed, and Christopher was to be followed by Little John. He was well known for his long history in the resistance. There were many tales of his activities, many originated by himself. He enjoyed relaxing with a beer and relating the many ridiculous events, dangerous escapes and gun battles he had experienced. If he told of a chase, he would creep around the room, hide behind a chair, leap out, point his finger and shoot with such a loud string of tongue-clicks that it hurt your ears. But he could also spend an evening in serious discussion of South Africa's trade union movement. In fact, he could talk all night on almost any subject.

When I met him in Amsterdam he had already been in the city for a couple of days, staying with friends. I came back from a short holiday with Tessel and my parents in our favourite little seaside hotel. He invited me out for a beer at a café terrace beside the River Amstel. To my amazement he was greeted warmly by a group of old men, and a Surinamese gentleman accompanied by his grandson immediately took up the thread of the conversation they had had with Little John the day before.

"How on earth do you know all these people?" I asked, the first time there was a pause in the conversation.

He laughed aloud, sitting with the grandchild on his knee.

"Old men are the same everywhere. They sit the whole day just talking. In Soweto there are old guys everywhere, hanging about together talking of old times. Just as the boys hang around in gangs talking about the future."

"And of course you belonged to one of those gangs?" I was reminded of Christopher's group of friends, trying to make some contact with the black kids.

"Of course. We were always together. Did everything together. We were so wild, such loud-mouths ... and very active. We wanted to do something militant, something clandestine. My God, but we were naive. We founded something called the Liberation Front. What did we know?" Little John laughed and passed the child back to its grandfather, who was listening with interest.

"The Liberation Front?" queried the old man.

Little John looked at each of us. "You want to hear about the Liberation Front?" he asked, and waved to the barman. Six beers arrived, three of them for the old men in the corner. "Okay. We, of the Liberation Front, were all fifteen or sixteen years old, living in Soweto in an area where a fair number of old ANC veterans lived. Ma Sisulu lived round the corner for example. I'd already kicked my football through her window before I was ten. Winnie Mandela lived in the street too. She let us have our meetings in her back room."

The old man nodded in approval. "Mandela," he repeated.

"My friend Tom," went on Little John, "had drawn a black fist on a piece of paper, with 'Freedom' written large underneath. We hung it up in the back room during our meetings. That was fine with Winnie.

"As I said, we were very militant indeed, so we'd elected Tacky as our commander. He could put a good speech together, and he already had a deep voice. He never missed a chance to demonstrate all his knowledge – about the Second World War and about Vietnam. We were always pretty much in awe of him. 'Comrades,' he'd say, and every time he used the word it sent shivers up our spines. C-o-m-r-a-d-e... It was such a forbidden word, loaded with so much meaning.

"One day he was extra solemn: 'Comrades, the time has come to make bombs. We shall break into a school to get hold of the

176

chemicals.' The rest of us were flabbergasted. Then he pointed me out as the one who'd have to break in. In my own school, mind you. I was still such a good boy, and now I had to become a burglar. I didn't dare protest. Luckily nothing ever came of the idea. Really, now and then there was something terrifying about those meetings."

I roared with laughter, but the old man threw me a withering look.

"One day Tacky arrived with a pistol. That was the first time I'd seen anything like it, and we were all allowed to hold it. We had no idea how it worked, but we polished the outside with a rag again and again until it shone. We hid it in Winnie's hollow bathroom scale.

'It's safe there,' we told each other, and peeped round the corner to make sure Winnie hadn't seen what we were up to, then went back again to re-check the hiding place.

'There are other ways to hide things,' Tacky said then. 'More ways than I can tell you about.' So then we got unsure of ourselves again. Maybe the scale wasn't such a good idea after all.

'Those chemicals you're going to fetch us,' and he pointed at me, 'we'll hide those in a much better place.'

"Then we'd sing freedom songs together, shout 'Long Live!' a couple of times, and hug each other. We felt so close at moments like that.

"After the meeting we'd drink tea in Winnie's living room, with her daughters. Winnie would pour, and then go back to her bedroom. She spent most of her time in there. She was under a banning order, and was harassed by the police almost every day. That got to her – you could see it. We wanted so much to protect her; that was our duty to Nelson, we felt, but we didn't know how.

"We didn't talk politics with the daughters. We couldn't tell them what was going on in the back room, we explained. It was very secret. We were so proud of that. I reckon they knew exactly what was going on. We said nothing to Winnie either; she didn't want to know. Sometimes she'd cook us terrific meals. If you didn't finish everything on your plate she'd be furious. We loved her and that house very, very much. The warmth was so special to us."

Little John ordered another round. The old man looked moved. He rubbed his hand through his short greying curls and sent the little boy off for an ice cream.

"One day the police came, the Special Branch. To Winnie's house. We were sitting in the front room having tea. 'What are you doing here?' asked the biggest of them, Van Niekerk. 'These are my children,' Winnie told them. The policeman demanded to see our pass books, but Winnie forbade us to say anything or to give him anything.

"We were pretty scared; we didn't know who we should obey any more. There we sat, the boys of the Liberation Front. And there stood a woman up against three white men who were demanding our pass books. She was standing there so fierce, so defenceless, and I was so very proud of her and so ashamed of myself. I'll never forget that.

"Van Niekerk bellowed: 'Give us your pass books!' We looked at each other. We had to choose between our fear of the enemy and our admiration for the woman. 'We'll take you in!' he yelled again. 'Just go ahead and try it,' Winnie shouted back. 'I'll sue the hell out of you!' So then all three of them left. Winnie was speechless with fury. She didn't say a word to us, just shut herself away again in her bedroom.

"All the time I was walking home I was just saying to myself 'What a woman. What a life she must live!' I still feel the love for that house and for her; I can still see the walls, and the little back yard where we kicked a ball around on Sunday afternoons. There was always washing hanging on the line."

Little John was silent, his eyes pensive above his glass. The old man was shaking his head, muttering something I couldn't catch.

"What became of the Liberation Front?" I asked, determined not to miss the end of the story. Little John looked up, pleased.

"Well, one Sunday Tom came running up to my house. 'There's this old man you've got to meet,' he whispered, all excited. I was sitting outside the house, polishing my football boots. The church bells were ringing and all the neighbours were passing by, wishing me good morning, with the children all dressed up for church. The juniors, in their team shirts with footballs under their arms, ran past calling to me. I was very popular on the field. Typical Sunday, as friendly as Soweto can be.

"And there was Tom with the news that he'd met this old man who had been in the resistance and could help us. I put down my boots and forgot about breakfast – my mother was already frying the eggs. We jumped over the fence and ran to the man's house. I knew it, it was Aunt Abenya's place.

"The old man was inside playing the piano. We told him about our Liberation Front and asked his advice. He was a bit hesitant. We asked him to tell us about the real liberation movement and confided seriously that we had a copy of the Communist Manifesto. He just shook his head, we didn't understand why. We kept the Manifesto hidden away in a brown envelope and made everyone we allowed to see it swear never to say a word. Then we told him about the pistol, and that did interest him. He promised to show us how it worked.

"We wanted to share the good news at our next meeting, but we were completely overshadowed by Thoki, another member of the group who'd just come back from Swaziland. He'd met real ANC guerrillas there, and now he milked the story for all it was worth. 'Men,' he whispered, 'I've struck gold.' And that became our name for him ever afterwards: 'I've struck gold'.

"He stayed quiet for a moment, looking around at our faces, and said: 'I met Thabo Mbeki.'

'Who is Thabo Mbeki?' we asked.

'His father's on Robben Island,' he said, annoyed.

'Whoooooh... his father is on Robben Island,' we all repeated. We were always very impressed by that.

'I met others too; some of them have got beards,' said Thoki. He paused significantly, while we all had exactly the same thought: 'These are the men for us!'

'Dlomo's got a beard, Mbeki's got a beard. Just like real revolutionaries!'

"We were very excited, and wanted to go off to Swaziland straight away for training. 'So this is really the ANC?' We wanted to be sure."

'Yes. Oliver Tambo's ANC,' said Thoki, very much the expert now.

"Then we decided that Tom should go to them with the message that the Liberation Front wanted to make contact with the ANC, that we wanted to fight and needed the training. So that's how the Liberation Front merged with the ANC."

The old man shook Little John by the hand, and we all drank another beer together.

Little John was a real challenge for the disguise team. His small stature led to long discussions, until it was decided, for one of his disguises, to emphasise his lack of height. He would become a bent old man, a smiling grandpa wearing thick round spectacles. His skin was darkened, with the liver spots of old age, and Yan made him a new body from soft and resilient material, which he could put on at will. He acquired a pot belly, high shoulders, and heavy footwear to slow down his movements. For his other disguise, as a young man, he was made taller. A tall wig of tight curls, clipped short at the sides, gave the impression of more height, and special Italian lift shoes were ordered for him. It all added up to make him ten centimetres taller. His skin was smoothed with film makeup and he learned to strengthen his eyebrows. Han Romer was amazed by the easy skill with which he played his new roles. "A born actor," he declared with satisfaction, and prophesied a golden future for Little John in the South African theatre world, "Once it's all over."

"I'll be picking you up very early tomorrow," Ivan warned me. He had just put his head round the hotel room door, in too much of a hurry to come inside. "Someone wants to talk to you at six-thirty."

There was only one person in Lusaka you'd have a meeting with that early: the ANC's president, Oliver Tambo, started his days while the doors of the other offices at headquarters were still firmly locked.

I stood waiting for him in the grey morning light on my second day in Lusaka. The city had started to come to life, but the atmosphere was still hushed and sleepy, as if no-one could face too much noise. The courtyard at ANC headquarters was peaceful. The

180

only people around were two young men guarding the steel gates and us, Ivan and me, sitting on a wooden bench outside the low, inconspicuously situated building. That bench had been standing there since I had first come to Lusaka some time in the early seventies. Since then I had sat on it countless times, because I enjoyed this inner courtyard which people in the ANC used as a village square. If you sat there long enough you'd encounter anyone you needed to talk to, as well as everyone you preferred to avoid.

The two young guards suddenly strode to the metal gates, threw off the bars and opened them. A car drove in at high speed round the sharp bend from the muddy side street, and a second vehicle followed. Three men leapt out of the first, fit and energetic, from their movements obviously bodyguards. Without a word they entered the building to check for anything suspicious. The car doors stayed closed, the interior concealed by the darkened windows. After a couple of minutes the bodyguards reappeared and signalled that all was clear.

The rear door of the second car opened and President OR Tambo emerged, approaching me with hand outstretched. I once again felt the slight shyness that came over me every time we met. I kissed him carefully on both cheeks. The eyes behind the spectacles showed his pleasure. We had known each other since 1974, and saw each other at least once a year, in various parts of the world. I never noticed any change in his face. Only if I looked at a photograph from years before did it strike me that he had indeed aged, and it seemed as if the long initiation scars on his face had become narrower.

He took my arm, and together we walked down the narrow passage to his office, as Ivan waited outside. At the end of the corridor the two bodyguards approached; they had again checked indoors. President Tambo stopped them with a small gesture, holding me back as well. His finger pointed to the floor, where a huge green locust was cautiously crossing the uneven red tiles, and we stood against the wall to give the insect plenty of room to pass. At a leisurely pace the creature reached the open air, hesitating in the bright sunlight and testing the sandy ground with one leg. The bodyguards waited patiently, hands hanging loose, saying nothing. Outside they probably crushed twenty to death every day under their boots. Lusaka was suffering from a real plague of the things. You could buy them at the market, toasted.

We went into his office at the back of the building. It was a small room, slightly better furnished than the other offices, and certainly less dusty. Very little light could get in through the heavy bars on the window. A large painted ANC emblem hung behind the desk.

President Tambo waved me to the sofa, and asked after the AABN. He had heard about the women's conference we were organising, and I gave him a book about Chota written by a Dutch journalist. He examined it closely, especially the photo of Chota and his two co-defendants printed at the back. Chota he knew, but he had never met the others. Then he laid the book on his desk and crossed the room to sit beside me. He wanted to tell me something; I saw it in his considered gestures and in the way he watched me.

He was taking his time.

"I don't want to talk about the work you're doing for us. Ivan keeps me up to date on that."

He paused again.

"I want to talk to you because I'm worried. I want you to be extremely ... careful.

"Very careful indeed," he repeated emphatically. "You must never underestimate the enemy." He tapped his fingers together. "They too are perfectly capable of putting two and two together, linking bits of information and drawing conclusions."

I wondered if he knew something I didn't. But I knew him well enough to be aware that, if he did, he certainly wouldn't tell me anything now.

"I want you to promise me that you will be careful and follow all the security procedures." He held my eyes with his.

I nodded, feeling very uncomfortable. Then he laughed, took my hands and shook them up and down. "Be careful, but don't lose your cheerfulness," he said, and accompanied me to the door. We said goodbye.

Ivan was waiting on the bench outside. He picked up his

briefcase quickly and we walked across the courtyard. "How did it go?" he asked, trying to be casual.

"Oh, fine. He wanted to warn me."

"Who against?" asked Ivan, stopping abruptly.

"Against the enemy, idiot!" I retorted, and we both burst out laughing.

That afternoon Lucia came to my hotel. She also carried a large briefcase, and looked the personification of an efficient secretary. Beside the swimming pool she pushed two reclining chairs under an umbrella, out of the hot afternoon sun, and ordered large ice-cold lemonades, with sandwiches. "Oh, I really need to talk," she exclaimed. "I've been so looking forward to you coming. Since I got here I haven't done a thing except work and work."

"Surely they gave you a bit of time to settle in?"

"Well, no. I was taken straight to the house when I arrived. There were piles of paperwork already waiting for me. It was two weeks before I finally went outside again, and I had no idea where on earth I was. All I had was a very vague memory of the route from the airport to the house."

After the sandwiches we decided to take the car to her place and talk further. I was impressed by the ease with which she manoeuvred among the ancient smoking lorries and dangerously reckless taxis, at the same time bringing me up to date with all the latest news.

The house stood in an exclusively black district; Lucia was the only white person. This had advantages and disadvantages, but more of the latter, as I quickly understood, making her life very hard. Running water was usually restricted to the night hours, and the electricity failed so often that she spent most evenings by candlelight. At those times it was impossible to cook, so at six she'd usually go to bed, getting up again at eleven to prepare a meal. The house was very small, with four rooms, each two by two and a half metres. Next door a couple with seven children lived in an identical house. There were no ceilings. You looked directly at the underside of the corrugated iron roof, and the doors were just a few planks held together with a couple of cross-pieces. The electric refrigerator and stove, however, made Lucia the most affluent person in the whole district.

She shared the house with a young man who was responsible for her safety. They each had their own rooms. Another was heavily partitioned off and barricaded to hold the computers and all the paperwork. It looked like a small bunker constructed within a shaky ruin.

"God, Luce, couldn't they find you anything better than this?" I burst out, angry and ashamed.

"No. Now don't get cross," Lucia said, calming me down. "It's not that easy. The operation is so secret that Ivan can't ask the ANC housing department for accommodation. There's a bad housing shortage here anyway. I'll be getting something better soon, Joe Slovo's promised me. Especially after what's happened."

"What's that?"

"Well, there've been two break-ins. One was just an attempt. But the first time they got my radio and all my tapes, blast them! That was the only entertainment I had. But the other time ... I'll tell you in a minute."

The house was spotless – no dust, not a scrap of paper anywhere. I had to laugh: this was Lucia, of course, the baker's daughter from a family of ten in Amstelveen. "So clean, Luce!"

"Has to be. There's no refuse collection around here. Everyone has a pit behind the house where you burn your rubbish every now and then. At night the rats and cockroaches creep in under the door."

There was a broken-down easy chair in one corner, and two wooden chairs stood at a small formica-topped table. That was all; there was no room for more furniture.

Lucia took one of the chairs at the table. "I'm not moaning too much, am I?"

"Go ahead and moan, for God's sake."

"Good. Okay, here goes. You know, losing my music was a real blow. I at least had that, even if the electricity was out and I was sitting in the dark. I'm alone a lot because my housemate goes out all the time. Then I'm stuck here with all the gear, whole weekends sometimes. I've complained about it, and I'm going to get someone else instead, especially after what's happened," she repeated.

"Come on, spit it out." I encouraged her.

"I don't mind, but you'll have to keep it to yourself. They know, Ivan and Joe, but I don't want it discussed any more."

I gave her my word.

"It was one of the evenings I was alone here. The others were out of the country, Ivan as well. Something was brewing near the border. I was in bed, with the bedroom door open as always so I could hear anything that happened in the rest of the house. Something strange woke me. I listened a bit, then got up. The kitchen door was ajar. I crept over, closed it and turned the key. There was a glimmer of light and I saw two men outside, heard them too. Kabalalas, thieves – they can be very dangerous. Poor wretches, they'll put a knife in you for a few cents. They're Lusaka's real outlaws.

"The door rattled, and I knew they wouldn't have any trouble breaking it in. I ran to the bedroom, pulled on a dressing gown and got out the AK-47. I've always got that handy, with two hand grenades, in case of a raid.

"Back in the kitchen I yelled through the window at them: 'Go away! Go away! If you don't I'll shoot.' I stayed well back, scared that they might grab the gun out of my hands through the window. They jeered back: 'Hey, shoot, go ahead and shoot!'

"I'd been told how the thing worked, but I'd never fired it. And I didn't want to shoot at Zambians if I could avoid it. That would mean problems for the ANC. I just wanted to warn them off."

She rose and moved to the middle of the room.

"I was standing here." She waved at the two doors, exactly opposite each other and about three and a half metres apart. "They'd taken one door each, trying to get them open. I yelled at them to 'get the hell out of here', looking backwards and forwards between the doors, AK-47 at the ready. Then I heard a window break behind me, and I could see them, wearing balaclavas, one with a machete and the other with an axe. I was so shaken by the sound of the glass breaking and the sight of the knife and the axe that I fired. It was such a surprise that the thing went off! I had it on automatic and the shots just poured out, I don't know how many, straight through the wall and the window. I didn't want to hit them, I really didn't. I'd been told: if they're kabalalas shoot to scare, not to hit them. I don't think I hit anyone. I reckon they ran as soon as they heard the gun...

"Then I put the big chair right in the middle between the doors and sat there for the rest of the night with the AK on my lap. I didn't dare go back to bed. They might come back, and both doors had been forced. It was freezing that night. I just had a blanket round me. At seven in the morning the woman from next door came round to ask if I was all right. She'd seen the men, but when she heard the shots she thought: 'Oh, she can take care of herself.' Everyone for miles must have heard. But nothing was ever said, and there was no sign of the police."

"Luce, you've got to get out of this house right away," I said, shocked.

"No need. Listen, two days later Ivan was back. My housemate lives somewhere else now and I was given a bodyguard immediately. Now he sits in the armchair all night with a machine pistol. I make a huge pot of coffee for him, then go to sleep."

"Lucia, I'm proud of you."

She giggled. "Well, it didn't do my reputation any harm. The bad side is, the whole district now knows that I'm armed and that this is an ANC house. Luckily I'll get another place soon, though. And Ivan tells me you're sending out a couple who're going to live with me. Is that right?"

"Yes, they should be here within a month. They're quiet Brabanders. It won't just make things safer, they can help with the work as well."

Lucia laughed. "Now I've got other people providing a safe house for me!"

It had been a rush to get to Harare on schedule. Preparatory discussions were being held there for a women's conference the AABN was organising in Amsterdam the following January. After the success of the cultural conference the ANC had called us in again. This time the aim was to explore and publicise the position of women in South Africa.

A delegation had arrived from South Africa, and the ANC contingent had a rough bus ride from Lusaka behind them. A school building had been provided where we could meet and in two days work our way through a colossal agenda. The problems were legion, but our spirits were high. Our experience with conferences assured us that everything would somehow come together on the day.

We had lunch on the playing fields outside the school, and already a few other women had gathered, South Africans living in Harare, to ask the latest news from home. That afternoon, during a tea break, I saw Totsi in the middle of one group of women. She gave me a brief, surreptitious glance. I strolled over to the group and introduced myself to those women I had not met, including Totsi. The conversation resumed. As we all walked back towards the building she casually walked beside me for a moment, saying quietly: "I've lost contact with one of the couriers. I don't know where she, Aaf, is now. Have you got the list of hotels she booked?"

"No, there was no reason to bring it. That's bad."

"Something went wrong. Our mistake. I'll be in touch." She turned quickly and drifted away.

A week earlier Aaf and her husband had left for South Africa on a courier run. In Cape Town they were to make contact with Sabata's group to pass on something that couldn't be sent over the communication network – passports or travel documents, I didn't know what. Aaf was not one to easily panic; what could have gone wrong? Couriers were travelling regularly between South Africa and the Netherlands, and up to now everything had gone pretty smoothly.

The discussions continued the next day. I concentrated as best I could, consoling myself with the thought that Aaf was well able to take care of herself. Late in the afternoon the South African women held their own meeting, and I was free to walk out over the grass and smoke a cigarette. Totsi came running up, and I saw from her face that all was well. We went to the toilets, to avoid being too conspicuously seen together.

"I reached her by telephone last night. All sorts of things had gone wrong, but we're back in touch now. Everything's going as planned again."

I was relieved, and very curious to hear the story, but for that I had to wait until Aaf returned to Amsterdam. She was to stay in Africa for a week longer than me.

Totsi told me that she was now stationed in Harare because from there it was faster and easier to reach the border area. "I travel as Diana Ross, and hang around at the border as my mother," she laughed, turning off the tap which had been running noisily during our talk.

When Aaf returned to Amsterdam she wanted to see me immediately. As we sat in her large, beautifully furnished house, her husband unpacked a huge flight bag full of maps, travel guides, stolen letter paper from hotels, Afrikaans study courses, books, periodicals – everything I had requested.

Aaf tossed a small packet of chicory onto the table. "I'd only come across that during the war," she exclaimed indignantly. "When you couldn't get coffee. It's for sale there now, in the shops for black people."

She pushed the great pile of paper aside, and sat down opposite me in a designer chair. She was over fifty, but could easily pass for ten years younger – good-looking, elegantly dressed, short skirt revealing shapely knees. She had been a nurse for years, and travelled everywhere. South Africa she had not visited before; her political convictions would not allow it. "What an awful country," she said, closing her eyes for a moment. She stood up, rummaged in her handbag, put it down again. I could see she was on the verge of tears.

"A horrible country," she burst out. "All those beautifully laid-out avenues, lovely gardens, boarding schools for the white children. And everywhere, everywhere you see the black people walking, trudging along the roads, kids on their backs, bags in their hands. Old people, sick people, and always carrying things –

everyone's lugging other people's rubbish about. 'How can I get this rotten fence post home?' I saw one man walking along with a broken car windscreen. What earthly use can that be?"

Han, her husband, brought us glasses and a bottle of wine.

"You can't get away from it anywhere. We were waiting at a red light in Cape Town and a small yellow police van stopped beside us. There was a horrible yelling and banging coming from it, as if there was a wild animal inside. An escaped circus lion they'd recaptured or something. I opened my window and asked a white man on the pavement what it was. 'Oh, just a black making a bit of a fuss.'

"But my last image of Cape Town is the worst. An old shrunken black man by the entrance to a parking garage. He had a placard hung round his neck, which said that the garage was full. They'd turned the old man into a living signboard. I'll never get that picture out of my head." The tears were now running down her cheeks.

Han went upstairs with a book. "Let Aaf tell you everything," he said apologetically.

"He read his way through thirty whodunnits," said Aaf, smiling. "I was so glad he came along. You have to have someone to unload your feelings on to."

"I'm really curious about what went wrong," I said.

"Well, we went to Harare first, as you know, to see our contact person and get our instructions. I waited in the hotel room for the phone call. It felt like being in the middle of a Pinter play. Second act: a telephone call is expected. Woman sits on edge of bed. When it rang I thought: 'Yes, right on cue.' A voice asked me to come down to the lobby, and watch out for two men. They would have my description. The first time it didn't work out – so back to my room. The next attempt was all right. They hadn't dared to speak to me because they'd expected a different type – older, I think.

"After that there were several meetings. They looked through my luggage and picked out a big pot of Nivea cream to take with them and hide a message in. And I was given a packet of biscuits which had something hidden inside. Cheap biscuits, from a supermarket. I didn't really think it fitted in with our luxury tourist image. There was a computer disk inside. I took it out and sewed it into the double back of Han's shirt. The shirt was straight from the cleaners, still in the paper packing.

"Just before we left they brought along a young woman. She was supposed to explain exactly where in Cape Town I would have my next meeting to hand over the stuff. The two men encouraged her to describe the place in as much detail as possible. She was from the city, and they weren't, obviously."

"And then you flew to Cape Town?"

"Yes, there was a hire car ready for us. Han had arranged everything through American Express. A room was reserved for us in an old colonial hotel, all the waiters and personnel were elderly black men. When we got to our room I looked in the Nivea pot, and was horrified to see that the message wasn't for me, but for someone else. The biggest blow was that now I didn't have a telephone number for contacting Harare. We'd been through all the rest so often, the place and the code words I had to say. They were no problem. Neither was what I should wear: black slacks, red top, and my round Marx Brothers glasses.

"That wrong message really had me worried. Should I destroy it, or hang on to it? It was incriminating material, after all. So then we quickly went to check out the meeting place, before I could forget the details. It was in an area called Belville.

"Belville is a bit scruffy, like a Belgian seaside resort. We drove down a long street with a lot of hardware stores, past a shopping centre, and over a railway line. It was fixed in my mind: hairdresser's, post office, second street on the left, and there would be a two-storey hotel. We'd worked out a story that I was looking for a friend. But no hotel. In the post office no-one had heard of it. There was a distillery which kind of fitted the description, but when we asked there they directed us to a completely different district. I felt so miserable – had I got it wrong? But Han said: 'Nonsense. You were given a job, you're not supposed to have to solve a riddle.'

"The next day, the day the meeting was supposed to happen, I was a nervous wreck. Back to the toilet every five minutes. My guts were feeling uncomfortable – and that always tells me I'm doing something that is at least out of the ordinary. We knew how long the drive would take, so we didn't have to hang around.

"We waited by the distillery, because it seemed the most likely bet. No-one came, nothing happened. I was so disappointed, really depressed.

"It turned out later that the other person had come to the place as well, but the hotel was long gone. It must have closed after the young woman in Harare had moved away from Cape Town. Maybe years before. It's so awfully complicated to organise something from so far away."

"So then you didn't even have a telephone number to report that it had gone wrong?"

"No. We were just talking about that when we got stuck in a huge demonstration. I read in the papers that August the ninth is ANC Woman's Day. I was thinking of getting out and joining them. At least I'd be doing something. But there was nothing left to do except follow our planned route, a real tourist's trip by car to Durban, where we'd catch our flight home. On the way we stayed in the prearranged hotels; I'd left a list of them in Harare. All I could do by then was pin my hopes on that list.

"We'd chosen to drive the Garden Route, although it was winter, with not a flower to be seen. We crossed hundreds of miles of bare, dry country, and we couldn't understand why American Express thought that this just had to be seen. Marienburg was our first stop, and the next day we went on through thick fog to the next boring place, where we stayed in a hotel whose big attraction was an ostrich farm. The two of us had to sit and watch one of the birds being called from the other end of a hundred yard track. Then they shut him into a kind of cage, and invited you to sit on his back and he'd give you a hair-raising ride back down the track. Of course Han had to try and get me on the beast: 'Do it! Don't miss the experience of a lifetime!'

"In our next stop, Kirkwood, we finally got a call from Harare. Such a relief! A new rendezvous was arranged with the man from Cape Town. Thank God our trip hadn't been for nothing.

"The meeting went smoothly and fast. He arrived by bus, a smart well-dressed man. So I gave him all the material, and a bag of oranges and apples for the trip back. He accepted everything politely, and we dropped him off by the bus stop.

Aaf looked at me with a 'mission accomplished' expression on her face.

"Do you want to hear the rest as well?" she asked hurriedly.

"Yes of course, go on."

"Well, in Durban we only had one thought: to get away from the circus along the shoreline as soon as possible. So we went looking for a botanical garden someone had recommended. But as soon as we left the city centre we got thoroughly lost. Where we expected to find the gardens there was just a huge rubbish dump. Beside it was a township spreading up the side of a hill. It looked like a huge ant colony, with lots of activity going on amongst the tiny houses, boys everywhere with wheelbarrows and trolleys fetching water from a tap. There was none piped to the houses. And people coming home from work, women carrying great bundles of wood. It was very cold; they needed the fuel all right.

"A bit further on we drove through sugar cane fields. The road had shrunk to a track by then. While we were trying to turn the car round we saw a group of people waving rather hesitantly that they wanted a lift. Han said immediately: 'We can't do that, we've got to get back to the city.' He felt we should stick to our instructions – as little contact with people as possible. We drove past, and saw that one of them was an old man, very ill. When we'd gone a few more yards I said: 'Han, we have to go back, now.'

'That's against orders,' he said again.

"We had a fierce little row, but then turned back. I knew that Han was expecting trouble. There were at least fifteen people gathered around the sick man, and the car would only take five. And then you start discussing what to do, and feel rotten because you can't take everyone. But when we stopped, all they asked was a lift for the old man himself.

"I helped him into the car, and got the feeling that I was holding a dying man – completely exhausted, so miserably ill. We put him carefully in the front seat. He wanted to go about six kilometres down the road, and up a steep hill; it would have taken him hours on foot. At the top he insisted on getting out. People appeared from nowhere to help him. The old man just kept saying: 'God bless you, God bless you, thank you baas.' Oh, imagine – 'Baas'! Aaf began to cry, her shoulders shaking. "We were absolutely devastated. If we hadn't gone back ...

"You just don't know how to act in that bloody country. I can't explain to twenty million people: 'Listen, I'm on your side; maybe I drive a posh hire car and stay in expensive hotels, and I'm white, and maybe you wouldn't think it. But I'm from the Netherlands and we see things very differently there.' "

Autumn 1989

Just outside Lusaka, Ivan and I waited in the shadow of a tree, sitting on yellow dried-out grass which scratched my feet, waiting for Sipho to arrive. "How are things with Mac and Gebuza?" I asked.

"Really starting to move, apparently. They've made cautious contact with the leaders of the 'above ground' resistance. Now they can co-ordinate their activities with ours much better. And of course there are still plenty of arms going in."

"Will there be action soon, then?" I had to move; the grass was crawling with small red ants and they were invading my trouser legs. "No. Everything's still being set up." He helped me brush the ants from my feet. "We're waiting for a definite decision from the leadership. But if it comes we want to be well prepared – trained people and weapons ready and in place. There are still minor actions going on – sabotage, for example, mostly railway lines. But those are just training operations, really."

I looked at him in surprise, he went on:

"But the most amazing thing of all is the success we've had in infiltrating the enemy's intelligence service. Our contacts warn us of danger, and that makes the work a whole lot safer."

"You're infiltrating them?" Astounded, I swatted a huge ant dead. The queen, perhaps? Or do they never come out into the open?

"Yes. Why, did you think that was impossible?" laughed Ivan.

A thin young man appeared in the distance, approaching with an easy stride. He came over the grass and stood, somewhat ill at ease. His serious face was reminiscent of an African ceremonial mask, with big, heavy-lidded eyes and high cheekbones. His expression remained reserved and suspicious; after a brief glance at me he kept his eyes on Ivan.

Wasting no time on introductions, Ivan repeated the story he'd told me earlier. A year before, Sipho had been attacked. A bullet had later been taken out of his shoulder, but it still pained him. His hand had also been hit, and was badly stiffened. "Perhaps it's better for you to tell the story yourself?" Ivan said encouragingly.

"No, it happened the way you said," Sipho answered in a deeper voice than I had expected.

"And you're having trouble sleeping, right?" Ivan tried again.

"Yes."

"Perhaps we can do something about that in Amsterdam, seeing as you're coming anyway for your disguise," I said, trying to look reassuring.

He nodded.

It seemed there was no chance of a real talk. He strode away.

"When he's in Amsterdam you should try and get his story down on tape. He's carrying a big piece of history around with him," said Ivan.

I had asked Peter, an old and trusted friend, if Sipho could stay with him in his large and peaceful house beside the river Amstel. Perhaps there he would feel at ease. Behind the house was a shady garden, and from the front was a fine view of the water. Peter lived alone, and was capable of giving more attention and understanding to others than almost anyone I knew.

The second day after Sipho's arrival I visited him. He was huddled in a big black leather chair, surrounded by the severe modern lines of Peter's house. He wore a woolly hat, and a jacket over his sweater, the sleeves pulled down over his hands. His legs were stretched out, and his head was pulled down between his shoulders, like a bird's into its feathers.

The room was boiling hot, over thirty degrees perhaps. The central heating was turned up as high as it would go. I wiped the perspiration from my forehead; it was very warm outside, even though September had arrived. The television was switched on, with a pile of videos beside it, and the remote control lay on Sipho's knee. The room was dark, with just one standard lamp burning in the corner, and the venetian blinds rolled down and closed. I looked at my watch; it was exactly midday.

"Have you been out yet, explored Amsterdam a bit?" I asked cheerfully.

"No. Why?"

"Well, it's safe here. And it's a beautiful city."

"Ivan said you wanted to interview me," he said abruptly.

"Yes. At least, if it's all right with you."

"When do you want to begin?"

"Whenever you like."

"Doesn't matter. You say when."

That evening Peter came by to borrow yet more videos. "My God," he said, "he's so withdrawn. It's as if he's afraid. The house is a steam bath – I can hardly stand it. He just sits there in the chair, or in his room listening to the BBC World Service. He knows all the wavelengths by heart. When I come home, he stirs himself and gets up for a bit, but then sinks down again as if he's just back from a long exhausting journey, frozen to the marrow."

I asked Peter to set up a good microphone in Sipho's room so I could make decent recordings. I wanted good sound quality; I wasn't sure why, but he seemed to me to be worth it. The disguise would just have to wait a little. He's carrying a piece of history around with him, Ivan had said; but Sipho himself gave me more the impression of dragging the history round like a great weight. Possibly, once everything was on tape and he had handed the burden over, as it were, he would find it easier to embark on something new.

The next morning we assembled cigarettes, coffee, and a jug of water in his room. Peter had hung the microphone above a small table, and set two chairs facing each other.

Sipho sat down, laughing a little nervously. I saw his teeth for the first time, small with prominent gums. I was also nervous; where should I begin? I had called the psychiatrist the evening before for advice. "Ask above all if he remembers what he was wearing, whatever the situation. What was the weather like, what could he smell... "

I began clumsily: "Can you tell me something about when you were young?"

196

Sipho moved his chair, rearranged everything on the table. "Not much, an ordinary South African youth. I didn't know anything; there were no books. I was seventeen before I got my first book – about Martin Luther King."

"But something must have happened to make you get involved in the struggle?"

"The Soweto uprising in '76 changed me completely. Then I wanted to fight. The people were all still so afraid, even then. If you mentioned Mandela they shouted that you were a politieker, and that you'd end up on Robben Island. But once I'd seen how they could shoot at children I wanted to get out, to fight.

"In those days I listened to Radio Freedom. I'd found it by chance on the radio dial. They urged us to join Umkhonto we Sizwe. So then I was in a real hurry to leave, and so were a lot of my friends. I had to go – I was making such wild plans; I wanted to attack policemen, raid their houses. I was virtually out of control, I hated them.

"So I went away, to Swaziland. I left a letter behind for my parents, telling them not to worry, because I was safe in Free Africa. The ANC sent me to Maputo, and then even further away, for training. That was in late 1977.

"And did they send you out on missions?" He coughed twice, and leaned away from the microphone.

"Don't you want to talk about that? I can promise you that these tapes will be kept very secure indeed, in a bank safe."

"You want to hear about the attacks on police stations?"

"I don't know. You tell me – if you want and as much as you want. But tell me from the beginning."

"A new group was being formed in Maputo. A new assault unit to attack the enemy. We would operate in a new way, surviving inside the country for much longer. Five of us were selected. We lived together in a house in Maputo. Undercover. For nine months. No one was allowed to know that we were being prepared for a long-term stay inside South Africa. It was very hard; we couldn't go outside, and we spent the days talking, and preparing for our mission. It was important to get to know each other. We were all

197

very nervous, but everything seemed to be going well, until a horrible thing happened.

"It was an ordinary day like any other, and we were making tea. As we started to pour it out we heard a shot. Benny had gone to the toilet and put a bullet through his head. That hit us very hard – we didn't understand it. He'd been the last one to join us, we got on well with him, hadn't noticed anything strange. We were really shaken, and couldn't stop talking about it. Was it the fear? Or because we'd been cooped up inside so long? Had we shut him out of things? He took the answer with him when he was buried. After the funeral they asked us if we still wanted to go on. We all said yes, but we still talked about Benny, still do sometimes...

"We left in May of '79. Leonard, our commander, had gone ahead to build an underground shelter for us and to smuggle in our weapons. You should understand that at that time it was still difficult for a fighter to survive in the community. The people were intimidated, and not ready to shelter freedom fighters. So the ANC had decided on a kind of Vietnam-style survival tactic in well-populated areas.

"In Maputo we'd worked out a way of living in a tunnel, a sort of dug-out. When the commander let us know everything was ready we set off. Me, Marcus Motaung and Thelle Mogoerane. He'd found good dead-letter boxes for our weapons, but we weren't so impressed with the dug-out; it leaked, and our sleeping bags got soaked. So we all decided we'd construct a better base, but first we wanted to prepare our first operation. A month earlier comrade Solomon Mahlangu had been hanged, and we intended to avenge his death. That way we could show them that we were back – the boys of '76. We'd left the country as schoolchildren and now we were back as soldiers, with guns in our hands. That had been our promise when we left, and we saw it as a duty to our people. So we were more interested in finding our first target than in a new shelter.

"It wasn't easy, though. We looked dirty and tattered from having to crawl in and out of that rotten dug-out. "Aaah ... *Malunda*", people called after us. *Malunda* means someone with no home, who sleeps in the fields. That was no good at all, we were too conspicuous. And my shoes had been stolen too, when I left them outside the tunnel for the night. I only had one pair after that, and I didn't dare take them off even to sleep.

"But we were in such a hurry! In the mornings we washed in a stream, and went into the township. We'd find some old woman prepared to sell us something to eat, then we'd start our reconnaissance.

"The Moroka police station was our first target. We studied the whole area, checked out the outside of the building, and even went inside, asking after someone who didn't exist. We talked over various ideas for the attack, and made sketch-plans – until we came up with a final strategy. The big problem was still how to get our weapons to the place. We didn't have a car, or anyone to help us. We were on our own, and still didn't dare ask for help.

"In the end we stripped the guns down, packed them in plastic bags, and hailed a taxi to take us to the target. The driver asked what we had in the bags, electric tools? 'No, we said, they're knitting machines we've just stolen.' That was fine with him, but when we told him where we were going he got nervous. 'Why so close to Moshaangani?' he asked. Moshaangani was a really notorious policeman back then.

'Hey, nothing scares us,' we boasted, and he dropped us off in Dlamini township. We hid the guns in the bush there, in the high grass. The next day we used another taxi, from a different township, picked up our weapons and checked them.

"Just after nine in the morning of May 4th 1979 we attacked the Moroka police station in Soweto. Our aim was to destroy all the files, which contained information on activists, and other people. We were carrying petrol, detonators and hand grenades. We split into two teams, went in through the entrance, and took the guards by surprise. We knew exactly where the files were stored, and threw the petrol and hand grenades. The whole building was on fire, hundreds of dossiers were destroyed. The attack was such a surprise that no-one put up any resistance, they just ran away. So the building blazed, and we left piles of ANC pamphlets there.

We'd made them ourselves. They said that we were avenging the death of Solomon Mahlangu.

"We pulled back, guns ready. The street was completely empty, and we ran off looking for cover. I was moving cautiously past one building when I saw a man standing there looking at me. He was on his way to church, with a Bible under his arm. I stood up and went over to him; all at once I wanted to let him know why we'd done it. "We're the June 16th generation. We've come back to liberate you," I shouted. He looked at me very calmly and said "I'll say nothing if they question me. I'm well aware that our lives depend on you."

I wanted to talk with him some more; "You should all help us, shelter us," I went on. He nodded, but then the others came up, furious at me. What was I doing, taking such a risk? I couldn't explain it.

Later we laughed about it. They imitated how I had stood, talking to the man. I hadn't realised that I'd been aiming my gun at him the whole time.

"The next day we bought all the papers. Front page news everywhere. There had been casualties, but they didn't print how many. We were satisfied anyway; now people would know that we had returned as soldiers, that we'd kept our word."

That evening I searched through the AABN's archives for paper clippings from the period. I found them in boxes at the back of our storage room. The very yellowed front page of *The Star* showed a picture of the burnt-out police station; hundreds of dossiers had been destroyed. "The attackers left ANC pamphlets behind" was the rather neutral caption. Another paper, the *Sunday Express*, reported that the "terrorists" had escaped, in spite of a huge search operation by large numbers of police. Minister of Justice Jimmy Kruger warned that these guerrilla actions would become more frequent: "They are entering the country in ever-increasing numbers to carry out sabotage."

"After that we could finally concentrate on a new base, and we quickly found something that seemed suitable – a disused gold mine," Sipho continued. "We were safe there, because it was deep and dark; no-one dared go inside. The entrance shaft was three feet high, supported by pit props, and dropped downhill a bit before levelling out. We could get more than ten metres underground. So we put our mattresses and other stuff inside, and hid our weapons well. It was warm in there at night. Our first real base.

"Our morale was high then, and we had plenty of motivation. That kept us together, because it was a very tough situation, and it was going to get tougher.

"No-one was allowed out of the base without the commander's permission. If it was your turn to go out scouting, you left before sunrise, often before four-thirty, and you couldn't come back until it was dark. Before you went into the base you had to go to a rendezvous where one of the others would be waiting for you. That was in case something went wrong, in case the hideout had been spotted during the day and everyone had had to leave.

"Everything was controlled, even smoking – once an hour, to avoid the smell of cigarette smoke coming out of the mineshaft. Footprints were brushed away, and we couldn't cook anything at all, because of the smell. We took turns with the radio headphones, passed on what we heard to the others, and discussed world news in whispers. We always whispered, and checked all the time if anything could be heard or smelt from outside the entrance.

"Oh, we were together for so long, we got very close. Any problems meant calling a meeting, where we had a chance to air grievances. We tried to resolve arguments all together. If someone was wrong, he'd know about it...

"For a while the mine was very secure, until we noticed that the props were disappearing from the entrance, one after another. We watched from outside, and saw an old man coming every day, knocking out a few posts and carrying them away. He was a poor old man, probably collecting the wood to sell it. We were stuck with him, and soon it became a real problem. It forced us to move deeper and deeper into the mine, and it was just a matter of time: the more wood he carried off, the deeper we had to go. He was more and more of a threat. We talked it over again and again, but couldn't think of a solution. Then one day he stopped coming. What a relief

– no-one had dared to say out loud what might have had to happen to the old man.

"So then we were dug in deep. We called that our second base, and it wasn't bad at all. There was an extra shaft we called our rubbish dump, where we got rid of old tins and other stuff. We lay in our sleeping bags by candlelight, discussing new operations, or making pamphlets with rubber stamps we'd bought, letter by letter. Hundreds, we made. We were pleased with our home, our toloko, our tunnel."

"And then the roof fell in. Between them, the old man and the heavy rain did us in. When the collapse happened there were three of us inside; our commander was away. The entrance was blocked completely, and we dug for our lives with our hands and the bayonets off the AKs. The only place we found loose sand was above our heads, so the earth was falling into our faces as we dug.

"Hours later, in the evening, the commander came back and realised right away that we were trapped. From above the mine, on the hill, you couldn't see exactly where the base was, and we heard him stamping all over the place. He shouted, but we couldn't make him hear us. It was easy to understand his panic. He'd been away all day and didn't know how long we'd been buried, or even if we were still alive.

"Hours later we finally broke through into fresh air. Then we had to quickly get our equipment and weapons to safety, and begin all over again building a new shelter. This time we decided to dig ourselves a tunnel."

Sipho turned off the tape recorder. He had needed no prompting at all, and now stretched like a satisfied cat. I suggested we go out, and we went for a long walk beside the Amstel. He had left his woollen hat at home.

When we got back he washed his face, and without a word walked back to his room and switched on the tape recorder.

"Were you getting ready for more operations at the time?"

"Yes, but we had some setbacks. We tried to blow up some railway tracks, but the detonators didn't work and the explosives were discovered. So for a while we concentrated on painting slogans on walls ... at night, along the motorway between Diepkloof and

Meadowlands. 'Viva Umkhonto!', Viva ANC!', 'Support the ANC!'.
Most of all we wanted to get the political message over. So we were
still making pamphlets: 'Free the Political Prisoners', 'Freedom for
Nelson Mandela'; we scattered them on the streets.

"Then came the attack on the police station at Orlando in
Soweto. We hit that at about twelve-thirty on November the 2nd,
1979. The main attack was to be at the front doors. So one of us
threw a hand grenade over the fence to try and bring the cops to the
entrance area. But most of them ran away in their underwear, from
the barracks to a rugby field nearby. Two cops were killed. We read
later that about sixty of them had taken cover under their beds.

"Gradually people were realising that we were a danger to the
state. The newspaper articles got more concerned. Questions were
asked in Parliament. Why weren't the police prepared for this kind
of thing? Moroka had been a surprise, Orlando was a shock. But we
had an even bigger one up our sleeves.

"After the attack we went along the railway tracks back to our
base, outside Meadowlands, behind the Mzimhlope hostel, and
further, over the river towards New Canada.

"The papers said that the whole of Soweto was closed off. There
were roadblocks as far away as Botswana border. We were proud of
ourselves – with that raid we'd even got into *The Times* in England.

"After every operation we'd go to bus stations and listen to what
people were saying. We wanted to know their reactions. If I heard
them say *Babuyile a Bafana* – the boys are back – then I felt really
good. I was very sensitive to those opinions. You're carrying guilt
feelings around, after all. You're a guerrilla, and you know why
you're doing it, but even so it sometimes hurts.

"We were so successful that the leadership in Swaziland decided
to reinforce us with three more comrades: Gordon, who was killed
later on, and became known as the Lion of Chiawelo, Bobby
Tsotsobe, who's doing life on Robben Island now, and Knox. He's
dead now too.

"Once they'd arrived and we'd expanded our base we discussed
new targets. 'Let's go white!' we thought. It was time for the whites
to feel us getting closer.

"The police station in Booysens seemed a good objective. It's in a white district, on the outskirts of Johannesburg. The whole Booysens complex is much bigger than Moroka or Orlando, and we'd need a car, because it was much further away. We couldn't trek back on foot from this one. We sent Bobby out to organise a car.

"It was the fourth of April, Good Friday. Bobby stopped a minibus taxi, pointed his revolver inside and told the two passengers to go home, saying: 'Sorry, but we're freedom fighters Umkhonto soldiers, and we need this taxi for a while.' He told the driver: 'I don't like to borrow your car with a gun at your head, but we're doing this to liberate us all.' The taxi driver understood, and said 'Okay, take it, as long as you leave it behind afterwards at one of the garages along my route.' Then he went off for a beer.

"Bobby came back with the minibus, we loaded up our weapons and drove straight to the target. We hadn't been able to study the building close up, because it was a white police station and as a black you couldn't just wander in. Our main target was the charge office.

"Bobby had training for rocket attacks, with an RPG-7. We'd all taken up our positions when we were surprised by a police car arriving from an unexpected direction. Bobby already had the RPG-7 on his shoulder, didn't hesitate for a moment, and yelled 'Fire!' I saw his missile flying. We hadn't allowed for the wall around the place being so high. The first rocket landed on the roof. The second hit the building, and everything shook. Then the third went over, too high. The rest of us had spread out, laying down ground fire with the AKs. The whole thing didn't last more than ten minutes before we withdrew, leaving more piles of ANC pamphlets. We drove the borrowed taxi back to near where we'd agreed, and left it there undamaged.

"Back in the base we waited for the next day's news. There were already a few progressive newspapers then. Their reports of the introduction of the RPG-7 were almost proud, and they linked our pamphlets demanding the release of Mandela and Sisulu with the general campaign for their freedom. That was great. Our operation had linked in with the people's actions.

"The *Sunday Post* had a big headline: 'The ANC assault on Booysens was the biggest since the movement's guerrillas began their operations inside the country ... Around 150 rounds were fired from AK-47 automatic weapons ... No one was wounded in the attack. Police Commissioner Geldenhuys said: 'Those who campaign for the release of Mandela and Sisulu are not doing it for political leaders but for terrorists.' *The Star* reported that '... white people reacted with shock – if they can get so close to Johannesburg, in a white area, then soon they'll be in the city centre itself.'

"After that we all attacked a rent collection office – there were protests being organised in the townships against the high rents. Then I was recalled to Swaziland. I'd been inside for fifteen months.

"I didn't go back until 1981. There were white elections going on, and our new unit carried out a whole series of attacks. First we stayed back in the mountains for a while, to build a new base. We were so skilled at it by then that we dug it in open country, near a railway station. And we put in good ventilation pipes, because I knew that a lack of fresh air could lead to all kinds of tensions. We had limpet mines smuggled in, and soon attacked a police station and a fuel dump, then another police station, transformers and power stations. We were so busy we used up all our mines.

"In May 1981 we were planning to blow up oil pipelines. It was an important target for us, because some other comrades who had tried it had been killed. We made a rendezvous in a township. I was to pick up Marcus Motaung on the way. We had a lot of contacts everywhere in the townships by then and he'd been staying in someone's house. I was already running late, and he was still in the shower. I yelled at him to hurry up.

"We took a taxi, which broke down, then another taxi, and with all that arrived much too late at the rendezvous. The others were nowhere to be seen. We decided to go find a friend in a house nearby which he sometimes used. No-one there except a little girl. She looked scared, and whispered quickly that our comrade, and someone else, had been arrested.

"Marcus said 'Come on, we've got to get out. There's something vicious going on.' We had entrusted all the group's money to a friend who had a shop in Stinkwater. It was safe with him and we picked it up as we needed it. So that was our next stop.

He came to the door. 'Something's wrong,' he said. 'Someone's just been here who looked like a cop, but he was pretending he wanted to cash in empty beer bottles.'

"We got out fast. After a few days we went back. We planned to pick up all our money and leave the area. There was an old woman wrapped in a blanket outside the shop, and she warned us, pointing a finger. We both saw the man, and I recognised him – Sergeant Selepe. He was gunned down later in Mamelodi. It looked as if he was scared about something. I told Marcus: 'Hey Broer, this is bad.' I watched Selepe's car, the only one around except an ambulance further up the street.

"Motaung and I have been through plenty, and we don't get scared easily. But that time our courage nearly killed us. 'Maybe it's just Selepe,' I said. 'We can handle him all right.'

"We wanted to take him from both sides, so we each ran round one side of the block. The distance Motaung had to cover was shorter than mine. I ran hard to make up the difference. Then I heard the shots.

"I stopped for a moment, then made a fast U-turn and went back the way I'd come, deeper into the township. Suddenly cops seemed to appear everywhere, steadily closing in on me. They cut off every street I tried, and their cars patrolled. I jumped over fences, further and further, until I reached open country, outside Stinkwater.

"Now there were police vans as well. They spread out steadily in the same direction, going very slowly. It seemed as if there was no escape. I made a decision: I'll go straight at them, go on firing until I've just one bullet left, and use that for myself. Just as I was about to charge them, I saw a donga ahead of me and I dropped into it, out of sight. I heard helicopters as I crept along the donga. My clothes were torn, and I was covered in mud. But I reached a village about five miles from that first ambush, and some people hid me for the night.

"I wanted to know what had happened to Motaung – I'd heard rifle shots. Marcus – sometimes he could really be reckless. He was so tall, we called him Biggs, because of his huge hands. He was so hot-headed, so stubborn, so afraid sometimes just like me – terrified even. We'd fought together for so long...

"I was scared then. The next day I took a minibus taxi back to Soweto. I had no idea what I should do. I looked for a friend of mine, but he wasn't home. I wandered around until I came to a yard where some skollies were drinking and smoking dagga. Watching them, I felt so angry and miserable. They just sat there stupidly, smoking and drinking, and here was I fighting for their freedom too ... and where was Marcus now?

"I sat down with them and drank some beer to become part of the group. I was shaken, didn't dare wander around any more. With them I was safe, at least.

"After dark I set off again to find my friend. He told me what had happened to Marcus. When he ran out to where we'd meet, they opened fire. He'd been taken away, wounded. It turned out that the whole operation against us had been controlled from the ambulance.

"From then on things were bad for me. I was being hunted. I couldn't turn up anywhere without putting others in danger. It was difficult, very difficult. Finally orders arrived from Swaziland that I should leave the country immediately. So once more, and so far for the last time, I climbed over the border fence."

In the AABN archives I dug out everything about the "Moroka Three", as Marcus Motaung, Thelle Morgoerane and Jerry Mosololi became known during their trial. Mogoerane and Mosololi were arrested in December 1981 in Hammanskraal. Motaung was wounded in Stinkwater. They had left him lying in his cell for two days without medical treatment. During the trial the doctor, Snyman, was cross-examined about this by the defence. She had declared that providing medical treatment was less important than providing assistance to the police.

I found photographs showing a long line of people in Amsterdam, demonstrating for the release of the three. They carried sandwich boards with the portraits of the three men, their names written underneath in felt pen.

The trial began in June 1982 in Pretoria. The state called one hundred and thirty-five witnesses over twelve days, mainly "experts" and policemen involved in the arrests. All three defendants complained of being tortured, being hung by the feet, having plastic bags pulled over their heads, and suffering electric shocks. In long statements they explained their choice for the ANC. Motaung said that when he had left the country he had been so bitter that all he wanted was to kill white people. The ANC had taught him that whites and blacks would have to live together in a free and democratic South Africa. All three men were sentenced to death. After the verdict they raised their fists, shouting "Amandla!" On the ninth of June 1983, Motaung, Mogoeroane and Mosololi were hanged in Pretoria Central Prison. Furious demonstrations followed the executions, inside and outside South Africa. In Amsterdam more than a hundred people gathered for an all-night vigil.

Sipho looked mistrustfully into the mirror at the huge full beard Winnie had stuck to his chin. She was experimenting with various styles of spectacles, and had shaved his hairline a bit higher. Against the wall hung a suit that Yan had substantially padded out. "He just doesn't believe in it," whispered Winnie when Sipho left the room for a moment.

Marloes was giving him massage treatment evening after evening, carefully trying to ease the pain in his wiry body. She was also cautiously trying to tackle the shoulder damaged by the bullet. "It's a block of granite," she said. "And there's nothing I can do for that hand."

Maybe it was time for a change of scenery, I thought, time for fresh air and distraction. We were all getting exhausted. We'd been working on the disguise every day now for over a week. Peter drove us out to the IJsselmeer. North Amsterdam, Durgerdam, waving reed beds, wildfowl and water, and past Uitdam we clambered up the dike. There was a strong wind blowing and Peter, Marloes and I, all under average height, had to hang on to Sipho. He gazed out over our heads at the water, and Peter explained the purpose and design of the dikes to him, shouting above the wind.

On the island of Marken we drank hot chocolate with cream, and in Volendam sauntered past the endless rows of identical model windmills and painted clogs. We paused in front of a shop where one can have a portrait taken, in traditional Volendam costume.

"Shall we have a group photo done?" I proposed.

"Don't be ridiculous," exclaimed Peter, trying to walk on further.

Sipho grinned, and I pushed him inside. Peter and Marloes hesitated, but in the end followed us. Inside the shop everything happened like lightning. Two assistants dressed us up with the speed of long practice, and asked us to search through a huge bin for clogs which fitted. Sipho wore wide black breeches, a fur cap, and the girl entrusted him with a long, slim clay pipe. Marloes and I had long full skirts and lace bonnets. We were grouped together in a side room in front of ready-made scenery – a painting of an old-fashioned Dutch tiled fireplace with large quantities of tulips.

Three days later a large colour print was delivered. We gathered round Sipho, laughing. He held the photograph at arm's length, shaking his head. I looked at him: "A real Dutch Boer!"

Disguising him was very much easier after that.

One evening I arrived at Peter's house on the Amstel to find it alive with people and noise. Cheers of encouragement and applause, laughter and chatter enveloped me even in the corridor. A dart game was underway. Peter and Sipho stood side-by-side, darts in hand. Marloes and her youngest son were leaning forward ready to throw.

"Peter's winning," cried Tessel. I had come to fetch her. Sipho was losing but did not allow my arrival to spoil his concentration.

There were more children in the house, shouting and squealing. Tessel put on some South African music. Sipho set down his darts, sprang in among the children and danced. He lifted his knees high, encouraging the little ones, in Zulu, to follow him. He was teaching them the toyi-toyi. The children watched the movements of his long legs, and leapt up and down around him, arms held high. They copied his chant, following him in a line. Three-year-old Noortje staggered round Sipho's knees, until he swept her up with a kiss and danced on, holding her in the crook of his arm.

"Have we finished the interview?" I asked him the day before his departure.

"Do you think it's enough?"

"Perhaps there are still things ..."

"You decide," he said curtly.

"Okay, last year. What happened?"

We went to his room. Coffee, water, cigarettes, a long bout of coughing and then he began:

"It was in September. I should have already been in Maputo, but there was no car available so I was still stuck in Swaziland, with my wife and two children. We'd just finished dinner one evening, and I was watching television while my wife did some ironing. My brother-in-law had gone out to fetch beer. Someone knocked. We thought: there he was at last. My wife opened the door. A man threatened her with a gun, and three more pushed their way inside, all armed. I heard a shout of 'Freeze!' and suddenly there were four men in the room. 'Freeze!' they yelled again.

"I jumped up, a reflex action, grabbed the axe from beside the fireplace and lashed out – a huge swing at the one standing nearest. I could hardly see anything, but I felt resistance as I hit someone. Then I hit out again and saw one of the men stagger. His gun fell on the floor, so I grabbed it and tried to shoot, but it jammed. At least I think it jammed. I was so surprised that the others weren't firing, just yelling at each other. They seemed completely thrown by my reaction.

"With the gun pointed at them I backed away slowly towards my bedroom, but before I got there I heard the first shot and a bullet hit me in the leg. I dived through the door, and tried to get the gun to work. When it did I came back out into the passage. There was a lot of shooting.

"Suddenly my little girl, just two years old, came running to me, calling 'Papa, Papa ...' I tried to shield her, and got hit again, in the shoulder. I yelled at the child 'Go away, go away!' But she stood frozen, staring at me. They were firing from the various corners

210

where they'd dived for cover, but most of the bullets were way off target. It was driving me crazy, the shots, the noise, I don't know why. I went berserk, firing back at them and trying to find some cover, with my daughter still following me. I was shooting like a madman. I felt the child hang on to my leg.

"Suddenly it got through to me that they'd stopped shooting back. Through the window I saw them running away, dragging the wounded with them. I searched through the house in case anyone was left behind, and came to the kitchen. Mosh was leaning against the refrigerator. I knew him – he'd worked with us in the ANC. He'd turned, betrayed us. I fired at him, I don't know if I hit him. He fired back, but missed me twice at short range. Then I saw he was wounded as well. I yelled in Zulu: 'Let's finish each other off, bastard!' But he turned and ran. I heard cars starting up and driving away.

"I found my daughter in the passage, still just staring at me. My wife and son had run to the neighbours and called the police. But no-one came. I finally realised how heavily I was bleeding; I'd have to find help. But I was still too shocked to manage anything. I didn't understand why they hadn't killed me. They must have had orders to take me alive.

"I couldn't stay in the house; there was blood everywhere, and the smears where they'd dragged someone away. I talked with my wife; she stayed behind with the children and I ran more than half a mile to a friend's house. My clothes were soaked in blood, but I still felt no pain. It wasn't until I tried to knock at the door and saw how my hand was ripped apart that I suddenly started hurting, all over.

"I stayed with my friend; going to a hospital was much too dangerous.

"The next day the Swazi police raided dozens of ANC people's houses, looking for me. I just lay there in my friend's place, passing out sometimes from the pain. I came to a bit in the afternoon, and saw Swazi cops bending over me. They arrested me, drove me off to a police station, later to a hospital. I was in a cell for three months before I came up for trial. I was just fined, and then I left Swaziland, with my family."

Sipho fell silent. I pressed the pause button on the recorder, but he said nothing more. I pressed stop.

"Shall we go for a last walk?" I suggested. "You want to get a radio, don't you? Let's buy it now. There won't be much time tomorrow."

He pulled on his jacket, and in a shop on the Ceintuurbaan, specialising in household appliances, we found a small world-receiver in a showcase. The shopkeeper brought it out. It was conveniently small, and had an enormous range. The man put the batteries in and looked for a station to show us how it worked. After some static, an old hit broke through loud and clear: "Free-ee-ee, Nelson Mandela", the number by the Special AKA group. Sipho turned to me, roaring with laughter. The shopkeeper looked at Sipho and then at me, mystified.

"A good omen – this is the one."

On the street he pulled the radio out again, and I prophesied that on that little set he would hear the news that Nelson Mandela would be set free.

My prophecy came true.

From South Africa there were more and more complaints coming back about the disguises.

The wigs were going bald. The moustaches had turned into grubby little pads full of old glue. The make-up was running out and a great many more activists now working for Vula urgently needed disguises. But it was far too risky to send large numbers of these people to the Netherlands, and there were no professionals available to them at home.

I discussed the problem with Winnie and Yan. They understood well enough. Their carefully hand-made creations needed a lot of care and maintenance. "Those wigs aren't bald! They just need a good wash and a brushing out!" said Winnie, her professional pride a little touched.

They put together a long list of instructions, but this would clearly not be enough. On-the-spot intervention was essential, by dedicated professional hands. We found these in Brussels. A couple, friends of Winnie and Yan, were remarkably easily persuaded to move to South Africa for at least a year: Daniel and Sylviane, theatre director and actress, didn't need much time to think. They'd had more than their fill of the Belgian theatre world, and the idea of disguising South African resistance people appealed to them greatly. Winnie and Yan could teach them the finer details of their skills.

The main problem for them would be to find work in South Africa. It would be impossible to stay in the country for a long period without paid employment. However, their English was poor, and although they took a crash course it would never be good enough to let them pursue their own profession there. We had to rule out the possibility that there would be a regular demand for an actress with a strong French accent – or for a Belgian director in South Africa's theatre world.

Finding suitable employment for our people was a problem I now encountered regularly. Two couples from Brabant had now departed with no immediate prospects, but they had been urgently needed. The quiet, serious couple who had flown to Lusaka to help Lucia did not worry me. They would find something, and they could both teach. The other couple, our exuberant hedonists, had left full of self-confidence to set up a safe house in Zimbabwe, but I did not share their optimism. If they didn't find something quickly they would finish up living on Vula funds.

One couple, on the other hand, were struggling with over-qualification. He was a biochemist and had already made a preliminary trip to South Africa, scouting for work. Much interest had been shown in his research, but in that steadily worsening economy no-one could afford him. His wife, a nurse, worked her way through piles of application forms, following one expensive course after another, and had to suffer the overwhelming attentions of development aid bureaucracy.

The difficulties were brought home to me even more clearly when Robert and Tina arrived back in Amsterdam. They had lived in South Africa for two years, storing large shipments of weapons in their house under very difficult conditions, and setting up caches. But they had had no luck at all in finding jobs. Now that they were home for a while they planned to study a variety of subjects to improve their chances of at least being able to provide for their own living expenses.

Some, however, managed to provide for themselves in the most surprising ways, finding the strangest jobs. Andre was an example. Before he finally became the manager of two sports shops, which gave him a more than adequate income, he had worked for a while for a natural gas company in Swaziland. He travelled from village to tiny village, trying to awaken interest in natural gas as a household fuel. But business was bad; the rural Swazis were not attracted to the product. To break the monotony he began selling helium-filled balloons, and thus became the amazingly popular balloon man at the markets, who for every balloon he sold would release two more, free, to fly up and away into the sky, to the great joy of the children and other market people. The natural gas company promptly dispensed with his services.

Occasionally I was assailed by another fear: that someone would lose their job: the air hostesses, for example. Elise by now had been flying to Johannesburg as a courier for more than a year, with great frequency. She was well overdue for a rest period. A colleague took over from her. We had to be extra careful, however, as I had no intention of risking her dismissal.

Shortly before Christmas Wilma was married. She was in Botswana now and had sent me another invitation, which I took as a gesture of friendship, for she must surely understand that there was no possibility that I could be present. She sent me a letter afterwards with a full report: "At first I didn't want it – a traditional wedding, it's so discriminatory against the woman. But when I understood that our Dutch marriage form wouldn't be accepted by the family or in the village, I didn't have much choice. I was also worried about them getting the idea that as a white I looked down on their culture; so on with the wedding after all. Everything was arranged well in advance by my husband's uncles. He's from a village. Everyone in Botswana is from a village, never from a town. Even my child belongs to that village, even though he's never been there.

"The mother, uncles and aunts were all told, and then permission was given. Then his mother spent days visiting all the cousins and aunts to tell everyone personally, very informal, very intimate. The subject of the coming marriage isn't mentioned too directly, it's brought up 'between the lines', but the news has to be shared person-to-person; otherwise they won't come to the celebration. Then they won't contribute to the feast or bring gifts, and that's their way of letting you know they don't recognise the marriage.

"In principle, everyone's welcome to the feast. It really made me think of old-fashioned country weddings in the Netherlands. The whole village comes, and there's plenty of eating, drinking and singing. But first I was 'told the law', which entails being taken off to one side by the women. You're wrapped in a blanket, shawl over your head, and you're told how you are expected to behave. This involves: never ask your husband where he's been, never contradict him, always stand up first and make tea for your mother-in-law. If you are in trouble never hesitate to go to your in-laws, because they are your family, and that entitles you to certain rights. That last one especially was really emphasised, and it was important to me, because I'm going to be living in Botswana for a long time and I'll certainly need that help.

"I didn't want to come over as a foreigner. There'd already been complaints about me. Old women had been saying: 'Look at her – how shamelessly she looks around her!' Because women are supposed to keep their eyes down, diffident and sad. The first time I went to a wedding and saw the bride like that I thought: 'Heavens, what's going to become of that? She's already looking so sad.' But luckily my brazenness was explained away – 'that's just the way white women are ...' When they saw me eating sorghum pap there were approving nods. When they saw me sweeping they knew I'd take good care of my mother-in-law.

"The preparations went on for weeks. My husband went to the village ten days before the wedding. The huts all had to be re-plastered with mud and cow dung, a new floor of mud and dung had to be laid – that's as hard as concrete. The walls were repaired and decorated, tents set up for the feast. They started slaughtering the four cows the night before the wedding, with a lot of goats, I don't know exactly how many, and around twenty chickens. It went on all night and through the day itself, behind the house. We wanted to have plenty of meat for everyone. Sometimes there's different treatment for the notables and the ordinary folk, but we weren't having that. Village children or white people from the city – they'd all get the same.

"It turned out to be a huge feast, with lots of contributions, which meant that it was all right – everyone was showing their approval. I still keep hearing: 'Yes, I heard that you got married. A cousin of my aunt's sister was there and she said you were wearing a lovely dress.' And in the end I did hire a white dress – it had to be white. We didn't like the idea, but it was made very clear to us that

216

otherwise we couldn't expect people to take it all seriously. So I capitulated, and at least the idea that I didn't think Botswana was good enough for me has been knocked on the head. I've been completely accepted. The word is: 'She got married here; we saw it for ourselves.'"

I was planning to spend Christmas in London. My daughter had left for a snowy family holiday in the Alps. I was feeling drained and dispirited, after months of nothing but work, shut away in my house. I hardly ever had a moment to see acquaintances, and if I visited a friend I couldn't think of a thing to talk about. I would become disoriented, and almost burst into tears if they so much as asked "What are you doing with yourself these days?"

Fortunately for me, Ivan arrived in Amsterdam; we were to travel on together to London. Complaining to him was at once satisfying and pointless. He also looked pretty exhausted. The problems confronting them in Lusaka were so much greater than mine. But his sense of humour, which could always put things in perspective, was just the thing to start my recovery, and his duty-free whisky continued the process.

Before we left he had long talks with all the new people who were to leave over the months to come. The Vula team was soon to be strengthened by the addition of more members of the ANC Executive Committee, and the first of these would be Ronnie Kasrils. So more and more safe-house keepers were needed inside South Africa.

A surprise was awaiting me in London. Janet Love had arrived there from South Africa on Vula business. Our reunion was ecstatic, as we threw our arms around each other with cries of joy, both chattering on so much that not a word could be heard. Tim had found a house where the three of us could spend Christmas. He was going to stay with his computers.

It was freezing cold in London, grey and disagreeable as only that city can be. A blanket of cloud hung low, with beneath it continuous, almost invisible drizzle. Everything in this unfamiliar cold house felt damp. The heating had been off for weeks, but Janet succeeded in persuading the boiler to come to life; it started up with a deep sigh and a loud "whhooff!"

It was the Saturday afternoon before the long Christmas weekend, and Janet warned us that we only had a couple of hours before London withdrew behind closed doors. The English shut themselves away with their puddings and turkeys, leaving the streets lonely and deserted. Almost nowhere else could one feel so much the foreigner. Janet had lived there unwillingly for years and hated the city.

In a nearby shopping centre's supermarket we loaded our trolley with coffee, cheese, wine, bread and vegetables, as if buying supplies for an expedition to unexplored territory. We checked our shopping list again and again – forgetting anything meant doing without.

Back at the house we unpacked it all, closed off the rooms we did not need, and turned the heating still higher. The lights had to go on before four o'clock. Ivan and Janet pushed two heavy armchairs over to the television set, leaving me the sofa. However much the boiler puffed and groaned in the basement, the house stayed chill and damp. We all wrapped ourselves in blankets. When at last we were settled, Ivan opened the newspaper, and read out the titles of all the films to be broadcast over the next few days. With much discussion and compromise we made a list.

The TV was switched on. The BBC's six o'clock news. Eastern Europe, East Germany, Romania. Pictures from the centre of Bucharest. "Since the fall of Nicolae Ceaucescu, troops of the feared Securitate secret police have occupied the former royal palace. After midnight they attacked the television building, and heavy fighting continues. The city's inhabitants are sheltering in cellars. Many Rumanians have already been killed."

Silent, we watched the screen. Thousands of demonstrators were gathered together. Not one face could be distinguished clearly, but the sea of heads radiated a massive anger.

"What are they doing?" asked Janet softly.

"Everything we were told was worthwhile is falling apart," said Ivan calmly. Janet had only left South Africa a couple of days before, and had read all the reports in the papers there about events in Eastern Europe with deep mistrust.

218

"There'll be nothing left. What was called socialism has turned out to be a lie," Ivan continued. Janet was staring in disbelief at the advancing tanks, as if unexpectedly confronted with the death of a friend. Ivan and I had been following these death throes for several weeks. We sat together, despondent, and not merely because of the tragedy of what was happening, the emergence of the bottled up anger and frustration, the crimes taking place; we were being forced to recognise that the deeper cause of the anger had been a complete lack of freedom. Freedom, the dearest idea of all to us, perhaps our highest principle.

Furthermore, there was good reason for serious concern. So much support for the struggle in South Africa had come from Eastern Europe: technical education and medical care as well as weapons and military training. These nations had always taken a positive stand where the apartheid system was concerned. The ANC was losing powerful allies, and would come to stand more and more alone against the West, whose policies were virtually exclusively determined by economic interests in South Africa. There was a sick irony in the situation. Now that the peoples of Eastern Europe were throwing off repression, it seemed as if the chances of freedom for the people of South Africa were becoming more remote.

For Christmas and Boxing Day we stayed inside with the television, read the papers and slept a lot. Sometimes a heated discussion would flare up. Tim came by with messages from South Africa and Lusaka, and then the talk would turn to the work, often until deep in the night.

On Boxing Day Ronnie Kasrils, whose family lived in London, threw a party. Only Ivan and I were to go, as Janet could not be seen in public. None of the guests were to be allowed to know that she was in the city, just as they would not be told that the party was a send-off for Ronnie. He was soon going back into South Africa, disguised and underground, to join Mac and Gebuza.

The house in Golders Green was packed to overflowing, and the atmosphere was strained. Everywhere people stood talking in serious groups – in the kitchen with plates of food, or sitting on the stairs. We had to wrestle our way through the passage to reach the living room. Television sets were on both there and in the bedroom. The BBC was showing the pictures broadcast earlier by Romanian television: the bodies of Nicolae Ceaucescu and his wife Elena in front of a bullet-scarred wall. "Last night there was almost no further shooting," said the newsreader. "Life is slowly returning to normal in Bucharest. The streets are being cleared."

On the sofa an elderly South African with a hostile glint in his eye was explaining to a young woman beside him that reactionary forces were undermining socialism, that fascists were manipulating the masses. The young woman looked from him to the TV screen and back, her own eyes puzzled. Loud voices rang from all the rooms in the house. Opinions were being put forward in an attempt to explain the unexplainable.

A shrill voice in the corner proposed that tanks should be sent in to crush the Romanian uprising.

I heard Ivan, shocked but in too quiet a voice, say that after all it was the people themselves who were protesting.

"Oh, people! Look at Hitler's Germany," the high voice retorted.

The young woman on the sofa finally spoke: "But for years they've had complete control of the media, the economy, everything," she said to the old man.

"Socialism is being stabbed in the back," the shrill voice rose once more before fading away into drunkenness.

"Well, I've got very different ideas about that ..." a polite young man began.

I went in search of Ronnie. He was in the corridor, and threw his arm round my shoulders. "Have you heard anything from Chota?" was his first question.

"Yes, a Christmas card." I wondered if anything was getting through to Robben Island of what was happening in the world.

After the Christmas holiday, Joop travelled from Swaziland to Maputo. He was in a hurry to get back, because he was expecting the arrival of a Dutch couple who were coming to take over his work. Just as he was planning to get everything ready to receive them, he was asked to pick up a load from Mozambique. The road was terrible, and he was using his own old car which was suffering all sorts of ailments. After the border there were a couple more checkpoints, and then he started onto the dangerous stretch where Renamo attacked regularly. The wrecked vehicles along the side of the road showed how things usually turned out. Using the road was only permitted during certain hours of the day, and even then only at one's own risk.

Once he was back in the Netherlands, he told me: "I'd just begun that dangerous bit when my horn started blowing, non-stop, I think because of all those potholes in the road. I couldn't have that – announcing my coming with a continuous hoot! I stopped, jumped out, opened the bonnet and pulled some wires loose, then leapt back in and drove away flat out. The whole electric system was shot to hell by all the vibration. But I made it safely."

In Maputo the ANC comrades had needed several days to weld a compartment into his car, to hide the guns. Joop got more and more restless; he did not want to miss the couple who were to relieve him.

"Finally I could head back to Swaziland. Outside Maputo, well before I came to that dangerous stretch again, it started to rain. Not rain, a bloody monsoon. The electrical system was still a mess; nothing had been fixed. So I had no windscreen wipers. Very slowly, bit by bit, I got closer to Renamo territory.

"This was hopeless. I couldn't wait for dry weather, so there was nothing for it but to use an old trick – wipe the windscreen with a potato cut in half. I'll spare you the story of how I managed to get hold of a potato in Mozambique, where there's virtually nothing to eat at all. But I found one, and in fact it did help a little.

"On the dangerous bit I really got panicky, with a car full of guns, no windscreen wipers, a tropical rainstorm and Renamo murderers on the loose. I got a real wave of longing for Holland. Then it happened – the weather cleared, the sun came through. Everything was fresh and green, and I whistled all the way home. I drove up right on time to go pick up the new couple and take them to their house. The next day I felt around in the secret compartment – cold steel, everything in good condition, ten AK-47s and a sack of ammunition. My last little job, for now."

February 1990

I WAS STILL DAZED, HANGING AROUND IN FRONT OF THE TELEVISION
set in the corner of the room, between the copy machine and a rack
of posters. Someone rushed into the AABN office with bottles of
champagne, and the television camera recorded my every move.

State President FW de Klerk, in his annual speech at the
opening of the South African white parliament, had just announced
the lifting of the ban on the ANC, and several other organisations.
From now on the ANC would be able to operate freely. De Klerk
had also promised that all political prisoners would be released –
that Nelson Mandela would be freed.

The telephones were ringing continuously. My colleagues Fons,
Fulco, and Bart were all busy on the lines, giving our comments to the
press. The text of the speech had now come in on the fax, and was
being analysed word-for-word by a group seated around the long
work-table. A copy was put into my hand and I quickly re-read the text.

The television set was already showing pictures of ecstatic
crowds on the streets of Johannesburg. Packed together, singing,
clenched fists raised high, they surged forward with ANC flags
waving above their heads. The same colours were flying from the
front of our own building. The news came in by phone that the
mayor of Amsterdam had hoisted the ANC flag on the town hall.

More and more people flowed into our office, with cries of
excitement and disbelief. I was hugged, kissed, congratulated. The
cameraman followed me about, recording everything. Fulco flicked
through the television channels with the remote control. There was
De Klerk again, a repeat of the speech, those same words. I had
already seen and heard it three times, but only now did I realise why
I was so very angry. That face, shameless and self-satisfied. I had
the urge to throw my champagne glass at the screen – not a single
excuse, not even one carefully formulated apology from those lips.

222

Someone threw his arms around me from behind.

"What a victory," he whispered into my neck.

It was indeed a huge victory. I turned round, joined in a toast. For thirty years this had been longed for: the ANC legalised, the exiles' return, the political prisoners free. Oh, God! Chota free!

The prison gates open, boat after heavily-laden boat crossing from Robben Island to Cape Town, celebrations on the quayside. Chota free!

I phoned my mother.

"Child, you've won," she said, warmth in her voice.

The television crew followed me around for a whole week. Everywhere I was filmed – at work, at home: a week in the life of a political activist. I tried to fulfil their expectations as best I could, and to hide my unease and discomfort.

Now we were waiting for the release of Nelson Mandela, and I called friends in South Africa, journalists and lawyers, for news. The police were already attacking demonstrators again, they told me. There was total confusion. Maybe it'll be in a couple of days, maybe at the weekend.

My faithful television director was lucky. Albie Sachs came to Amsterdam to give a lecture which had been arranged weeks before. Our first meeting since the attempt on his life in Maputo was recorded on film. I saw for the first time his damaged face, his missing arm, and felt it as a kind of betrayal to allow the camera to thus spy on our emotions.

During that week I gave more newspaper and television interviews. Everyone wanted to know how I felt now. "Happy and concerned" was my simple reaction. I came face to face with my own picture on newsstands, people called out to me on the street, and the greengrocer round the corner asked if it was all right to start selling grapes from the Cape again.

For years I had tried, as far as it was possible for a chairperson of the AABN, to lead a relatively secret life. I had closed the door of my home to friends, and built up a facade behind which I could work in peace and safety; now, suddenly, I was caught in the spotlight.

In the evening, once the television crew had left, I brought out my computer. I wanted to know what the reactions were in Lusaka, and hear those of Mac and Gebuza. But the message which quickly came through was cool and reserved. This is a step forward, it said, an important step; its implications can't yet be fully estimated. However, the work must simply continue.

Then followed a whole list of questions and instructions. Maarten Vis, the electrical technician from Castricum, had left early in January to set up a safe house in Durban for Ronnie Kasrils. They had lost contact with him. It was urgent that I track him down. The Belgian couple had left, their luggage full of wigs and makeup, but they had urgently requested extra material which would have to be purchased and sent out. A carpenter from Zeeland was ready to leave. All the instructions for him to meet his contact in Johannesburg were listed. Tim was going to bring extra computer disks to Amsterdam.

On February 11th, at seven in the evening, thousands of people streamed out of Dam Square for a joyful, exuberant procession through the streets of Amsterdam, with music groups and choirs. A few hours earlier Nelson Mandela had been released from Victor Verster prison. Beside the canal two elderly women released white doves; cars stopped, hooting their horns, to let the crowd pass. The waiting trams flew small ANC flags on each side. There was shouting and laughter; people hung from their windows giving thumbs-up signs.

The city had a strong anti-fascist and anti-racist tradition, and there were often demonstrations against injustice. But this was the first time I had ever seen a joyful demonstration. I walked somewhere in the middle, together with the mayor of Amsterdam. He was surrounded by a large group of cheering children, most of them black. They held his hands, and pulled at his coat. Smiling shyly, he had to struggle to stay upright. Shortly before eight, we approached the Leidseplein, where more thousands were already waiting.

At that same moment, in Swaziland, a short distance from an army patrol, four ANC fighters and two old men clambered over the border fence. They walked in close single file in the pouring rain, over treacherously slippery mud, through the reeds, close by a white farm, to a chorus of barking dogs. Totsi and Rafael were guiding Sipho and Charles covertly into South Africa.

In Cape Town Nelson Mandela appeared on the balcony of the town hall, to be cheered by hundreds of thousands of South Africans, and by millions more spread across the world, who were hearing his voice for the first time.

On February 2nd, Peter and Sipho sat on a porch in front of a holiday house in the Swaziland hills. Peter had rented the house to provide a secure base for Sipho and another ANC guerrilla, Charles, until the moment came for them to cross the border.

Later, back home in the house beside the River Amstel in Amsterdam, Peter remembered:

"It was oppressively hot over those few days, and we got what relief we could sitting on the porch, under the umbrella. That was your best chance of getting a little cooler. The house was in a beautiful position, halfway up a hill, and we could look out over a big green fertile valley. No-one knew how long the wait would be, so we played darts, day after day. Sipho won every time. But we couldn't keep it up for long, we'd collapse back into the porch chairs, all sweaty, and listen to the news every hour.

"It was the same on February 2nd. We didn't expect anything special. Sipho was sitting with his elbows on the table, head in his hands, and Charles a bit in the background. He was a quiet guy. Sipho's little world receiver was on the table; we were listening to De Klerk's speech. So then we heard it: ANC legalised, Mandela was going to be freed.

"We were all staring straight in front of us. The news was repeated. There was just an amazing silence. Sipho could only whisper: 'Hey, man, hey man ... '. Charles stared at the radio. After a couple of minutes we all stood up, and slapped each other on the back, a bit awkwardly. Then we sat down again. It was still dead quiet. You'd think there'd have been a cry of joy sort of swelling up softly from all around, that the trees would sway with pleasure.

Sipho had looked around briefly with a beaming smile, but a

moment later, so quickly I couldn't understand it, his face dropped again, grim. 'It's a trick,' he said, a couple of times. 'Now it's going to get tough. The rest of the world will think it's over, now. But the struggle won't be won this way.'

"The evening before they left, Totsi and Rafael, who were to lead the infiltration, prepared a traditional meal. Totsi stood in the kitchen cooking the pap for hours, because it had to be boiled, cooled and heated up with more water, over and over again. I suggested maybe slicing it, with some cheese and garlic. Totsi just gave me a look – this is the way to cook pap, and that's it.

"We sat on the porch in the dark, with the smell of singed meat and the boiling pap in the house. Rafael had made a huge fire and stood rubbing his hands over the crackling sparks. He looked really fiery, in the glow. He explained to me how that kind of traditional meal is important for your morale.

'Tomorrow we're going into enemy territory,' he said.

"And then the weather broke. It began to drizzle. We'd been a bit noisy, and a night watchman wearing a cloak came to see what was going on. That damped down the party a bit, and we sat quietly, eating the pap from the pot with our hands.

"The temperature dropped quickly, and there were short, heavy showers one after another, drowning the fire. Totsi and Rafael stood up looking at the rain, worried. I could see that this wasn't the best weather for them to cross the border.

"It was still pouring down when I watched them leave the next day, in their bakkie. Before that, the last few hours, you could cut the tension with a knife – Sipho irritable, Charles more silent than ever, Totsi and Rafael touchy and curt. The goodbyes were short and hurried, there wasn't much more to say. They drove down the track, and I went in to clean up the house."

Totsi: "I left for Swaziland with Rafael just before Christmas to get things ready for the crossing. I don't know why, but I was very tense; maybe because I was pregnant, or maybe because things had been going so well for so long. I didn't understand it. I took some Valium now and then, and put my trust in my disguises, and did the relaxation exercises that Marloes had taught me.

"As soon as we arrived we went as quickly as we could to the border area, to Baba Nsibande. I must tell you about Baba, he's a fantastic old man. Old people like that shouldn't be forgotten.

"Baba is sixty, or maybe much older. He's very tall and fat, and actually he's very ill. Diabetes and a lot more; he doesn't even know himself everything that's wrong with him. He's South African, but for a long time now he's had to live just over the border in Swaziland, because something went wrong once. He did all sorts of work for us, for years, going back and forth across the border.

"One time we'd asked him to pick some comrades up in South Africa. Everything was arranged, the contact person and so on, but a couple of things happened on the way which made him uneasy. He felt so unsafe that he hired a truck, loaded his car inside it, and drove on like that. It didn't help – they arrested him. They tortured him horribly for a good ten days, but he didn't say anything. Well, that's Baba Nsibande. In the end they had to let him go, and from then on he's been helping us from the Swazi side of the border.

"So I went to Baba for help, if he was well enough at least. When I'd introduced him to Rafael we set out to find a good place for the crossing. Baba managed to surprise me again – I'd been doing that work for so long, I knew the border like my own hand, but even so he'd found another new place.

"We watched the soldiers' movements for weeks, and checked out five other locations, but in the end we decided that Baba's proposal was the best – close to passport control near Amsterdam. It would be a difficult route, and pretty dangerous, but it had some important advantages. Baba's brother, a sangoma, lived just across the border there. He knew the way on the South African side well, and we asked him to come over to be our guide.

"The evening of the actual crossing, Sunday, February 11th, we sat in Baba's house talking everything through once more. Before we left, the sangoma wanted to perform a ceremony for luck. He scattered herbs over our shoes, so our path would be safe, and drank some home-made beer. Then he took a couple more swallows, and while we pulled on our overalls and boots he had a good bit more. Rafael took me aside, and asked me for the umpteenth time if I was sure I wanted to go along, because I was pregnant. I told him angrily what I'd told him before: I was only pregnant, that was all.

"Then we set out, the six of us. Rafael and me, the two old men, Sipho and Charles. The sangoma had had one more drink to our success. I could understand it; the security police can be vicious all right if you fall into their hands. Baba Nsibande can tell you all about that.

"The weather was awful; it had been raining all day. There were holes in the ground everywhere, full of water, and the going was slippery. We were wearing boots, but the old men went barefoot as ordinary country folk. That's the way they wanted it. It was a pitch-black night, no stars, you couldn't see a metre in front of you and we had a long way to go to reach the fence. The sangoma was drunk by now, staggering about and wanting to discuss everything. 'Hey, hey Baba man, what you coming this way for? Why you doing this?' he said, in a loud voice.

"So we told him:
'Sshhh! Voices travel at night ...' I was terrified that the soldiers would hear him.

"We had to stay very close together so as not to walk into trees or get lost in the scrub. Baba stopped us and whispered that we were taking a difficult route. He explained that the easiest routes were the most dangerous. The more impenetrable the terrain, the safer it was; the soldiers would rather not venture into it.

"At the border fence he gestured for us to be as silent as possible. 'If they see us they'll shoot us on the spot.'

"I was irritated that he was going over that again. Sipho and Charles were tense enough already. They're trained guerrillas, man, they're not just going to stand there and be shot. They'll shoot back. I said quickly: 'Boys, it's after February 2nd, we don't shoot any more, we agreed, right?'

"'Have you told them too?' said Sipho, sarcastically.

"I didn't dare say any more. I'd never been shot at. Then we climbed over the fence – with a lot of difficulty. Baba went first. I could see him hauling his great body slowly upwards. Then all the rest of us heaved the sangoma up, he was frozen stiff with fear.

228

Right at the top he grabbed wildly at the air, and then we all heard a soggy thud. The boys and me went over, Rafael last. When we were all down, he gripped my arm tight, and whispered to me, very moved: 'I can feel South African earth under my feet again. You've no idea how long it's been.'

"The really heavy going began on the South African side. We had to hold on to each other, and feel with our feet for grip on the rough ground. We walked through scrub – you could feel the branches and sticky leaves grabbing at you – then back into open country. We waded through a river. I felt the icy water fill my boots and creep up to my hips. Quickly, almost too late, I pulled the pistol out of my trouser band and held it over my head, hoping the boys would do the same. All I could see, just, was the faint silhouette of Sipho ahead of me. Over his head he was carrying the holdall he'd insisted on taking with him.

"On the other side we had to clamber up a sandy bank, and I was covered in mud up to my armpits. There were woods around us now. The rain had stopped, and ribbons of mist were drifting through the trees. The sangoma fell to his knees, raised his arms high and called '*Izipoko ... izipoko ...* Spirits, Spirits! They're coming for us, we're lost!' Well, this time Baba was really angry. He turned round and hissed: 'If it was up to you we'd all fall in a ravine next!'

"We all had to laugh at that. Rafael helped the old man to his feet and we all trudged on out of the woods, through the mealie fields, skirting a white farm. We could hear the dogs barking – maybe they'd scented us. I could feel that there were people close by, and sometimes I thought I could see the lights of Amsterdam, way off in the distance.

"Baba was manoeuvering like a genuine guerrilla, circling and making detours to follow the lay of the land, using every little ditch or piece of cover, every hill and valley.

"After three and a half hours – I was exhausted – we reached the sangoma's house. It was the early hours of the morning; everyone was asleep. Just his wife had waited up. She lit a fire and made tea for us. We sat there, gradually getting warm again. I watched Sipho and Charles side by side, lost in their own thoughts. The first stage of their journey was over. A car would be coming for them soon, to take them further into the country, until they could contact Gebuza.

"We couldn't stay long; we wanted to be back over the border by dawn. Sipho and Charles gave us their overalls and boots, and their pistols as well – reluctantly. They were to go the rest of the way unarmed, those were the orders. We said goodbye. The sangoma could go and sleep off his home-brew, and Baba Nsibande would come with us again for the three and a half hour hike back to the border. But this time he took a shorter route. In two hours, at the end of our strength, Rafael and I were back on the Swazi side of the border fence. We were covered in burrs – *wag-'n-bietjies*.

It was getting light as we drove back to the city. We didn't even know yet that Nelson Mandela had been released the evening before."

I wanted to go to Africa, to try and understand what had been happening. After the great party around Mandela's release came the doubt and confusion. What was it that had changed, and who would be the key figures in the changes yet to come? And why had it all happened now? Only a few months before, De Klerk had railed against the ANC, accusing white liberals of treason for being in favour of negotiations. He had not said a word to explain his about-face. And no-one dared to ask; no-one wanted to be disillusioned. Only conservative Afrikaners howled their fears. They would rather fight to the death than live under a black government.

The messages coming in on my computer were still very cautious. The underground work should simply continue. The resistance cells were being briefed on the new situation. I should see the legalisation of the ANC as an anticipated step in a progression which had been worked at over a very long period. Nevertheless they too were surprised by the speed with which De Klerk had played his hand, and uncertain about the cards he might still hold.

In South Africa, black people strode proud and defiant through the streets in their ANC T-shirts. "We forced him to it," was the general opinion, but there was also some respect for his courage. An Afrikaner worthy of respect. Under the euphoria of victory there grew up an urge for appeasement, even for understanding. We should forget what has happened in the past, said those who had not suffered, and look to the future.

Mass meetings were held in the football stadiums, where ANC speakers called for patience, and where everyone joined in songs banned until so very recently, which gave an impression of liberty.

For the first time I was struck by an intense longing to go to South Africa; but Lusaka was as far south as I could travel.

I arrived very early in the morning of March 2nd. Ivan picked me up.

"Mandela's in town," were his first words. "In a couple of hours he's meeting ANC people in Lusaka. If we hurry we can get there in time."

We took my luggage to the hotel. I quickly washed and changed, then had to sit down, sweating, to recover from the exertion. Although it was early, the heat had hit me hard, and I had not slept at all.

But Ivan was in a hurry. He drove very fast to a hall just outside the city. Hundreds of ANC members were waiting at the doors, and many more were spread across the grass, sitting in groups under the trees. Complaints were being voiced. They had waited long enough.

Mandela was giving an international press conference; cameramen and sound technicians were still pouring into the building. Journalists already leaving were interrogated about how much longer the press conference would go on. A few South African exiles tried to see inside, through the open doors. They were impatient to know what was in store for them. When would they be able to go home, when would the rest of the political prisoners be released, and what were the prospects for negotiations?

Hours later the doors finally opened, and they pressed inside, ANC cards held high. Ivan steered me forward; I am not a member, but the ANC head of security had known me for years, and looked the other way for a moment.

We found a place high at the back of a gallery, not too conspicuous. It was oppressively hot. At last the sound of animated conversation everywhere, of hundreds of people moving about, blended and rose into one great roar of welcome.

Mandela entered, followed by the entire ANC leadership. Everyone was shouting, arms held high. I saw an old man stamping his feet with emotion. High women's voices broke into song, and Mandela began to toyi-toyi, leaning forward, knees lifted in rhythm. The auditorium shook with the force of thousands of pounding feet.

Then he was standing at the microphone.

"I am a member of the ANC, just as you are," he cried out to them.

"It is up to you to decide what role I shall play. If you ask me to sweep the floors of the offices, I shall do so."

They cheered and applauded again.

Ivan and I left the hall before the meeting was over. It was better not to be seen together too much.

Once outside, I asked Ivan to what extent Mandela had been in the know about Operation Vula.

He laughed briefly, standing beside the car.

"Oh, he knew for a long time. He used our communication system inside Victor Verster prison to keep in direct touch with Oliver Tambo and the others in Lusaka. I can't tell you exactly how it was done, but thanks to that line his reports reached Lusaka very quickly. Of course it was a little while before he trusted the system completely, and before he realised that with it he could discuss everything with Tambo down to the last detail.

"Before his release, when the press were implying that he was having talks on his own with government ministers, he was actually in continuous contact with the ANC leadership outside. And that's the way he wanted it, anyway. Pretoria, naturally, wanted to create the impression that they were only dealing with him. They were hoping to split him off from the rest of the ANC. But throughout 1989 there was direct contact between him and President Tambo, about the possibility of negotiations, about State President PW Botha – who

232

was already ill and due to be replaced by De Klerk, about the other ministers and security service people he met in the prison.

"We realised from his reports that the Pretoria crowd were struggling a bit with their earlier declaration that they would never come to the table with the ANC. They wanted to get out of that without too much loss of face. And he reported at one point that they were coming round to the idea that the ANC had a key role in normalising the political situation in the country.

"He warned Tambo that Pretoria might well move faster than expected. A lot would depend on the results of the white elections in '89. A comfortable victory would give the government enough courage to move towards negotiations.

"Then he told Lusaka not to expect that the main stumbling blocks would be the armed struggle, foreign pressure, or even the alliance with the Communist Party. Majority rule and group rights were going to be the hottest items on the agenda. He told Oliver Tambo that Pretoria would fiercely reject the principle of majority rule. Mandela was really indignant about that. He wrote: 'They reject that principle, even though it is fully accepted by the rest of the world. Now that it is clear to them that their apartheid system has failed, and that the black majority will win a clear voice in government, we are told that majority rule must be avoided at all costs. As long as it can be adapted within the context of white politics it is acceptable, but if the demands of the black population have indeed to be met, another formula must be found to avoid the black people assuming a position equal to the whites.'

"Mandela explained to Pretoria in no uncertain terms that majority rule and peace were inseparable, and that white South Africa would just have to accept this, and that negotiations were the only way forward, that without them the country would go under.

"There's still a direct contact, even now that Mandela is free and Mac and Gebuza and Ronnie are still underground. But there's a good chance that Mac and Ronnie, as members of the Executive Committee, will come into the open soon."

Ivan leaned his arms on the roof of the car. People were streaming out of the hall now.

"Come on, time to go." He opened the door and we reversed over the grass to the road, while hundreds of excited ANC members, still in animated discussion, spread across the great empty field.

The next day, unexpectedly, I found myself in the company of Mandela's delegation from South Africa. I was invited to lunch where they were staying in the government guest residence, and after coffee we had to hurry to be in time for a mass official welcome being prepared for Mandela.

On the front seats of the bus which took us to the football stadium were his old comrades from Robben Island: Ahmed Kathrada, Andrew Mlangeni, Raymond Mhlaba, Elias Motsoaledi.

The younger generation of ANC leaders occupied the back seats: Cyril Ramaphosa, Mohammed Valli Moosa, Jay Naidoo, Trevor Manuel. I was meeting most of them for the first time that afternoon. The atmosphere in the back of the bus was that of a school outing. They made uninhibited comments on everything which passed by outside the windows. They teased and scuffled with one other like overgrown schoolboys. A cigarette was smoked surreptitiously, passed from hand to hand, after the elders in the front of the bus had imposed a smoking ban. Cyril was beaten over the head with a newspaper, the penalty for dozing off amidst the exuberance of his comrades.

I wondered how long they would succeed in keeping their high spirits and spontaneity. All of us travelling in the coach that day were still political activists, together forming a tiny part of a huge movement for reform; our actions and behaviour sprang from shared ideals. We were the new force. But for how long? Soon these men would become players in the great negotiation game, with power in South Africa at stake. Perhaps De Klerk and the think-tank behind him thought they would be able, through the age-old sport of division and manipulation, to entice these men to their side; thought that these men were open to temptation and corruption. I knew too little about the enticements of power.

Our coach brought us right up to the covered podium inside the stadium. The playing field was packed with Zambian song and dance groups in brightly coloured costumes, each group singing a different song. We shuffled into our places among the other guests, a short distance from Mandela, who sat next to Zambian President Kenneth Kaunda. Mandela nodded to us as if we were his grandchildren, arriving late for a wedding.

At a sign from a soldier carrying a gun, the singers and dancers fell silent and sank to the ground. President Kaunda opened the proceedings. His speech rang out with three-fold echoes from loudspeakers in each corner of the stadium. The distance between the Zambians, gathered on the opposite side of the field, and the podium was so great that there was a delay before the crowd's lukewarm reactions to his slogans could reach us. We clapped our hands politely.

Mandela then spoke, talking of the heavy price the Zambians had paid for their defiance of the Pretoria government. He spoke of the necessity of democracy. Outside the fences of this same stadium, over the previous months, the first cautious demonstrations had taken place, for more democracy, for a multi-party state. He spoke of equality, of the fair division of wealth. Valli Moosa whispered: "Not all the rich people here are white, but all the poor are black."

I looked at him. "Would you be in the opposition if you lived here?"

He laughed in surprise: "I think so, yes."

Mandela again thanked the people of Zambia for their support. I could not see the reactions on the faces so far away. Had anything been said that afternoon which had any significance at all for the majority of poor Africans sitting there? I wondered. All those words: democracy, freedom, dignity, humanity. Hadn't they recently been chased out of the stadium with their pro-democracy placards months ago? The choirs resumed their earlier competition, and we were ushered back into the bus, fists clenched high for a last time.

Then came a ceremonial drive through Lusaka, Mandela and Kaunda in an open Jeep, our coach following behind. The windows of the bus were open and the boys leant out, returning the greetings of the Zambians along the route. It brought us through a suburb, past the market with its rats and beggars, the absurdly big cathedral, past one of the rare bookshops stocked with four-year-old periodicals, bad American paperbacks, *Reader's Digest* and Bibles. The native culture had been so fiercely repressed, even outlawed, over decades by colonial rulers and missionaries that Zambia had finally become merely a dumping ground for the West's cultural refuse. The effects were easily seen; Lusaka had no face of its own, not even a mask of its own. It was just an ugly old colonial city, abandoned to its present poverty-stricken inhabitants.

Our enthusiasm for hanging out of the windows and waving gradually waned. We sat quietly in the back of the bus, looking out at Africa.

SUMMER 1990

IN SOUTH AFRICA, PRELIMINARY TALKS ABOUT NEGOTIATIONS WERE now underway. Everyone was holding their breath; after the wave of expectation and hope that had flooded over the country, calm was being urged. De Klerk was demanding an end to the huge ANC gatherings. If they wanted to sit across the table from him, they would have to keep the people outside under control. And De Klerk was now considered honest. He had promised democracy, and no-one now remembered that he had always claimed that South Africa was a democracy.

A great silence had fallen. The prisoners sat mute in their cells, the exiles were too distant to be heard. The resistance stayed underground; too high a profile and you could still be arrested. South Africa's security apparatus was working overtime.

The ANC leadership from Lusaka had returned to Johannesburg, and the papers showed pictures of how the ANC's top people slapped their former enemies on the back; on television you could hear them make familiar use of each other's first names. The smiles were self-assured, and everything pointed to a swift resolution of the business at hand.

'Wait' was the new watchword for me also. Perhaps, Ivan told me, everything would go so fast that an extensive underground network would no longer be necessary.

I had started to clear out my flat. Papers, notes, lists of codes appeared everywhere: in books, behind paintings, inside an old family album. Great heaps of manifestos, pamphlets, the texts of speeches – I sorted them all by date, and made two piles: one to burn and one to keep.

All the windows were open wide to the hot, windless summer air. Each little corner I had cleared had to be thoroughly soaped and scrubbed. I was determined to have everything clean and fresh, determined that I would no longer have to ask myself fearfully, whenever someone casually picked a book off the shelf, whether some secret little piece of paper was going to flutter to the floor.

I had completely emptied two bank deposit boxes, and come home with bags full of passports, photographs and hand-written reports – all given to me for safekeeping over the last years. The great black box hidden under my floor, containing the dossiers of all the Dutch people who had gone out there during those same years, emerged into the light of day. But to go through them all once more, as I had planned, was too much for me. I made them up into bundles, relegating them to the archives with the string I tied around them.

Assorted leftovers from the disguises – spectacles, make–up, tufts of grey hair, a man's suit – were all thrown into a grey rubbish bag which was stuffed away on the top shelf of a cupboard.

Once everything was cleared out, and my home smelled of assorted cleaning liquids, there still stood, against one wall, a mountain of papers that could not be thrown out.

I brought a large quantity of brown cardboard archive boxes back from an office stationers', folded them into form and stuck on blue labels; from year to year, sorted by subject. But boxed or no, the papers could certainly not stay in my flat. This was material that could still put others in danger. That evening, flustered and miserable, I phoned Peter. He came straight over and we lugged all the boxes down to his car, and hid them under his floor, well wrapped in plastic.

Back home, I was seized by a veritable fury of sorting out and cleaning. Everything must be scrubbed and polished; everything must go into boxes – my daughter's toys, dolls, drawing things – into boxes with labels. Magazines were sorted, numbered paper markers indicating the places for missing issues – all stacked and in sequence.

Utterly exhausted, I gave in to Peter's urging and went to the seaside for a week with him and Tessel; but in the holiday cabin among the pines I was still restless, troubled by feelings of guilt. I wanted to go home; something wasn't right. Why on earth had I cleaned everything up?

Peter stayed, with Tessel and a few friends. The weather was far too good to go back to the hot and sticky city. But I somehow had no choice, and I felt a sense of relief as I again turned the key in my front door.

There were three messages on my answering machine. One from my mother, and two from Tim. He had an urgent message for me; would I please read it as soon as possible?

"Pick it up. Hurry!" was all he said the second time.

In one lightning movement I pulled the computer from its hiding place, plugged it into the telephone and pushed in the decoding disk, then dialled the number and heard the message come through. Decoding always took a little time, and just then the phone rang again – my mother. While she chatted to me I pushed the keys which brought the decoded message onto the screen. No greeting, just tiny green letters saying:

"Disaster ... a lot of comrades involved in the operation have been arrested, including Gebuza ... We believe that the enemy has got hold of one of our code disks, plus a large number of recorded messages ..."

My breath stuck in my throat. I could still hear my mother talking on, as if from a great distance, as I read the message again: "Disaster ... " I broke in on her rather bluntly, promising to call her back.

The rest of the message consisted of instructions. The communication lines had to be switched over to the emergency system. I should, as quickly as possible, ask the computer expert to help set up the new system. Tim ended with: "Work fast!"

A lot of comrades arrested! Who else? Where were the others – the Dutch, the Belgian couple?

I sat frozen on the chair, staring at the screen. Outside, a tram bell rang, and some children shouted. I was suddenly struck by an excruciating headache; even my eyes hurt.

It was July 15th; my friends had been arrested. What would that mean now? Interrogation? Beating? Surely that couldn't happen any more. Weren't there agreements, deals, between the ANC and Pretoria? Negotiations – bargains around the negotiations – the two sides were talking to each other on the phone all the time now, after all. Surely it would all be sorted out...

Gebuza arrested. I saw his tall proud figure before me, and couldn't conceive of him in handcuffs. Who would dare to hit Gebuza, to kick him, or to humiliate him?

The phone rang. Through heavy static I heard in the distance: "Hello ... Hello ... " Suddenly the voice sounded close by – Ivan. I began to cry. He just kept on urging me: "Don't panic, don't panic. You mustn't forget, we've had the second of February. This will be sorted out. Mac and Ronnie are above ground now, and they've got indemnity."

"Do you believe that yourself?" I asked him.

"I hope it. Come down here quickly. There's a great deal to be done."

A few days later I left for Harare, as Ivan had asked. There was no word about the arrests in the Dutch or English papers I had bought; just reports that South Africa had been hit by a wave of bomb attacks by white extremists against blacks, and that Mandela had been threatened with death when he returned from abroad. In Durban, unidentified assailants had shot up a bus carrying black South Africans – twenty-six dead.

After the seemingly endless flight, my first sight of Ivan was like a homecoming. He looked so dependably familiar, standing there slightly bent, briefcase in hand, shyly positioned at the back of the crowd waiting at the airport.

And he had news. Charles, who had gone into the country with Sipho the previous February, had been the first to be arrested, along with someone else I didn't know, a Vula activist from inside.

"As far as we know, they were arrested on July 12th, or maybe a day earlier. We can only guess exactly what happened; but we suspect that they were working together to recruit new people, and fell foul of a police spy. Their interrogation must have been very bad, because it looks as if they gave away the addresses of some safe houses. Gebuza was arrested about three days later. They forced his car off the road. They got the two girls as well."

"Which two girls?"

"Catherine and Minor, who came to you for disguises. How and where they were picked up I don't know, but they're definitely inside. A whole group of people were arrested in Durban, including Raymond Lalla, who's a good friend of mine. But when it comes down to it they've only caught about twelve. The rest have gone deep underground. The greater part of the Vula network is still there."

"Is there still normal contact, through the communication system?"

"Yes. That wasn't broken. We don't know exactly what they got hold of, in the way of communication stuff. Apparently they found a couple of floppy disks during the arrests. Dumb luck – our people were actually busy storing information on a file disk, to send outside. Right now Lucia is going over everything recent, to see how bad the damage is."

"What happens now?"

"Personally I expect they'll be released pretty quickly. I mean Pretoria can't expect to happily sit opposite us at the negotiating table if they're throwing our people in jail at the same time? It must be just a few rogue security police, having a last fling. They must have stumbled on Operation Vula by chance, through Charles; otherwise we'd have known. We've built up a really fine espionage network, infiltrated deep into their security networks. So we always knew if one of us was being watched, or if there was other trouble brewing; we were tipped off by their own people. What probably went wrong is that we just got too relaxed. We let ourselves get lulled to sleep by all the palaver about negotiations, and by how straight De Klerk was supposed to be."

We drove into Harare down a fine avenue of trees with grey trunks. On the corner of a street we always passed stood an old decaying English mansion, empty for years. I craned my neck to see how far the undergrowth had invaded the veranda. The house was still uninhabited, the window beside the front door broken now.

Ivan accelerated again, drove through a suburb and around a shopping centre into a cul-de-sac. We stopped in front of a house. Out of it, into the garden, came Totsi – a baby on her arm and a wild-looking light-brown dog bouncing around her feet.

Inside, looking worried, she held out some fax sheets just dropped off by Rafael, who was also in Harare. He had already left to see if more had come in. Faxes of newspaper articles. *The Sunday Times* carried a headline three centimetres high: "ANC secret cell shock – militants arrested and arms caches discovered by police."

The journalists Potgieter and Venter wrote that armed ANC insurgents had secretly penetrated inside South Africa. The police had seized large quantities of weapons including mines, firearms and rocket launchers. We looked at each other. We had heard nothing at all about them finding a single weapon.

The Star announced, across the full width of the front page: "Communists on the run," and reported forty arrests. "This unit was top secret; only a small group of top people were in the know," a police informant had told the paper.

According to *The Citizen*, the people arrested belonged to a clique which was against the negotiations, and which had planned an armed coup. Walter Sisulu responded on behalf of the ANC: "We have never made a secret of the fact that we send people covertly into the country; we have been doing this since the 1960s, when we adopted armed struggle." *The Citizen* expected more arrests within the next few days. Four thousand pages of communications material was supposed to have been seized, which revealed the size of the clandestine network.

"A highly-perfected system had been developed," Ivan read out, "employing high-tech equipment. The operation involved complex structures. The leadership consisted of around seventy people, subdivided into twelve regional commandos. The operation was under the direct control of ANC President Oliver Tambo."

The next day the papers reported major foreign involvement in Operation Vula. Dutch nationals, Belgians and other foreigners were named in the seized documents. All were supposed to belong to an international wing of the ANC.

"The foreign involvement is substantial. Their tasks included setting up safe houses and arms caches. The names of a number of foreigners involved are known from the computer print-outs ... "

I looked at Ivan.

"They haven't got any of your people," he said shortly. "I think the only vulnerable ones are the Belgian couple. We'll have to try and get in touch with Johannesburg tonight."

We listened to the radio – the same stories: "Communist conspiracy ... seizure of power by force ... Pretoria demands exclusion of Joe Slovo from negotiations, as secretary of the Communist Party." We all sat around the room. Totsi was breast-feeding her baby, Rafael slumped down in the big armchair and re-reading the newspaper articles. Ivan sat on a straight chair, repeating what he had already said several times: that everything would soon be sorted out. That Mac and Ronnie, along with Mandela, were probably at that very moment already talking with De Klerk.

"This will all blow over. It's just old habits dying hard. They just want one more chance to let out their anti-communism. They just want to use this to get at Slovo, to shut out the Communist Party."

Rafael came across a report saying it was known that many of the infiltrations had been organised through Swaziland.

"We've got to warn the people there – especially Andre!"

We drank tea, lots of it, strong and dark with plenty of milk. Then the telephone rang; Totsi went to answer it, baby in her arms. We heard a shriek, and she reappeared in the doorway:

"Mac's been arrested ..."

No-one spoke. Ivan's face was ashen. He stood up:

"I think we've got to talk through the seriousness of the situation." He seemed to have gone through a complete change. He made no attempt to speak further but just sat back on the chair, hunched over, turned in on himself.

"Where are the others? Where are Little John and Sabata, Christopher and the others?" asked Totsi.

No-one answered.

"Now we can expect anything," she went on.

"Right." Ivan roused himself, stood up and clapped his hands together. "Let's do some clearing up. If they know all that much, we'd better be ready for visitors..."

Tasks were quickly shared out. That evening Rafael and Ivan, with the help of two others, carried cases outside – big, heavy cases.

They were loaded onto an open truck and driven away. Totsi and I had piles of documents to burn. We had made a fire in the grate and she picked up papers one after another deciding what should be done with each. Some went straight into the flames; others went into a 'can't go' pile, and in front of me there grew a heap of 'doubtfuls'. The fire crackled as we sat on the carpet, the baby rolled in a blanket beside us. She gave me some papers to tear up and consign to the flames.

"Little pieces," she said knowledgably. "Big pieces sometimes leave traces."

"Let's not burn everything," I said hesitantly. "We can't throw a part of your history in the fire like that."

Totsi paused, looking again at the report in her hand.

"Let me take it back to the Netherlands. I can make sure it's stored safely. If we can smuggle documents into South Africa surely we can take them north safely too. Maybe one day someone will want to write a book about it all."

"About me, yes." She laughed aloud, and stroked the dog that had come to sprawl beside us. But she nodded, and we began the sorting all over again.

The radio was on – the news. Ivan and Rafael appeared in the doorway.

"The security police have raided a house in Mayfair in Johannesburg, and arrested a top ANC official, Sathyandranath 'Mac' Maharaj. It is expected that another highly-placed ANC official will be detained at any moment..."

"That must mean Ronnie," said Ivan.

"According to an eyewitness, Maharaj arrived at the house, which belongs to United Democratic Front council member Mohammed Valli Moosa, at 5.30 in the afternoon. Two carloads of police were lying in wait for him..."

"In Durban, Billy Nair and Pravin Gordhan have been detained... "

In the doorway, Ivan's head sank lower.

"If they're arresting NEC members now, who's ever going to trust these people an inch any more?"

I suddenly realised that Ivan too must have been hoping he would be able to go home, to Merebank near Durban, to the sad and dirty township whence he had come.

Next morning, Rafael went out for the morning papers. The ANC had reacted angrily to Mac's arrest. The papers closest to the government continued their furious denunciation of Joe Slovo, and it was suggested that the Vula conspirators had asked Lusaka for big shipments of arms to allow them to incite the people to a general uprising. The security services had informed press and diplomatic corps that a Belgian couple, a Dutch person and a Canadian had aided Operation Vula. At least seven ANC leaders were involved, including President Tambo, Joe Slovo, Mac Maharaj, Ronnie Kasrils, Siphiwe Nyanda (Gebuza) and Ivan Pillay.

I read out the list of names. Ivan shook his head.

Over the days that followed, a shift could be discerned in some quarters. *The Daily Mail*, in an editorial, wondered what was in fact so sensational about the case. It was no secret that the ANC was pursuing its underground struggle, any more than that the Internal Security Act was used to hold people in solitary confinement. The detainees were in no position to refute the allegations, lawyers had no access to them. There was no possibility open to them to defend either themselves or the movement to which they belonged.

In *The Citizen*, Nelson Mandela hit back hard:

"... the assumption that these outstanding sons and daughters of our country are harbouring ideas of undermining the peace process through armed action, is an insult thought up by the enemies of democracy..."

Over the first few days of August I travelled home. Just before I left, news came in from Johannesburg that the two Belgians had reached safety; but there was an urgent need for new people who could arrange safe houses for the Vula activists who were in hiding. Could I work on it with the utmost speed?

Autumn 1990

THE TWO BELGIANS, DANIEL AND SYLVIANE, WERE ALREADY IN Amsterdam, and we met in a house where I had never been before. Now that the Dutch Vula connection had been so openly and exhaustively covered in the newspapers, I intended to be extra careful. I had no idea what action the South African security network might be able to take against us in our own country, but they worked out of the embassy in The Hague, which was as close as I wanted them.

Daniel and Sylviane were very emotional. They hugged and kissed me very thoroughly, and I too was justifiably happy to see them safely back. Daniel, two good heads taller than me, held me suffocating against his chest, while Sylviane had already launched into their story. They both talked at once, shouting at each other in French that just one of them should tell it.

"Everysink was going soo kood ... " sighed Sylviane. As my French was so bad, and they were from Brussels, we communicated in English.

They had found a fine house in Johannesburg, and were well on the way to finding a job. Their contact with the resistance was entirely through one woman. I gathered from their description that it must have been Janet.

Everything went well until July 13th, a Friday. Janet had arrived, and told them that she was in danger. She couldn't rule out the possibility that the police were already following her, and in any case she dared not go back to the safe house where she usually stayed. So she had brought her things to their house: a portable computer with disks and a modem, a portable telephone in a suitcase, and some personal luggage. To their surprise she had also brought along a small parrot in its cage. The bird could talk – one sentence – but their English was not good enough for them to understand it.

"I think she felt safe with us," said Daniel. "Until July 16th; then she phoned at eleven at night that she no longer dared come to our house. We'd agreed what to do in that kind of situation, and we met her the next morning at a coffee shop in Rosebank. She was very tense. It looked as if the danger to her was getting worse all the time. We worked out what would have to be done if she was picked up.

"The same evening we saw her again, in a multi-storey parking garage. She had bad news for us. She knew that the police had our names. We didn't ask how she'd found that out. So now there was a very serious danger that they would quickly be on our track. Janet thought that we should get out of the country as soon as possible, and promised to call us that evening.

"We booked tickets straight away, but didn't hear from her that night. So we were sure she'd been arrested, but we didn't dare call Amsterdam. She finally phoned us the next morning, and we met her one last time to hand over everything we had – money and disguise stuff. The only thing left to do then was clear the house and pack our bags.

"It wasn't until we were ready that we noticed the parrot in the corner, and sat down again to discuss the problem. We couldn't take the bird on the plane, could we? But who knew how long it would be before someone came to the house? It dawned on us finally that the police might arrive at any moment."

"And then that bird," Sylviane broke in impetuously. "It spoke a sentence, clearly. We still couldn't make it out! Then Daniel said: 'Oh, what does it matter if the police take it? It's already a prisoner in that cage anyway!' and we just left it in the middle of the table, so they'd see it straight away."

So that was how Sylviane and Daniel left South Africa. Not long afterwards their names and code names appeared in the South African papers, as well as a photograph of Janet's safe house in Rockey Street, a flat above a restaurant – Mamma's Place.

Names of some Dutch people were printed as well. The newspaper articles alleged that they had aided and abetted an attempt to overthrow the government of South Africa by force.

There was wild speculation on who was still inside the country, and who was already safely over the border.

About the carpenter from Zeeland it was written that his job was to recruit agents for Vula. In fact he had been back home for some time, and was on the point, until his name appeared in the papers, of returning to Durban.

Maarten Vis was named. It was known that he had organised a safe house for Ronnie Kasrils. "He is still being hunted," wrote one Afrikaans paper.

The owner of the house in La Lucia in Durban that Maarten had rented was interviewed:

"He telephoned me at nine o'clock in July 21st to say that he had to go back to Holland unexpectedly. A week later the police came, searching for weapons; but they didn't find anything."

I read the papers with growing amazement. Maarten had already flown home in June, because Ronnie was coming out of hiding.

Happily, news quickly came that Ernest was safe in Cape Town. He had been keeping his head well down for some time anyway, because his house had been broken into three times. He had no idea of Christopher's whereabouts.

The Dutch in the front-line states had been warned. They were spread across Swaziland, Botswana and Zimbabwe. Although we had the impression that not much was known about them, and that the South Africans would no longer dare raid across the border, we had no desire to take risks and had asked everyone to be extra cautious.

I talked with the airline stewardesses also. Elise in particular was strongly affected by the news of Mac's arrest. She had read about them all, but had not known that Maharaj was the man she had met so often. I had to convince her that there was nothing she could do.

Reports from South Africa became steadily more distressing. The violence in the townships was taking horrific forms. Sinister death squads operated in black townships. People were shot down in bus stations, or thrown from moving trains. This type of violence was unprecedented. Masked men, always coming and going too fast to be recognised, carried out slaughters while the police kept their distance. Mandela called on De Klerk to put an end to the violence. De Klerk authorised the police to shoot down "agitators".

Immediately on my return to Amsterdam I had begun preparing people to help with the massive concealment operation inside South Africa. There were now two people ready to leave at short notice.

Jesse, an energetic young woman from Nijmegen, was self-reliant and courageous enough to be able to work under these new and dangerous conditions. She left in early November. She was soon followed by Robert, who would be in familiar territory. During the year since he had returned home he had completed enough courses to be able to get straight to work. His wife Tina was to follow him in the new year.

Janet and Ronnie had escaped arrest and were deep under cover, but through the computer link they were still in touch with Lusaka and London. They were delighted by the news of the imminent arrival of Jesse and Robert. They were in desperate need of more help and immediately made a new request: someone was urgently needed to take care of some urgent jobs in the next couple of weeks.

I had to rack my brains to find someone suitable. I was afraid to send out another Dutch person. After all the press coverage of Dutch involvement, I assumed the South African embassy in The Hague would be somewhat more alert with regard to people from the Netherlands asking to travel to South Africa at short notice.

There was only one person among my immediate circle of acquaintances with a different, and suitable, nationality: Brian, an Englishman who had long been resident in the Netherlands and worked as a translator. He still had a British passport, and therefore did not need a visa.

Brian was intelligent, but also very sensitive. His first reaction was positive; he felt honoured, and felt that it was his duty to go. Then the doubts set in. He asked himself if he would be capable of doing the job, and if he had enough knowledge of the country and the politics involved. His girlfriend and I worked hard to encourage him. He had so many abilities. Not only was he good with his hands, but he had worked for years in England as an actor before coming to the Netherlands, and he had taught courses for businessmen. He was more suitable than any other person to travel to South Africa as an entrepreneur. For that was what we wanted of him. The time was ripe for it; white South Africans hoped above all that De Klerk's promises would attract new investments to the country, and this, we calculated, would mean a warm welcome and plenty of co-operation for him, arriving as a British businessman with big plans.

He left in mid-October, and a month later I heard the whole story.

"The first thing to do in Johannesburg was to find the place where the first meeting was agreed for the next day. I wandered out of the hotel, into a pleasant, sunny city, dressed in the business outfit that Yan had picked out for me, expensive leather shoes, short-cropped hair, black leather document case under my arm, trying to get into my part as much as possible. I walked past parks, and the art gallery, caught sight of my unfamiliar reflection in shop windows. On the way I had lunch in a restaurant which was clearly frequented by other business people, and then strolled comfortably on, with my self-confidence nicely boosted.

"I passed a long line of minibus taxis, with a big crowd of black people standing waiting. There were black women selling all sorts of things, which were spread out on the pavement. So the street scene was getting more and more exclusively black, and I could feel I was being stared at, from all directions. Maybe I looked even too much like the white businessman, with that awful army-style cropped hair.

"A short black man came up beside me. He stroked my leather case, with a quick movement, and grinned: "Heey, niice!" I put one hand up to warn him off, and in a flash my watch was off my wrist. The little chap was round behind me. I turned quickly, and he stood there, in a straight challenge, with my watch between two fingers and a big knife in the other hand. He was holding his arms spread apart, and looking at me, laughing.

"I turned again, and walked away, as if to try and save face, expecting to hear loud jeering from behind me. But I knew the little chap was going to get a sad surprise. The watch may have looked expensive, like gold, but Yan had bought it at the market back home, for a few bob probably.

"So that was my first day."

Brian couldn't laugh about it. He ran his hand nervously through his hair, which was still extremely short.

"The next day was the meeting. That was a pleasant surprise because my contact, about whom I'd built up a whole set of expectations, turned out to be a bright, attractive young woman, with a good sense of humour. She told me straight away what they expected of me: rent a house and furnish it. Transport two people and a message to another city, hire portable telephones and post office boxes, and a whole lot of other little jobs. It seemed like a lot for just a couple of weeks, but the plus side was that I could get out of that suit, and the first thing I did was buy myself jeans and a T-shirt.

"It all went pretty well. I rented a house, and bought furniture in second-hand shops. The woman joked about that. She said the police had carted away so much furniture from the safe houses that their storage warehouses must all be overflowing.

"I made two long trips with the rental car, to Durban and Cape Town, but the most fun I had was setting up a clandestine woodwork shop. I drove about all over town in a pick-up, buying tools and materials. I was just lugging machinery around all day, looking gloriously scruffy. But I did manage to get pretty much everything ready in time.

"The last few days were tricky. Apparently the newspapers had published a list with the names of wanted 'Vula terrorists'. What was worse was that their pictures were shown on television. The woman I was working with asked me not to buy newspapers and not to watch television any more. I realised that it must be to avoid me knowing her real identity, and maybe the identity of the others too. So things were a bit strained while we sorted out the last few jobs. When I left I saw the newspapers with the portraits at the airport. I bought one, and didn't open it until we were well up in the air. I recognised her straight away. Her name's Janet Love."

On October 29th, the trial of the Vula people opened. Mac Maharaj, Siphiwe Nyanda (Gebuza), Raymond Lala, Catherine Mvelase, Susan Tshabalala, Dipak Patel, Pravin Gordhan and Amnesh Sankar appeared before the judge. Billy Nair failed to appear in court. The other defendants named included Joe Slovo, Ronnie Kasrils, Janet Love and Ivan Pillay, along with Maarten Vis, the carpenter from Zeeland, and the Belgian couple.

There was also a long list of others charged, who were only known by their code names. Some Vula personnel, Dutch as well as South African, were mentioned as many as three times, under different code names.

Oliver Tambo, long since named in the press as the head of Operation Vula, was not charged; they must have been afraid to go too far. Moreover, no mention at all was made of Charles Mbuso and his friend, the first two to disappear; there had been no trace of them since. The lawyers had now made enquiries, but the police refused to admit ever having the two men in their hands. The chance that they were still alive was becoming very slender indeed.

The indictment claimed that the accused had intended to arm and train a people's army, and overthrow the government with an armed uprising. They were also accused of establishing safe houses and a covert communications system, of smuggling weapons and explosives into the country in specially adapted cars, and recruiting members of the South African security apparatus.

Even the involvement of couriers including air hostesses from Amsterdam was mentioned.

The newspapers dubbed Umkhonto commander Gebuza a "master of disguise". Thanks to the disguises he had evaded the police for two years, while working under their noses. A whole series of forged passports, wigs, moustaches and beards were displayed during the trial. The journalists were impressed. Photographs of Gebuza as four different characters were published.

"The only thing these men had in common was their brown eyes," was the caption. I could not help laughing when I read that. I had known he would never wear those contact lenses, specially made for him.

The prosecutor spun the case out at great length. There were detailed descriptions of how communications were sent abroad in code. Examples given included the fact that "Lucy's place" was really Amsterdam, and "Jessy" was the code name for Johannesburg. One of the transmitted code messages was read out during the trial. Carl, one of the code names for Gebuza, had to meet a new air hostess. Her coming was announced in code, with the exact time she would leave Amsterdam. It was stressed that she should be treated with some kindness, as it was after all only the second time she was doing this. [The first time, Gebuza had been rushed and curt. I remembered the angry message I had sent, and the cool answer I had received.]

The Citizen printed a huge headline: "Seven foreigners have infiltrated South Africa". They were all supposed to have entered the country in 1990, and to have established fourteen safe houses.

"Were whites from abroad Vula agents?" wondered *Beeld*, which had learned from security force sources that some of the foreigners named had left the country, but that others were still in hiding, being hunted by the police.

The greatest shock, however, was that Operation Vula might have recruited at least seven moles within the South African security apparatus, who were still operational because they were only known by their code names. Mo Shaik of Vula was named as their handler. Fortunately Mo was in very deep cover, because if he were ever caught he would be in very deep trouble.

The security police had admitted to *The Sunday Times* that the foreigners had only escaped as a result of a huge blunder. The Vula people still at large, furthermore, were only still free because police in Durban had been too late in contacting their colleagues in Johannesburg. The prosecutor admitted that ninety per cent of the Vula activists could not be traced.

On November 8th, unexpectedly, came news that the Vula defendants had been released on bail. The ANC had had to pay R300 000 for each of them. They had to report daily to the police, and were not allowed to change address. All their travel documents had been withdrawn. The trial would reopen on January 15th.

The newspapers of November 14th published the photographs of wanted Vula personnel. They were also shown on television. Ronnie Kasrils, Janet Love, Little John – but also Charles Ndaba, who had disappeared. All were described as: "Armed and dangerous".

Winter 1990

The decision to go to South Africa had been slowly maturing in my mind for twenty years. Now that I had fixed a date, applied for a visa and bought my ticket, I became anxious and uncertain. I asked Ivan for advice, had long telephone conversations with Tim, and sought the opinion of my colleagues in the AABN. They all felt the risk was acceptable. I wasn't yet convinced, however. I called Wolfie in London, again asked all my friends what they thought, until Ronnie and Janet sent a message. They were wondering if my longing to see the country was actually worth the risk. Then came more doubts – one AABN board member thought there was too high a risk I might be arrested, and did not want to share that responsibility.

But I knew by then that my decision had been made. I had to go; there was no avoiding it. Before the end of 1990 I wanted to set foot on South African soil.

I left on December the thirteenth. I had never before been such a nervous traveller. I had no book with me, had bought no magazines at the airport, and just followed with my finger the track of the plane as we left Europe and approached the continent of Africa. After the sea came the desert. Unseen during the night hours, the Sahara gave way to tropical Africa; we flew for hours over the huge expanse of Zaire. Early in the morning we crossed Zambia, for so many years my regular destination in Africa, and above Zimbabwe the first light of dawn came through the windows. The aircraft started its landing approach over Matabeleland, and crossed the South African border.

I felt sick with excitement, and tried to see out, past the heads of my fellow passengers. But there was nothing to see. The wheels thumped down, and with a loud roar the plane approached Jan Smuts Airport. When it touched the ground I felt the impact as if

I'd ridden a long way on the back of someone else's bicycle, with the same kind of cramp in my legs.

I was stuck in my place for a long time before the other passengers finally started to move and shuffle towards the exit, rumpled from an uncomfortable night in their seats. Everyone had different plans – my aim was simply to somehow get through immigration. After twenty years' work with the AABN and five for Operation Vula, I was now to have my confrontation with South African officialdom. The embassy in The Hague, after some hesitation, had granted me my visa, but it might just as easily turn out to be a form of invitation from the South African Police. My nerves were trying to break out in laughter; why was I so frightened? The last thing they would do was arrest me.

In the cold, forbidding arrival hall there were long queues at passport control. After all my years of waiting to visit the country this extra half-hour of waiting was hard to bear. But finally I could lay my passport before an unsmiling immigration official. He examined every page, with extra attention for the large visa stamp within which strings of numbers had been filled in by hand. I saw him pass the document to a colleague, out of sight beside him, and heard the soft tapping of computer keys. And then an excited voice saying: "Hey, hey ... a fish on the line."

I froze. This was bad! He pressed a button, and two extra-tall characters came into the booth. They glanced at me briefly, and took the passport away. The minutes passed; the official ignored me, and unfriendly comments started to reach me from the queue. Then they returned and smacked my passport down on the desk. "Let her go."

Hardly breathing, I walked to the baggage area, and found my things. I was now in South African territory; I did not feel at all safe. But there were no further controls as I walked out and threw myself into the arms of a waiting friend. "Welcome to South Africa."

For the first time I was seeing the country with my own eyes, not through those of a cameraman. We drove to the city along a motorway with huge traffic signs, amongst trucks loaded with black labourers, Jeeps with agricultural equipment and the occasional sports car. I was surprised by the hills. For me Johannesburg had always been a map, a city split into districts, crossed by red printed lines, with grey blocks on a white background – and flat.

I was staying in Hopkins Street in Yeoville. Before my departure everyone who knew Johannesburg reassured me: "You'll enjoy Yeoville. It's not a typical white area, it's mixed with black and white living next to each other. The atmosphere's a bit like Amsterdam." The second day I plucked up the courage to go out on my own. I wanted to learn to feel at ease in South Africa: go shopping, buy a paper, chat with someone. I planned a route on the map, memorised the street names and set out. My first solo outing was to Rockey Street, three blocks away – Yeoville's shopping centre. I hadn't left Hopkins Street, however, before I already felt a bit lost. It's such a huge country. I crossed a small park, and was laughed at by some older black women sitting under a tree. At the bottom of the steps leading out of the park sat a beggar. I gave him R10. I did not yet know the value of the currency, and feared making a bad impression. I made one friend, at least.

I walked along Rockey Street past the shops, and within fifteen minutes had encountered the whole spectrum of the country's people: black, Indian, white yuppies, uncouth Afrikaners, poor whites, beautiful black women, brown street kids, Orthodox Jews, Portuguese shopkeepers, dirty old men of every skin colour, hippies, and one sangoma in traditional dress. There were flower stalls, jazz cafés, posters everywhere for Bob Dylan-style performers, and from one dark entrance the scent of hashish. You could eat food from any continent, and on every corner stood a group of boys willing to carry your bag for you. I fell a little in love with Rockey Street, but never for a second relaxed my surveillance of any white man in sneakers. It was some time before I realised that they couldn't all be working for the Special Branch. Even Pretoria wasn't that rich!

And so I found myself on the corner of Cavendish, outside a restaurant called Mamma's Place. I recognised it from a newspaper photograph. Above it were flats – Janet's former safe house. I remembered suddenly, almost guiltily, that Janet and Ronnie were still in hiding somewhere in the city. Where might they be? But even if they were only one street away it might just as well be the other side of the world for me.

Mac was in Johannesburg, released on bail. At the new ANC headquarters, which I sometimes visited, Mohammed Valli Moosa had given me his telephone number. He knew I was in the city and was waiting for my call. So Mac and I met again, after almost three years. Suddenly there he stood, on the veranda of the house where I was staying. He strode forward with that well-remembered grin, and greeted me enthusiastically. We sat down on a wooden bench between huge green shrubs with red flowers, and giving me no chance to find out about him he asked after all the people he'd met in the Netherlands: Diderik the dentist, the wigmaker, the makeup artist, Floris, and especially the air hostesses. He seemed unchanged, except that he spoke faster, with less expression in his voice. His good humour seemed brittle; something had changed in him. The months of prison, and of the hospital where he had been treated for a neck injury, must have left their mark. We went out in his car, and had coffee in a shopping centre. Here and there people nudged each other and pointed. He was a well-known figure without his disguise. He wanted to know everything about my daughter, about all the AABN people. I was feeling more and more uncomfortable with this formalised friendliness. "What do you think about the trial, Mac?" I interrupted him.

The smile disappeared; now I could see bitter lines around his mouth. "They've set it up just as you'd expect them to, exactly according to their racist thinking. There are six Indians on trial, and three Africans. But we know that in Durban alone five Africans have already been arrested. Where are they? They're trying to make it look as if Vula was thought up by whites and Indians. As if Africans couldn't really be involved in that kind of operation. That way it all fits their communist plot theory much better." He lit a cigarette.

"And look at the situation in the country." His voice had an angry edge now. "In the Transvaal alone more than a thousand lives have been lost. The security force involvement is blatantly obvious. We can hardly defend ourselves any more. They want us to hand in our weapons, and to stop our protest actions. They want to turn the ANC's leaders in the negotiations into accomplices in the repression, so they'll be dealing with a badly weakened ANC. That's their idea of democracy!"

"Do you have to report to the police every day?"

He nodded. "They're still afraid of us. They know that not all of us have been arrested – far from it. Vula is still a threat to the regime, that's why the trial is taking so long. They're holding us as hostages, tools for blackmail in the talks."

"What are you going to do?"

"Rest and think, first. Then I'll see."

We went back to the house and said goodbye. His wide smile had returned. His wife and children were on their way to South Africa.

I had telephoned Gebuza at his father's house in Madadeni, a township near Newcastle. "You'll have to come to me. I'm not allowed out of the area," he said sullenly. But I had already heard the pleasure in his voice when I had first said my name.

"Would you really like me to come?" I asked, to make sure.

He just roared with laughter and called out: "See you tomorrow."

Next day, after a three-hour journey, I saw him walking towards me – thinner, a bit stooped, much older than I remembered. We stopped still for a moment, with a few yards between us. Then followed a silent embrace. Tears came to my eyes. He rested his hand on my shoulder and led me into the house.

It was a large living room, filled with heavy furniture and cupboards. The success of his father's liquor stores could be clearly seen. You'd expect to find this luxury house in a Johannesburg suburb. But black businessmen too lived in the townships. Gebuza stood in the middle of the room, looked round him awkwardly. "It's not my house," he said. His children rushed in, then withdrew again shyly with the presents I had bought for them on the way. He watched them with pleasure, and pointed to some photographs in a sideboard. "My sisters." I wanted to ask if there was a photo of his brother Zweli, who had been murdered in Swaziland, but he was already walking out onto the terrace.

"I do nothing all day, just sit here in this house." He sat on the edge of the concrete terrace, and wrapped his arms round his legs.

"How badly did they treat you?" I asked carefully.

"Rough. But not as rough as they'd have been before the second of February. I don't think I'd have survived if it had happened before then. They were a bit more careful, maybe because I've got a certain rank in the ANC. They'd have had to think twice before beating me to death."

"And the prison?"

"Solitary confinement until we appeared in court. Five months. I was transferred to a quiet wing with only white guards. They were worried that I might influence black guards, or that the black cleaners might smuggle messages outside for me." He picked a long dry stalk of grass and put it between his teeth, stretching his long legs and leaning back.

"And now you're home."

"Yes, after so many years. When I left the country in '76 I thought it would be for six months, twelve at the most. Get training, come back, fight, liberation celebrations in the stadium, and we'd all be heroes. God, how easy it seemed. But it all took a bit longer, and turned out a bit differently. When I think of what we said about comrades who'd left the country in the early '60s: 'In the time you've been away you could have dug a tunnel from Lusaka to South Africa,' we used to say. Oh, we still talked big then. I've always wished I'd stayed here. I should never have left South Africa."

That afternoon I went along when he had to report to the police. I stayed in the car while he went inside, watching the white policemen going in and out. As he emerged from the building I recognised him once more. The commander, straight as a poker, chin up, light springy step – the man who speared the sky.

I had to leave soon afterwards, and saying goodbye was rather sad. He stayed by the fence, his hand raised. I looked back, waving until Gebuza, caged now, was out of sight.

I saw Oliver Tambo again, in a huge football stadium near Soweto – me and sixty thousand South Africans. It was his big

260

welcome home. Wild youths in T-shirts printed with militant slogans sang impatiently, pushing each other off the benches. Right in front of me five dignified old men sat side by side, very still, wearing traditional hats from Lesotho. Behind me was a restless group of black labourers in bright yellow safety helmets with Operation Vula written across the front. I grinned at them, unable to resist giving a thumbs-up. They answered my greeting, waving and yelling all sorts of things I didn't understand. For the first time I was feeling at home in South Africa.

A car surrounded by officials drove out onto the grass. The huge sea of people rose as one, and burst out in a huge cheer. There he stood, Oliver Tambo, returned to the land of his birth. He stood there so small – I had never before seen him at such a great distance – with his clenched fist raised. The old men removed their hats, and a boy waved a wooden gun. "Viva Comrade President!" called a hoarse voice into the microphone. "Viva!" roared the stadium.

Just before Christmas I flew to Cape Town, the city that more than any other had featured in my fantasies about the promised land. I stayed with Amy, a friend, in an old secluded house with a garden where the trees carried outrageously huge flowers. As I gently lifted a thick cluster of them in my hand Amy looked at me as if to say: "So, I was exaggerating?"

She poured me a glass of Cape wine, and indicated the great mountain rising behind the house, Devil's Peak. "Table Mountain is right behind there," she told me proudly. I sniffed at the breeze, but couldn't catch any smell of the sea.

The next day Garth, just recently back from exile, drove me round the mountain in his rusty Volkswagen, and at last – the interior is so very dry – I saw water, the ice-cold Atlantic Ocean. We stopped beyond the port and sat on the rocks, the south-east wind blowing in our hair, and watched the breakers forming thinner and thinner white lines as they neared the horizon, until they merged with a thin grey-green strip of land surrounded by water, far away in the haze of spray.

Robben Island.

Chota.

Such a significant but disconcerting distance. You could not call across it, or swim across it. Just look.

And look I did, until the sun's reflection made the island appear to be swallowed up by the sea, and Garth led me away.

He drove along the coast, around Hout Bay, to Noordhoek, then turned past the Cape of Good Hope over the mountain foothills to Vishoek. Further still, inland from Valsbaai, the landscape became bare and sandy. Here and there children ran about among rickety buildings, and the white sand drifted between shacks packed close together. An endless collection of sad shelters sprung from the plentiful refuse of the nearby city. Khayelitsha, where Pretoria had dumped Cape Town's black population, had a few small toilet buildings as services, and huge floodlight masts which lit up the ghetto at night so that no activity would be hidden from the eyes of the police.

We drove for more than an hour past tens of thousands of poor shacks. They seemed endless – Cape Town's open, sandy wounds.

Christmas day was hot, with no breath of wind. Amy had hung some glittering Christmas decorations over the paintings in the living room, and on the table were piled gifts for the children. Her friends gathered in the garden, elderly people who between them could boast over a hundred years' membership of the ANC, dozens of years in prison, and at least as many of exile. Talk was of those still abroad, and how they could be housed when they returned, which of them were ill, and how everyone had the right to die at home.

During the afternoon joyful celebrations followed the arrival of a lawyer bringing a young man who that morning, totally unexpectedly, had been released from Robben Island. He had been given exactly fifteen minutes' warning that he was being released. The ferry ride had taken thirty minutes, and the lawyer had been waiting for him on the dock. Now he sat in Amy's garden, after seven years on the Island. He had not been permitted to take leave of his comrades. He was the only one released, leaving two hundred and three fellow prisoners behind. I had not the courage to ask him for news of Chota.

I was wondering where my other friends might be, Sabata and Little John. All I knew was that they were hiding in the Transkei under difficult conditions. No-one had any means of contacting them; they were having to survive with no money or support. Little John had been declared a target – fair game to shoot on sight, after his photograph had been shown a number of times on television, once in a programme where the viewers were asked to help in tracking down criminals. And where were Christopher, Ronnie and Janet, Ernest, Jesse, Robert and all the others, hidden at many different addresses? Were they in touch with each other? Would they be feeling especially lonely during these days when others were so busy creating their artificial Christmas spirit?

Sipho told me later that he spent Christmas alone in a township near Johannesburg: "It was an awful time. On Christmas Eve I heard police banging on the doors of the houses next door to mine. There was shouting, and I heard them take some people away. I didn't know if they'd come for me as well, and all I could do was wait for them with my revolver in my hand. But they didn't come, and I never found out who or what they were after. Late on Christmas Day I'd had enough, and I went out in disguise to a place where you can get a glass of wine. I sat there and drank, among people who knew me, but didn't recognise me. I didn't stay long – the urge to speak to them was getting too strong."

Two days after Christmas Garth came running into the house, excited. "We've got a surprise for you." He looked at me, a little nervously. "You can visit Chota on Robben Island."

I sat down. He explained how he and Chota's lawyer had worked out a clever trick. Two older ANC people had been given permission to visit Chota, and they were prepared to let me go in their place. At the last moment the lawyer intended to switch the names, and then we just had to hope that no-one would find out. The chairperson of an anti-apartheid movement would never be given permission.

"It's the holidays. The ministries are all working at half strength," he said. I looked at him very doubtfully. I would have to be patient until the very last moment. It wouldn't be clear whether or not I could go until just before it was time to leave. Nervous and fretting, I called the lawyer to ask what I could take to Chota, what was allowed, how I should behave, what could I say and what not?

"Say as few words as possible until you're on the boat," he advised me. "Your accent could give you away."

The visit was to be on the twenty-ninth of December, a *kontakbesoek* – not separated by glass, therefore. I would be able to touch him.

Garth drives me to the dock in Cape Town harbour. He drops me by a high fence, slaps me on the shoulder in encouragement, and points to the office where I should announce myself. In a plastic bag I have fruit, fresh orange juice and various Indian delicacies the lawyer has suggested. In my bag are a few postcards with greetings from friends. There are soldiers everywhere, and behind the counter a tall blonde young man in uniform. I give my name as quietly and innocently as possible, and he checks it against a list. For one eternal second he looks at me, but he asks no questions, waving me to the waiting room.

A group of people, all white, waits there. Children with inflatable toy animals, women in low-necked beach dresses, men in shorts, with sunglasses pushed up on their heads and cameras slung round their necks. On the wall is a sign stating that it is strictly forbidden to take cameras over. I start to wonder if I'm in the right place. Who are these holidaymakers? Is someone playing a cruel joke on me? A soldier stands near the door and I ask him to direct me to the toilet. Up the stairs I find another waiting room, with exclusively black men, women and children. Yes, they nod, they are going to Robben Island. I want to ask who are the people downstairs, but resist the urge.

I hang about by the stairs because I have no desire to be with the whites, and don't really dare go upstairs, which would call attention to me. At a quarter past one we board a small white ferry, and I walk through to the upper deck where the black visitors are sitting together on a long bench. The white holidaymakers have taken noisy possession of the rest of the deck. As soon as the engines start and the lines are cast off I go quickly to sit with the blacks. So what can they do? Throw me overboard? The soldiers in their brown uniforms stand together

264

whispering, looking in my direction, and just as the boat pulls away still more soldiers jump aboard.

We sail out of the harbour. At the end of the pier a group of seals are piled half on top of each other on a small rock. Their hides are scarred as if by frequent fights or because they have been wounded by boats' propellers. Above our heads a big flock of seagulls follows us. Every boat provides them some refuse.

I look back. Cape Town is getting smaller and more insignificant against the great bulk of the mountain. Then we reach the open sea and the weather changes suddenly as a strong wind begins to blow. I feel the anxiety in the young boy beside me. "Is it worrying you?" I ask, and he tells me that this is the first time he's ever seen the sea, and the first time he's visiting his brother on the Island. He has travelled for twenty-six hours on the train for a thirty-minute visit.

It is getting steadily colder, we are showered with sea water, and I spread my coat over the boy and myself. I catch the hate-filled glances thrown at me from the white group under the plastic canopy, and then we arrange the coat over our heads so we have a small viewing hole through which we can just see the strip of land growing bigger ahead of us, and the sharks that are circling the ship. It is not the ice-cold water that for centuries has deterred the prisoners from attempting to swim to freedom, but these highly dangerous predators, the real prison guards.

We approach the harbour on the Island. The holidaymakers pack up their foam mats, parasols, inflatable toys and picnic baskets, waving happily to the uniformed men on the quay. I understand that they must be relations of the guards, coming over for a day out. When the ferry is secure they run down the gangplank and clamber into the waiting cars. The crew and soldiers have also disappeared. On the Island no-one needs to be guarded. Escape is impossible.

I stand on the quay with about twenty other visitors. I can see no living thing on the roads or in the fields. All that is visible is a group of barrack buildings in the distance. Beside the water lie the wrecks of cars, some of them models dating from the 1950s. Further on there is nothing but sand and dry undergrowth. We all stand staring around us, until one woman starts to walk – she has been here before. Close together and silent we approach the barracks, passing a gate with 'Welcome to Robben Island' painted above it.

In the nearest building we wait in a sort of classroom, everything white, with just two benches in the clean and sterile room. No-one comes.

After at least fifteen minutes a guard – big, fat and bearded – appears in the doorway. He doesn't look at us, but stares with hostility at the list in his hand. He shouts: "Braam!"

My name echoes round the space like a cannon shot. I step forward. "Kom".

I follow him down the corridor; the others remain behind. We pass rows of empty little rooms. Halfway along he turns suddenly and strides back past me without a word. I see movement from the corner of my eye, and half turn towards it.

Chota.

For a moment we just look, then he spreads his arms. I run to him and he swings me round. He seems taller and stronger than I remember. We sit down, facing each other. Two guards take up positions in the doorway and Chota pulls my chair closer to him. He takes my hands. His face is very close now. They had only told him the evening before he was to have a visitor, and he had wondered who else he knew who was called Braam. He had lain awake all night, just as I had.

I want them to go away, those men by the door, those voyeurs. They're distracting me, they're the last ears I want to have listening. I long to shut the door. But whenever my eyes glance in their direction Chota tugs at my hand as if to say: 'Concentrate on me.' He is now, after eighteen years, an experienced prisoner, accustomed to being watched, and determined to take full advantage of his time.

I examine his face in curiosity; the eyes are so large and clear, he seems so much younger than fifty-five. And his hands. I have forgotten his strong, fine hands. I stroke his leg and feel the rough prison cotton, something hostile that belongs with the men at the door.

He talks and talks, about his kidnapping, about the cruel interrogation and torture. For twenty-four hours a day they bombarded his cell with a high shrill noise.

"You're convinced that you're going insane, the only thing you want is for it to stop. There's no escape from it."

266

There had been moments, two in fact, when he though he was going to die. They had kept him alive only because they thought he might be useful; perhaps in the end, they thought, they'd get some information out of him.

Chota kisses me quickly on the neck, asking in a whisper if I had noticed whether the adjoining rooms were empty. I nod. He signals with his eyes and I understand that there are probably others besides the guards listening in.

More than an hour passes. The guards let us run over the time limit, and when they are not looking I quickly give Chota the postcards and a photo of Tessel and me. Is he hungry? No, he wants to take it all back to the others. Perhaps things will be a little less strict during the days of the Christian festival.

I ruffle his hair, run my hand down his back. I want to touch him as much as I can – kontakbesoek. He pulls me to him.

"Five minutes," shouts the guard. I become nervous; what do I still have to tell him? What have I promised his friends in Cape Town I'll say? What are the things I absolutely must not forget? But Chota is calm, he knows the horrors of the last five minutes. At some point during the remaining time he stands, picks up the plastic bag, holds me close again, turns and walks away.

The other visitors are already outside. After I had been called they had waited another half-hour. The prisoners had been told that no-one was visiting, and only after protests were they again brought out of their cells. By then only thirty minutes were left.

I walk beside the boy who had never seen the sea. His head is hunched between his shoulders.

"How did it go?" I ask. He shakes his head violently and I put an arm round him. On the quay another group of people from the beach are waiting, and as the wind is now blowing a gale we all have to go below, whites on the seats by the windows, blacks in the middle. The boy is weeping now. All I can do is hold his hand.

The boat plunges through the waves, and the Island quickly fades back to a smudge on the horizon. The holidaymakers are having a ball, laughing loudly with every dive off a wave. The picnic baskets roll about the aisles. Next to me on the other side is a black woman. She has pressed her face into her hands, her shoulders are jerking, and a child sits close against her.

When we reach Cape Town harbour the last drops of salt water run off the windows and I see Table Mountain appear. So huge and powerful, such an ancient mountain – its summit shrouded in white cloud. Surely that summit reaches on up forever, hidden from us down below.

Postscript

In 1991 THE VULA DEFENDANTS APPEARED BEFORE THE SUPREME Court in Durban. The case was immediately adjourned until March. On the twenty-fifth of that month all the accused were granted indemnity, and the case against them was closed. Mac Maharaj and Siphiwe Nyanda then demanded clarification of the circumstances surrounding the disappearance of their Vula colleagues Charles Ndaba and Mbuso Shabalala. In March 2001 Hendrik Botha and Gerhardus du Preez were granted amnesty for the murders of Ndaba and Shabalala, whose bodies were dumped in the Tugela River and never discovered.

On 22 June 1991, ANC President Nelson Mandela introduced some of the Operation Vula members to the press at his Soweto house. This meant an end to underground life for Ronnie Kasrils, Sipho (Solly Shoke), Little John (Christopher Tsie Manye), Janet Love, Sabata (Charles Nqakula) and Christopher (Max Ozinsky).

Early in July 1991, Mac Maharaj, Ronnie Kasrils, Ebrahim Ismael Ebrahim (Chota), Joe Slovo and Siphiwe Nyanda (Gebuza) were elected to the ANC National Committee. Oliver Tambo was chosen as chairman. Ivan Pillay, Janet Love and Tim Jenkin all took part in the CODESA negotiations. Oliver Tambo died in 1993, and Joe Slovo in 1995.

I regret that I was not able to include everybody who was involved in Operation Vula in this book. Many other South Africans were involved. Between seventy and eighty Dutch people made a contribution to Operation Vula. Most of the Dutch people who worked for Operation Vula in South Africa or in the frontline states returned to the Netherlands.

This book is an attempt to recall the unique co-operation between South Africans and Dutch people in the struggle against apartheid. I have done this from the perspective and position I held during the struggle years.

Now, more than ten years later, I still feel strongly that given the historical ties between The Netherlands and South Africa, it is important for new generations to realise that standing side by side against an evil system such as apartheid was an important experience. The fight for justice, humanity and democracy has enriched us all. I can speak for all Dutch participants when I say that we are proud to have been in a position to support the heroic South African freedom fighters. We have done so in the tradition of international solidarity. You are always in our hearts.

Conny Braam
Amsterdam, 2004

2004

1. Sipho - Solly Shoke, now mission director in the South African National Defence Force
2. Little John – Christopher Tsie Manye
3. Gebuza – Siphiwe Nyanda, now head of the South African National Defence Force
4. Chota – Ebrahim Ismael Ebrahim, Special Advisor to Deputy President Jacob Zuma
5. Oliver Tambo – former chairman of the ANC; died in 1993
6. Sabata – Charles Nqakula; now Minister of Safety and Security
7. Tim Jenkin – now Director of Unwembi Communications
8. Ivan Pillay – now South African Revenue Services General Manager: Special Investigations
9. Totsi – Totsi Memela-Khambula, now works for First National Bank
10. Christopher – Max Ozinsky, now Cape Town regional secretary of the ANC and member of the Provincial Legislature
11. Rafael – Jabu Moleketi; now MEC for Finance and Economic Affairs in Gauteng
12. Minor – Dipuo Mvelase
13. Catherine – Susan Tshabalala
14. Mac Maharaj – former Minister of Transport and non-executive director of First National Bank
15. Ronnie Kasrils – now Minister of Water Affairs and Forestry
16. Joe Slovo – former Minister of Housing and chairman of the South African Communist Party, died in 1995
17. Janet Love – former Member of Parliament and Special Advisor to the Minister of Water Affairs and Forestry, currently works at the South African Reserve Bank

OTHER JACANA BOOKS

Inside Out: Escape from Pretoria Prison by Tim Jenkin
The astounding tale of how Jenkin and two other prisoners planned their escape, made their own duplicate keys and managed to make their way through ten locked doors to freedom.

They're Burning the Churches by Patrick Noonan
A meticulously written and moving account of the disturbing events leading up to the downfall of apartheid. They're Burning the Churches elucidates the Sharpeville Six trial, the Delmas Treason Trial, the 1984 uprising that led to international sanctions against South Africa, as well as the Boipatong massacre.

Drive Out Hunger by JJ Machobane and Robert Berold
JJ Machobane is a farmer, novelist, social visionary and self-taught scientist. In the 1940s and 1950s, as a young man in Lesotho, he spent 13 years researching an agricultural system which would allow the poorest people to harvest food all year round. Working entirely on his own, he perfected his farming system and then founded a college to teach it.

Lucky Fish! by Reviva Schermbrucker
Lucky Fish! is a novel set in Johannesburg in the 1960s, and is told by a 13-year-old boy named Steven. This account of Steven's life during the apartheid regime, when his parents, Ivor and Lucy, become political prisoners at the same time, is remarkable for its authenticity and freshness.

Did you enjoy this book? Email us or write to us and tell us what stories we should be publishing, or send us your story.
marketing@jacana.co.za
Jacana Media
PO Box 2004, Houghton, 2041